SWAN RIVER

'An exquisite work of memory . . . in turns funny, sad and moving; it's a book that will stay with the reader long after the final page'
Jeremy Poolman, *Daily Express*

'Unsensational and deft . . . Out of his bedroom, into the wider world and back into the past, gently, Reynolds leads the reader on, immersing you in his ancestors' world until you begin to think they are yours, too'
Philip Hoare, *Independent*

'The unflashy prose and downbeat candour are disarming . . . His family's story matters to him. Stubbornly, against the odds, he makes it matter to us, too'
Blake Morrison, *Guardian*

'A beautifully written family memoir'
Real Magazine

'A remarkable portrayal of the love between father and son . . . a fabulous, moving book'
Will Self

'Entertaining and readable, written with great warmth and shrewdness . . . The sense of personal satisfaction, of some kind of closure being achieved, is strongly conveyed. It is a mark of Reynolds' skill that the reader shares it'
D J Taylor, *TLS*

‘[An] evocative family memoir, in which the stories of three generations intersect until the mystery is resolved’
Fanny Blake, *Woman and Home*

‘That the author can still think of them like this (after his mother has divorced her husband for cruelty) shows how well he has kept his balance, and is probably why the book is so immensely likeable . . . readable, engaging, wholly appealing’
Globe & Mail

‘A profoundly moving story about fathers and sons’
Vancouvre Sun

SWAN RIVER

A FAMILY MEMOIR

DAVID REYNOLDS

PICADOR

First published 2001 by Picador

This edition published 2002 by Picador
an imprint of Pan Macmillan Ltd
Pan Macmillan, 20 New Wharf Road, London N1 9RR
Basingstoke and Oxford
Associated companies throughout the world
www.panmacmillan.com

ISBN 0 330 39197 6

3 5 7 9 8 6 4 2

A CIP catalogue record for this book is available from
the British Library.

Typeset by SetSystems Ltd, Saffron Walden, Essex
Printed and bound in Great Britain by
Mackays of Chatham plc, Chatham, Kent

For Martha, Grace and Rose

He appeared to suggest, however, that there was something debilitating that haunted human society. He implied that the knowledge he conveyed was crucial to survival, that Armageddons loomed for us, always. The threats he saw to civilisation were vague. They had to do with the failure to remember, which explained some of his devotion to the study of history, and the failure to honor.

Barry Lopez, 'Theft' in *About This Life*

The more a man is, the less he wants.

Maxwell Perkins
(painted across their living-room mantelpiece by his wife)

Contents

Author's Note

While the events described in this book are essentially true, they stretch back more than a hundred years and have been recalled not just from my memory but from my father's and from those of other members of my family. My father died many years ago and cannot be asked for verification, but it is worth noting that he was quite taken by Aristotle's view that 'poetry [by which, in modern terms, Aristotle meant fiction] is something more philosophical and more worthy of serious attention than history'. Though I have much respect for history, I am inclined to go along with my father and Aristotle on this – and with Nietzsche: 'There are no facts, only interpretations.'

The names of certain people have been changed to protect their privacy.

Prologue

In northern Manitoba the winter of 1906–7 was hard, but not exceptionally so for that part of Canada. The snow began at the end of the second week of November, and within a fortnight lay deep throughout the valley and all around the new buildings and shacks that made up the town of Durban. The homesteaders, who had been in the district for seven or eight years, knew that the freeze-up could be endured, but the newcomers drawn to the booming town by the new railway shivered in the dry, cold air and thought of returning to the east or the south. There were two trains out every week, so for some it would be easy. Others had no choice.

In the middle of a night in early January Tom was woken by the cold. Since winter began, he had slept fully clothed, but the fire had died. He had forgotten to replenish it before retiring; he had been too drunk to think ahead. Wrapping a blanket around him, he forced his stiff limbs a few strides across the floor; then returned to the bed to pull on his boots. He took two mouthfuls of whisky from the bottle, stared at the thermometer which showed 60° below zero, the coldest since his arrival the previous summer, and began to remove the ashes from the stove with a shovel. He quickly built a fire, and walked up and down his tiny board cabin, flapping his arms as he waited for the warming blaze.

He sat down with the bottle and a packet of biscuits; then remembered that he was due to take the sleigh to his workplace on the track at 6 a.m. He put the whisky down and gained comfort from the biscuits alone. He sipped a little freezing water instead, holding it in his mouth until it was warm enough to swallow. He was close to the kind of desperation that produces total inertia, and had a headache that stretched from the front of his head to the nape of his neck. He was forty-seven years old and had spent most of his life in north London.

1

A Quiet Day at the Lock

THERE WAS NOTHING happening at the lock that afternoon. Two swans, their wings arced upwards, paddled upstream towards the bridge. The lock-keeper looked up from a pile of ropes and waved. It was the end of March. In a few weeks there would be sunshine and pleasure boats. Then we would push the grey-painted beams against the current to close the lock gates. And the ice-cream van would wait where the gravel path met the road.

It was our favourite place to hang around, kids let out from school at 3.30, mostly boys though Richard often brought his little sister, Kay. Adam, my other close friend, sometimes came with his big sister, Sarah; at thirteen, she was taller and stronger than any of us. Patrick and Dennis, the Irish brothers, who went to the Catholic school, were often there before us. Dennis was our friend. Patrick would walk with Sarah and even put his arm round her shoulder to show off.

That day I sat on one of the beams and waited, but no one came. The swans flapped up from the water and flew under the bridge, necks urgently outstretched, heading upstream. Staring down into the water outside the lock gates, where brown foam and waterlogged sticks collected, I had an idea. It was nothing much, the product of boredom, curiosity and just a little affection, but years later I see that this was a moment – an arbitrary decision – whose consequences would endure.

I had met the old man hundreds of times, usually with my

dad, sometimes with my mum, occasionally with both, but I had never seen him alone or really talked to him.

The red-brick mansion was a little way up the road behind a huge, billiard-table lawn, featureless at this time of the year but for a giant cedar at the further corner towards the house; in summer it would be dotted with chairs, tables, and green-and-cream umbrellas. A young nurse opened the door and led me down the polished corridor to the day room. She said he'd be glad to see me; no one had been since the previous weekend.

Four old people were playing cards. Others were sitting about reading, chatting quietly and drinking tea. Uncle George was in his usual comfortable chair by the window, a book in his lap, a pot of tea and a slice of fruitcake at his side. He was gazing across the lawn to the river and the wooded hills beyond.

'David! Did you come by yourself?'

He was a little old man, terribly old, with brown skin and thin white hair cut short at the sides. He heaved himself up on the arms of the chair and craned round to see if I was alone.

I told him I was and that I'd been to the lock. 'There's nothing happening there, so I thought I'd come to see you.' Not very polite, I realised too late, but he didn't seem to mind.

'That's very nice of you. You must come more often, whenever you like. I'm always here.'

He had been living there since 1951, almost ten years. At first, he had treated it like a hotel, always out around the town, shopping, calling in for a half of bitter at the George and Dragon, dropping in on friends most of whom he had met through my father; he had joined the local fishing club and a bridge club.

My father was his nephew and, when Auntie Marie died, had suggested this luxury old-people's home instead of the house in which the old man couldn't bear to be alone. Even though it had meant moving a hundred miles to Marlow, a town where he knew no one except us, Uncle George had made a quick decision and had got on with enjoying the rest of his life.

Now well over ninety, he stayed at the home all the time except for an excursion by taxi every Tuesday to his friends, the Browns, a couple in their sixties who ran the grocery shop in the High Street. There he played bridge, always partnering Mrs Brown's spinster sister, whom he called Miss Robson. He even stopped coming to see us, although he would have been very welcome; my father's theory was that he was 'sweet on Miss Robson', a handsome, somewhat melancholy retired nurse.

I fetched an upright chair and sat in front of him, though I was careful not to block his view through the window. He pushed a button that dangled across the arm of his chair on the end of a lead attached to the wall. A foreign man in a white coat appeared.

'This is my great-nephew, David. He'd like orange squash and some cakes.'

When the man had gone, Uncle George smiled and leaned forward. 'Tell me, David. Are you a happy boy?'

I told him I was. Like all adults he asked if I liked school and we talked about my efforts as centre forward in the school football team. Then he asked about our house, which he hadn't visited in four years, though it was less than half a mile away. Which room did I have? Did my father still write in the room at the top in the front, and paint in the room at the back? Did my mother still work in the shop? What job was my father doing now? Was he still repairing televisions?

Repairing televisions had been my father's job before last. He had moved on from that to driving an ice-cream van about three years before: Eldorado ice cream. There had been three vans and because he was new my dad had had the oldest, which didn't play music. He had to stop the van, lean out of the window and ring a bell. I had often gone with him, rung the bell, and served ice cream and lollies from the other side of the van, back to back with my father, when things had got busy.

Now though, he worked for a nation-wide company driving around selling seeds to farmers, and, again, I went with him sometimes, just for fun. Uncle George seemed interested, though it surprised me that he didn't know this, since my father visited him at least once a week. I told him through mouthfuls of sponge cake where we went, at what time and for how long. His wiry white eyebrows waggled up and down as I spoke.

'He's always been full of energy, your father. Never gives up. Keeps on trying.' He tapped me on the knee, then leaned back and lowered both eyebrows. 'A bit like his own father, poor man . . . but different.'

'Why was Dad's dad poor?'

Eyebrows up again, he gazed out the window, then turned to me. 'He had a hard time, married to my sister. Your father doesn't really understand, but it's not his fault. Not Tom's fault either, not entirely, come to that.' He spoke slowly and thoughtfully, as though unsure whether he should say such things to an eleven-year-old boy.

'What happened to him? Dad hardly talks about him, except he says he drank too much whisky.'

'He's right about that. But why did he? That's the question.' He looked out of the window again, before turning back and staring at me as though this was a matter of importance. 'Your father should think about that. I've told him, but he won't listen.'

'Why not?'

'It upsets him. He was very young when Tom went away.'

Some rooks cawed loudly somewhere outside. A swan

rose from the river, straightened out and glided away over the weir. The man in the white jacket appeared again and filled my glass from a jug, without being asked.

'Why did he go away?'

Uncle George stared at me for a few moments, and then spoke quietly. 'Because he drank too much, too often.' He drew a long breath, while still looking me full in the eye. 'He sometimes', he breathed deeply again, 'upset your grandmother, my sister. We had to make him go away.'

I was interested in this family mishap, even though it had happened such a long time ago. My father hadn't told me about his father upsetting his mother, whatever that meant. Uncle George was looking across the river to the hills again; his thoughts seemed to be many years from now. I interrupted them. 'How do you know about it? Were you there?'

He smiled and raised one eyebrow; the other seemed to droop as if to balance its partner. 'I was there. We all lived together, you know.'

I did vaguely know that, a very long time ago when Queen Victoria, whose face was on the oldest, smoothest pennies, still reigned, my father had been a child in a house full of adults, and that when he was ten his father had disappeared from his life for ever. 'So who lived there? And where did Dad's dad go to?' This last question interested me particularly; where would a person go – a person who for some reason had to leave their home and family – what would a person like that do next?

The eyebrow went up again and Uncle George leaned sideways towards me. 'All right. I'll tell you all about it.' The foreign man appeared again; this time he filled the teapot with hot water and poured tea into Uncle George's cup. Uncle George just went on talking. 'My mother died when I was nine, in 1878. My father, your great-grandfather, had the same name as me, George Thompson. I had a younger brother, Ernest, and we had an older sister, Millie, which was short for Amelia, but everybody called her Sis. She was your grandmother, though you never met her.'

'Why was she called Sis?'

'When he was very small, my brother Ernest called her that because she was his sister. After that everyone called her Sis, even our father.'

I waited as he drank some tea and gazed out of the window.

Eventually he put his cup down on the saucer with a clatter. 'When my mother died, my father rented a new house – almost new anyway. It had been built about ten years before, in a road full of new houses in Dalston, east London.' He tapped my knee. 'That's why your dad supports the Spurs. He grew up a penny ride from the ground, and Tom took him before he went away. The Arsenal were still in south London then. That's why the Spurs supporters have always disliked the Arsenal supporters; they're interlopers, you see.' He chuckled quietly which made his eyebrows shoot down; he peered out at me through the stiff white hairs.

I knew my dad had supported the Spurs since he was a little boy. He had taken me to a match for the first time a few months before and I was a fervent fan. He had bought me a rosette and a blue plastic, star-shaped badge with a tiny photo of Danny Blanchflower stuck in the middle of it. Then he had bought a glossy white, wooden bird-scarer, carefully painted a dark blue stripe down it and presented it to me as my Spurs rattle.

'He would have gone to White Hart Lane first in the late 1890s. I took him myself sometimes after Tom left.' Uncle George paused. 'But that was all later, you've got to understand. I'm telling you about when *I* was a little boy which was even longer ago. It's a long story and we won't get through it all tonight. You'll have to go home soon I should think.'

I had a small Timex watch, of which I was very proud. It was ten past five. I could stay a little longer.

He told me how he had lived in the same house with his father, his brother and his sister from the age of nine until he got married in 1900, when he was thirty-one; that, after his mother died, his father's sister had come to look after them, and how they had had two servants who lived in the attic. After a while his father got fed up with the sister because she drank too much gin, but by then Sis, my grandmother, was a teenager and she took over the running of the house. She was a bossy type of person and bossed the servants and everyone else, except for her father, but then her father was often away selling furniture which was how he earned his living.

It took Uncle George a long time to tell me all this. I was fascinated – I had never heard anyone talk about things that happened so long ago – but what I really wanted to know was where did my grandfather go when he had to leave all the rest of them, and what did he do then. Eventually, though, I just had to have a pee and that made Uncle George think that it was time for me to go home. He would tell me more another day, he said.

Walking home, I thought about Uncle George and his eyebrows and my long-dead grandfather, whom Uncle George had called 'poor'. At the corner of Lock Road and Station Road I met Patrick and Dennis; they were leaning against the wall sharing a cigarette. Patrick held the packet towards me, but I said I was in a hurry and just took a quick pull on theirs.

When I got home I told my mother that I had been to see Uncle George. She told me I was sweet, and asked how the old man was.

'Fine,' I replied.

She had just got in from work and was standing at the kitchen table with an apron over her work skirt. It was

Tuesday, so she was mincing the leftovers of Sunday's joint to make rissoles.

'I'd better go and do my homework.'

'Just a minute.' She quickly rinsed her hands; then kissed me on the side of my mouth. I could smell her lipstick, and hoped that she couldn't smell tobacco smoke. 'It's so nice of you to go to see Uncle George.' She reached into her handbag and gave me a Penguin biscuit. 'Here – a treat.' She smiled and went back to turning the mincer.

Penguins, which cost threepence each, were an extravagance; squashed flies or bourbons from a packet were an acceptable expense. My mother was not mean – in spirit, she was generous – she was simply parsimonious, the product of the times and of years of living with a man who saw money simply as something to spend, preferably as soon as possible.

I took the Penguin up to my room and ate it slowly, staring out at the few cars parked in the street.

~

I called in on Uncle George a week later, again at about teatime. Orange squash and cakes were produced again, and he seemed pleased to see me, but he looked tired and was less talkative.

We talked about school and football and my father and mother, especially my mother this time. He told me how fond of her he was, and how my father and I must look after her. There were silences while he stared out of the window across the river to the tree-covered slope beyond, and he held my hand some of the time, something he had never done before.

After a while, he screwed up his eyes, stared at me and said, 'You know, I first met your mother in 1933.' He closed his eyes still tighter. 'Your father brought her to Sudbury to meet me and dear Marie.' He opened his eyes and smiled. 'Such a polite, quiet, gracious woman.' He tapped my knee.

'Now, is she happy? . . . I know she was upset when she had to sell the shop.'

She had sold the shop two years before. It was in the High Street and we had lived in large, airy rooms on the two floors above. I told him that I thought she was happy. I didn't tell him my worry about the way my father was sometimes unkind – even cruel, I thought – to her.

'Good. She deserves to be happy. She's a woman with a great sense of duty . . . It comes from her upper-class English upbringing.'

I had an idea of what he meant, but he seemed to have forgotten that my granny, my mother's mother, was American.

Uncle George continued to smile, though he looked tired. 'You've made her very happy, David. You know that, don't you?' He leaned forward and poked at my knee again. 'They were married for sixteen years before they had you, you know.'

'I know,' I said wearily. My father mentioned this fact almost every time we met someone new, especially new farmers: 'This is my son David. We were married sixteen years before he came along.' Depending on the response, this was often followed by: 'My third marriage. My eldest son's forty-five and this one's eleven . . .' His arm would then be placed round my shoulder. 'Remarkable.'

They had married in 1933, and I, their first and only child, was born in 1948. My father was then fifty-six and my mother forty-two, but I could never understand why this should be of such interest to people, especially complete strangers.

Uncle George took my hand again and leaned back in his chair. He shut his eyes for a minute, and I wondered whether he had gone to sleep. When he opened them, they were watery, and he spoke about his wife, Marie: how pretty she had been and how he still missed her. He pronounced her name with a long 'a' sound and the emphasis on the first syllable.

The same foreign man refilled his teacup and my glass, and then I asked him about my whisky-drinking, disappearing grandfather and where he went after he had to leave home.

He took several sips of tea while staring at me over the rim of the cup. He put the cup down slowly and carefully, and turned his eyes back to mine. 'When you are grown-up and can afford to travel, you must go to Swan River, Manitoba.' Despite his obvious tiredness he said this with great earnestness, nodding, waggling his eyebrows and tapping my knee quite hard.

I felt a little strange, as though I had heard bad news, although he was smiling at me now. I had never heard of Swan River or Manitoba, but I felt that I had to obey this curious instruction, as if suddenly I had a duty. I asked him why and where was it, but he was looking down at the floor and didn't seem to be listening.

'Is that where my grandfather went?'

He looked up at me, nodded and smiled; then he looked at his old Omega watch and said he was tired and that it was a long story and Billy Cotton's *Band Show* would be on television soon; he would explain next time I visited him. 'But remember, Swan River, Manitoba.' Again, he said the words with emphasis and then smiled.

It was a quarter to six; Billy Cotton would not, in fact, start up for another fifteen minutes; the sun had long gone off the river and the trees. He said no more about Swan River, but talked about his brother Ernest's first wife who had worked in the music halls around the turn of the century. There was clearly a connection in his mind between her and Billy Cotton whose show was a variety show, the closest thing on television in 1960 to the kind of entertainment Uncle George had loved as a young man.

Ernest's wife had earned her living in the music halls by

playing the violin with her feet while walking around on her hands. She could even do this while going downstairs, Uncle George said, and sometimes practised at home in the house where they all lived. This amazed me. I found it hard to picture; I could see her only as a still image, but not in motion. She had an exotic name, La Frascetti, he told me, although she was English and came from the East End of London, and her real name was Rose Porter.

Just before six o'clock Uncle George asked the foreign man to turn on the television. A thin old man with a stick walked slowly past and raised his hand to Uncle George in greeting; he sat down near us and stared up at the television, sitting very straight with his hands on his stick. As I finished my orange squash, I watched the opening number, Billy Cotton's band playing their signature tune while the Television Toppers kicked their legs. I left after that, kissing Uncle George on the forehead as I went. He smiled, squeezed my hand tightly and muttered, 'Good boy.'

Walking home, I repeated the word 'Manitoba' so I wouldn't forget it. I didn't tell my parents what Uncle George had said; it seemed to be something that was just between me and the old man, for the moment, anyway. Later, lying on my bed, I wrote 'Swan River, Manitober' in the red, soft-backed notebook that I kept for my very few secrets.

Uncle George died unexpectedly in his sleep six days later, for no particular reason. I had planned to visit him again the following day. My mother told me that the foreign man had found Uncle George when he took in his early-morning tea; he was in bed as if asleep, but not breathing. 'He died peacefully,' she said.

Through the crack in our living-room door I saw my father sitting alone crying with a handkerchief in his hand. I went away because I didn't want to embarrass him, fetched my satchel and left for school. My father took the day off work. When I came home, he was standing in the hall, speaking on the telephone; my mother came back from work and said he had probably been standing there all day and that we really ought to put a chair in the hall.

~

The funeral was a generous occasion, conducted in the church by the white suspension bridge, a short walk from Uncle George's home by the lock. There were crowds of people, lots of them very old; children; flowers; a halting address by Mr Brown from the grocery; the choir singing 'Jesu, Joy of Man's Desiring'; the vicar in white with shimmering purple extras. I sang loudly, sandwiched between my parents in the front pew, and my mother stolidly held my hand. All around us were cousins of all ages, most of whom I didn't know: Uncle George's children, grandchildren and great-grandchildren. My father, a lifelong atheist, but then in the middle of his brief religious phase, wept not quite silently and knelt, head in hands, longer than anyone at the end.

As we walked down the aisle I was introduced to two elderly women who were Uncle George's nieces, the daughters of the long-dead Uncle Ernest. I was disappointed to discover later that they were not the daughters of the fascinating La Frascetti, but of a piano teacher who had been Uncle Ernest's second wife.

In the churchyard, a weak, late-winter sun lit the grass around the red-brown rectangle; brass and varnished pine gleamed; spoonfuls of earth were thrown with a polished spade – first by the many cousins, then my father, then my mother, then me.

Later, still holding my mother's hand, I wandered among the graves, past an ancient yew, to the river. Two swans glided in small circles near the weir. A car's horn sounded from the bottom of the High Street.

'Where is Swan River, Manitoba?'

My mother looked at me curiously. She was wearing her calf-length black tweed suit. 'Manitoba is in Canada. Why?' She swung her black handbag with the gilt clasp from her right hand to her left.

'Uncle George told me to go there.'

'Did he? You'd better ask Daddy.'

I took her arm and pressed my cheek against her shoulder as we wandered back and out of the churchyard to the street. It had been my first funeral. That Uncle George was in that smart box under the ground now seemed less strange than when I had first seen the coffin, covered in daffodils and lilies, and had asked my mother, 'Is Uncle George actually in there?'

~

Uncle George's wake, or 'the do afterwards' as people called it, was at Burger's Tea Shop, a little way up the High Street. A long table for us children at one end was matched by another for old people from the nursing home, at the other. In between was an uproar of polite adult chatter which I carefully ignored, although I was pleased and stood up when the foreign man approached me hesitantly and said how much he had liked Uncle George.

I sat with my friend Deborah, whose father ran the sweetshop further up the street and who was the only person privy to the secrets in my red notebook. Out of earshot of my mates, Richard and Adam, I asked her whether she'd come with me to Swan River, Manitoba, Canada.

She was slim and had short brown hair, and showed her gums when she smiled. We had been friends since we were five, had, indeed, shown each other everything when we were five, and had been caught in the bathroom together by Deborah's mother – a shameful discovery which had led to a row between our fathers, mine liberal and fiery-tempered, hers conservative and kindly.

'Yes. When we leave school.' She forked in a rectangle of Welsh rarebit, chewed, swallowed, tilted her head sideways and gazed at me from under her hair. 'We'll have to go on a boat, won't we?'

'Probably, I'm going to ask Dad where it is.'

'Canada is in America. You have to go on a boat to get there.'

My father had flown to Australia and back four years before and had made a tremendous fuss about it, filling a complete photograph album with tiny black and white pictures of a silver aeroplane with four propellers and even more of himself standing under palm trees dressed in white wearing a curious hat that looked like an oval fruit bowl, but everyone else who went anywhere abroad seemed to go by boat.

Deborah didn't ask why we were to go to Swan River; she loved an adventure, and had been an avid reader of Arthur Ransome. If I had suggested a trip to somewhere with a less watery name, San Francisco, say, or Staines, she would probably have wrinkled her nose and said 'No'. When we were younger we had often had fantasies about what we would do when we grew up, and had made detailed plans which we wrote into my red book.

Richard and Adam, currently separated from us by a crowd of my young cousins, had little imagination and no thought for the future; they seemed to live solely in the real world and in the present. But Deborah's ability to fantasise frequently dovetailed with my own. On this occasion, though, I had a new, scary feeling; going to Swan River wasn't just an imaginative game.

2

On the Road with the Seed Salesman

MY FATHER HAD GLASSES with thick black rims in those days. He looked not unlike Harry Worth and was often just as funny, but he had a serious side – a very serious side – as well.

The next evening he and I watched *The Brains Trust*. I didn't understand much of what *The Brains Trust* talked about, but I liked the people's names – Bertrand Russell, Dame Edith Sitwell, Doctor Bronowski, Lady Violet Bonham-Carter – and I found their serious faces and their accents somehow entertaining. And this was a rare time when I could be with my father while he listened to someone else talk instead of talking himself.

When the programme ended I spoke before he did. 'The last time I saw him, Uncle George told me to go to Swan River, Manitoba, once I'm grown-up.'

My father leaned back in his loose-covered armchair and stared at me intently for a few seconds. He took off his glasses, pulled out the handkerchief he always kept in the breast pocket of his tweed jacket, waved it about a bit and blew his nose loudly and thoroughly. Stuffing the handkerchief back and replacing his glasses, he looked at me again. 'My father spent the last part of his life in Swan River, Manitoba.' Unusually, he fell silent – and stopped looking at me. He stared at the carpet instead.

'Why would Uncle George tell me to go there?' I asked this a little tentatively – it was clearly a sensitive matter.

He got up and poked the Cosy Stove vigorously. Yellow

and blue flames appeared on top of the anthracite. Still standing, he said, 'My Uncle George was a very kind man, a very liberal man – if you know what I mean. He found it hard to think badly of anyone.'

He walked back to his chair and sat down, throwing one knee over the other. He picked up his tin from the table and began to roll a cigarette. 'Uncle George thought there was good in my father.'

He licked the Rizla paper and stared at the floor again. 'It's what they call a long story.' He lit the cigarette with his shiny Ronson and inhaled. 'Very long indeed. I'll tell you it all, but not all at once.'

He blew blue smoke towards the ceiling and it gradually formed a horizontal cloud above our heads. 'It's complicated . . . Or it's very simple, depending on your point of view . . . Where's your mother? Let's play Cluedo. I'll be Professor Plum.'

~

I knew we would talk about it, because I spent a lot of time with my father and talking was his great talent. Though he was sixty-eight years old, he worked hard at his job selling seeds, driving from farm to farm all over Buckinghamshire in an Austin A35 supplied by his employers, persuading farmers that his varieties of wheat, barley and oats were better than those of his competitors. He was very good at this – he was his firm's nationwide champion salesman for the whole country that year and the next. I often went with him in the holidays and in the afternoons after school, map-reading, finding farms he had never visited before. We talked a lot on these journeys, and we talked early in the mornings before my mother got up.

As well as being a generation older than my friends' dads, my dad seemed to have had a more complicated life than they had. Richard's father was in the RAF and had been ever since his call-up during World War II; he was 'ground staff' and my father referred to him as 'the man with the ping-pong bats'. Adam's father taught politics at the London School of Economics; my father approved of him and they had frequent, reasonably friendly arguments. Deborah's father ran a sweet-shop and always had done as far as I knew.

These three men had been married only once. My father had been married three times; had, I understood, been very rich and very poor; and had had more jobs than he had had cars, which was a lot. He had once written me a list of all the cars he had ever owned; it began with something called an Invicta, which he had bought in 1912 when he was twenty, and continued over two pages.

During World War II he had done three jobs at once: he had managed his own furniture business in High Wycombe; had, with no previous experience, run a farm on a hill just outside that town; and had written a series of autobiographical books about life on the farm – they were sub-titled 'One Hundred Acres Farmed by an Amateur'. He had been 'too old to fight' in that war and told me without shame that he was 'a coward' and that, had he been young enough to be called up, he would have avoided fighting anyway, as he had, fortuitously, during World War I.

The books – four of them – had made him quite wealthy. In the three years between the end of the war and my birth, he had owned a Rolls-Royce and a yacht. I had seen photographs of both, and there was a model of the yacht in a glass case on top of the cabinet containing the *Encyclopaedia Britannica* in our living room. When I asked my mother about this period of their life, she downplayed both these signs of riches: the Rolls-Royce was an old second-hand one, and the yacht was not what some people would call a yacht – it was a large sailing boat with room for eight people.

These days, he wasn't wealthy. He had spent the money from the books, sold the yacht and the Rolls-Royce, and wound up the furniture business long ago. After the war, his publishers had brought out four more books with decreasing success and had, in 1950, declined to publish his ninth. Despite this, he still woke every morning at 5 a.m. and wrote for about three hours, either with a fountain pen, sitting up in bed, or on a black portable typewriter at his roll-top desk, wearing his dressing gown over his pyjamas.

When I was younger, before I liked reading, I would go to his room every morning as soon I woke up and he would stop writing and play games with me, or I would climb into bed with him and he would tell me exciting, made-up, adventure stories. He taught me chess, cribbage and bezique, and he made a board on which we played shove ha'penny. He liked to play with me, his late child, born late in a late marriage, and I took it as the joke he intended when he said that his writing career ended when I started to demand his attention.

I loved him, and I loved being with him, but he had a demon. It showed itself in frightening outbursts of rage, sometimes vented on strangers in shops or in traffic, only rarely on me; I had learned to recognise the stirrings and to back away. But my mother couldn't escape; she was the enduring receptacle for his wrath. In his presence she was quiet and subdued; away from him she came to life and laughed. He seemed compelled to destroy her spirit – and he succeeded in dulling her brightness – but I knew that it would never leave her altogether. I loved her unreservedly, and couldn't understand why this otherwise clever, funny and kind man should attack someone so innocent and so perfect.

The mood came upon him most frequently during breakfast, as my parents sat with their newspapers at opposite ends of the table, with me in between. Often he would read out something he had written that morning and ask for her opinion. But no response was ever adequate. A positive comment provoked a sneering shrug, as if her opinion were of no consequence; a critical one led to an interrogation as he pinned down with ruthless logic precisely what she meant and proved – to his own satisfaction at least – that she was both stupid and wrong. The exchange might end with him shouting 'I cannot suffer fools gladly' in the ugly tone I had heard him use to bank clerks and shop assistants, and with my mother gently sighing and drawing her paper up in front of her face. My hands and arms and shoulders would tingle with the fear that he would hit her. And I wondered what would happen then. And I wondered why and I wished it would stop.

He was always Professor Plum, but we didn't play Cluedo that day because we couldn't find my mother. At first neither of us could think where she was. We had gone into the garden to look for her and were gazing at the budgies when my father said, 'I know. She's warbling . . . She's gone to practise warbling in a bonnet.'

'What's that? What's warbling in a bonnet?'

'*HMS Pinafore*. You know, the opera. They always wear bonnets in *HMS Pinafore*. She's in it, God help us. Mrs . . . Whatsername persuaded her.'

I remembered then. She was at the Liston Hall in Chapel Street, rehearsing.

'She has to learn how to warble in a bonnet,' my father said abstractedly. 'You don't have to learn, do you?' He was talking to one of his budgerigars.

'She left us a shepherd's pie.'

He didn't seem to hear me. 'How many will be purple? That is the question.' He was looking at a small wooden nesting box, high up at the back of the aviary. 'What do you think, Sunny Jim?'

'Three out of four,' I replied.

The budgerigars had been an enthusiasm for about two years; my father had built a lean-to aviary out of two-by-one and chicken wire, installed nesting boxes and bought four adult budgies, two of each gender. Despite minor setbacks – tiny, blind, pink creatures falling to the ground and being tended to in the house, often unsuccessfully, with eye-droppers filled with warm milk – the aviary was now packed with budgerigars and, reluctantly at first, he had started to sell them by advertising in the *Bucks Free Press*. The next stage had been to specialise in budgies of a certain colour; he and I both liked an unusual pastel purple; he had isolated two birds of this colour and we had waited expectantly to see if their children would turn out the same.

To prevent my hopes from rising too high, he had read out loud to me long sections of *The Origin of Species* and tedious articles from the *Encylopaedia Britannica*. He was expecting 'throwbacks' as detailed in these two publications, and we got them: of the three surviving children, one was purple and the other two were green. The purple youngster, who turned out to be a girl, had taken ten months to reach adulthood and had then been isolated with a purple cousin – not with her father, because that way we might produce a new colour altogether, if we carried on long enough, according to my father and Darwin – and we were now waiting to see what would happen.

'All right. Two bob. I'll give you two bob if we get three out of four.'

Two shillings was a lot of money, but I tried for more by looking disappointed and saying, 'Oh, go on. Five bob. There might not even be four.'

He looked at me sharply. 'No, two bob. Two bob's enough.'

My pocket money, paid to me by my mother, was one shilling a week. My father gave me money sporadically when it occurred to him, which tended to be simply when he was feeling flush, or when he heard that I had done something good, scoring a goal or getting high marks at school; he gave me sixpence if I found a new farm on the Ordnance Survey map, but only if it led to a sale, which had happened six times in his two-year career as a seed salesman.

And then there were the bets. The odds were against me, but then, I never had to pay out. 'What colour will the next car we see be?' 'Red.' He would then think for a couple of seconds. 'OK. A penny.' Red and blue were usually a penny; black and white twopence; green threepence; and wishy-washy colours like beige and maroon might go as high as sixpence. We also betted on types of car, types of people – 'lady with grey hair' – animals, traffic lights, pubs – defined by brewer – and any random thing that entered my father's head as we drove around the lanes of Buckinghamshire.

On a cold, sunny afternoon in the week after Uncle George's funeral my father and I drove up a long gravel drive, lined with new young conifers. At the end was a large, dull, red-brick house; roses were sprinkled in geometric patterns across recently mown grass; and several girls and a very small boy were trotting around a horse-filled paddock while a bossy woman in a sleek headscarf shouted and waved a whip about.

Although he knew he had to do business with the farm manager who would be in the farmyard round the back, my father stopped the car and walked across the gravel to the front door. He wanted to greet the owner even though he didn't like him; he was one of what my dad called 'the idle rich', but he paid the bills and, more importantly, might easily be induced to buy his seeds from the competition for the price of a few gin-and-tonics. My father had to maintain a presence and he was at a disadvantage in this one respect; he hated alcohol and would only visit pubs if this was absolutely essential to further business; inside a pub he would order bottled Carlsberg and drink it as slowly as possible.

On this occasion I stayed in the car while he talked to a small, aggressive man in a tight checked jacket, cavalry twills and a flat cap that looked as though it had just been ironed. He soon returned exclaiming, 'God *strewth*, that man thinks he's God almighty!'

'And he's a bloody fool,' he added as we drove round the back through some small cypresses, past a garage containing a highly polished, bottle-green Jaguar 2.8, to the farmyard. Here the gravel became tarmac, streaked with just a little mud. The bailiff appeared immediately. He had neatly brushed hair and no mud on his clothes, but he did know about farming and my father enjoyed chatting with him about 'yields per acre', 'straight ears', 'one-year leys' and endless stuff, some of which I had begun to understand.

That this man respected and trusted my dad went without saying; more unusually, he remembered me and my name and called his sheepdog for me to pat. He ordered several hundredweight of Koga 2, at that time my father's revolutionary new line of wheat, signing the order that my father wrote out in his order book. As we drove back past the house, the man in the checked jacket was standing on the gravel talking to the woman in the headscarf. My father lifted his hand from the steering wheel and waved rather formally; the man nodded. My father glanced at me. 'Never forget, Sunny Jim: no person of quality esteems another merely because he is rich.'

'Yes, Dad.' I had heard this before.

The speed and success of this call left my father wondering what to do next. We sat in the A35, deliberating. We could go home or we could visit someone else. I knew we were close to my favourite farmer and his wife.

'Can we go and see Dor and Narby?'

He turned and smiled at me knowingly; he liked Nobby and Doreen Cox as much as I did. He pushed his hat backwards so that it hit the ceiling of the little car and removed his glasses while continuing to smile to himself. He shut his eyes and pulled his thumb and forefinger across them to his nose; then he opened his eyes, blinked and replaced his glasses.

'All right, Sunny Jim. There's no sale in it, but it's good customer relations . . . And we'll get some tea.'

He turned the ignition and flicked the black plastic knob under the windscreen, unnecessarily activating the indicator. With only average grunting and cursing, he performed a seven-point turn in the country lane and we were off down a gradual curving hill with the Chilterns high above the hedge to our right. We passed through a long straggly village without speaking.

'Could you tell me more about your father?'

He felt inside his overcoat, pulled his handkerchief from the breast pocket of his jacket and blew his nose noisily. Then he held the steering wheel and his handkerchief with his left hand while gently drumming with his fingers and thumb on the black plastic spoke beneath his right hand. The drumming meant that he was thinking.

'It's a story about my mother as well. There are two sides to every story.'

He replaced his handkerchief, changed down a gear as the car began to slow on a hill, rummaged in his side pocket and handed me a small, shiny tin. 'Roll me a cigarette; there's a good chap.'

I often did this and took some pride in my prowess. My friends' fathers seemed to smoke ready-made Player's Navy Cut, or not to smoke at all which I found very dull. In the shiny tin was a little machine comprising two rollers with waxed cloth stretched over them. I pulled a Rizla paper from the green packet, placed it in the cloth between the rollers, tugged tobacco from the silver paper packet labelled 'A1', crammed it down on to the paper, pinched the rollers together, twiddled them so that only the gummed edge of the paper stuck out, licked the gum, twiddled some more, pushed the rollers apart and there was a perfect cigarette.

It took me less than a minute on this occasion. Meanwhile he was telling me that it was hard for him to know whether to begin with his father or his mother. I suggested he start with his father and why he went to Swan River, Manitoba.

'But that's the end of the story, you see.'

He turned and looked at me, then looked quickly back at the road. I handed him the cigarette which he stuck in his mouth while searching in his jacket pocket for his Ronson.

'And once he goes, there's no more to tell about him.'

His voice quavered a little and his eyes were watering. I was embarrassed, and part of me wished I hadn't asked the question. He had cried in my presence many times, but we had usually been watching a film, either at the cinema or on television. I put my hand on his forearm, and he lifted his other hand from the steering wheel and put it on top of mine for a few moments.

As we drove towards Nobby Cox's farm he began talking about the house, his grandfather's house, the one Uncle George had told me about, and the people who had lived in it while he had been growing up in the 1890s.

His memories were of a house crammed with people – his grandfather who was called George; his mother, Amelia, usually known as 'Sis'; his father, Tom; his uncles, George and Ernest; his aunt, Rose – the astonishing La Frascetti – Uncle Ernest's first wife; and two servants, both called Alice. He described most of them at some length. It seemed that he had the fondest memories of his grandfather, his mother and Uncle George. Uncle Ernest and La Frascetti had been intriguing characters, but away from home a lot performing in music halls in Britain and abroad. Last of all he mentioned his little sister, Gladys.

Not only had all these people lived in one house, but

numerous relations had dropped in all the time because his grandfather had been the eldest of seven brothers and sisters, most of whom had lived nearby with their spouses, children and grandchildren. The house had been run, somewhat imperiously, by Sis, my father's mother, who had taken charge in her teens and who had deferred to no one except her own father, to whom she, and all the rest of them, had deferred a great deal.

By the time my father had told me all this, including naming and describing all his great uncles and aunts, we had been parked in the lane outside the Coxes' farm for almost an hour. All the time I had expected that the next minute we would get out of the car and change into our wellingtons for the tramp through the Coxes' sticky farmyard, but there was always just one more person, or another detail, that my father had to mention. Eventually we picked our way past derelict farm machinery to the Coxes' back door. It was the kind of home where the front path, the front door and the front room were clean and neat but barely used. My father speculated that the Coxes would have people they regarded as superior – such as their landlord, or an official from the Milk Marketing Board or the vicar – in their front room, but not friends or tradesmen.

The half-hour we spent with the Coxes took my mind off the story of my grandfather Tom, and Uncle George's curious instruction; but later, in bed, I thought about all my father had told me in the car. He had given me a quick but vivid account of his childhood. It seemed a magical time to me with horses instead of cars, gaslight instead of electricity, singsongs around pianos, family parties with numerous aunts and uncles and cousins, and servants to help with the work. And I could imagine the people who had lived in that house in Dalston: the grey-haired, bearded patriarch; the strong young woman; the handsome, moustachioed man who had married her and turned to drink; the two brothers, one slick, talkative and witty, the other introspective and kindly; the young, pretty, servant and the blowsy, larger one. I had had a picture in my mind of the music-hall artiste since Uncle George had first described her; I saw her more fully now: brash, determined, physical and friendly. I could imagine the house as well; it was like ours but on a grander scale and with an extra floor – the basement, where the kitchen was.

There were two things I didn't know, and Uncle George had in different ways asked both questions: 'Ah! But why did he drink so much? That's the question,' and what had he done in Swan River, Manitoba?

3

Deborah and the Outsiders

DEBORAH AND I HAD known each other since we were four, when my mother had used money left to her by her father to open a shop selling china and glass two doors from Deborah's father's sweetshop in the High Street. She was one month younger than me, born on the same day as Prince Charles, the little boy on our savings stamps. We had much in common. We both lived above shops in which three of our parents worked long hours, and neither of us had siblings.

We fell into a sister-brother relationship with none of the bad bits; we didn't have to compete for our parents' attention and we could get away from each other if we wanted to. As we grew older and went to different schools, we found friends of our own sex with whom we spent more time, but the closeness remained, even after my mother's shop failed and we moved to our house a quarter of a mile away in Station Road. My mother became the bookkeeper at what had been her own shop, which meant that I went on spending time among the china and glass.

We met in the library the next Saturday – it was the first time we had seen each other since Uncle George's funeral – and later we walked through the back streets towards the lock. I told her that I had found Swan River in my father's atlas and that Manitoba seemed to be right in the middle of Canada, with Swan River about half-way up it, on the left-hand side.

At the lock, leaning on one of the beams, staring down at

the water, I said, 'What I really want to know is what Uncle George thinks – thought, rather – I'll find in Swan River.'

'We. I'm coming too. I am, really.'

'And when are we going to go?'

She looked up at the sky. 'When we're eighteen, nineteen, something like that . . . When we've saved some money.'

This meant seven or eight years' time, and it seemed like for ever. But we solemnly agreed that we would go there together as soon as we had enough money after we left school. Deborah said that this seemed like a Famous Five adventure. To me 'Two Go to Swan River' was more real than a story in a book or our other wild schemes, because I believed that, one day, it would actually happen.

There was a solitary motor launch waiting to enter the lock, and we helped the lock-keeper open the gates and sluices to let it through; then we walked along the towpath downstream past the bird sanctuary, an ancient wood beside the path where humans were forbidden but which I had frequently entered with Richard and Adam. We were silent most of the time, but spoke whenever one of us had an idea.

I told her that, now that I had time to think about it, Swan River, Manitoba, was beginning to seem more of a worry than a potential adventure. She took my hand, turned to me and said that it couldn't matter that much; Old Tom, as she called my grandfather, was dead; Uncle George had been very old when he made his odd request; it would just be something interesting, rather than worrying or important; besides, she'd come with me, she really would. She put her arm round my shoulder.

The conversation meandered on, confused and inconclusive, as we walked back to the lock and on to my house, which was distinguished from the others in the street by its bright green window-frames and doors, the work of its previous owner. My mother had wanted to paint them white, but my father had said he liked the green – it reminded him of a cricket pavilion near Oxford that he had once slept in – but, to please her, he had painted the picket fence in front of the privet a brilliant white.

The house was three storey, late Victorian, end of terrace. The front door and the back door, which led into the kitchen, were down a path at the side where there was more green paint. Inside it was neither spacious nor poky; the furniture was mostly old, comfortable rather than elegant. For some reason, perhaps to avoid a disagreement between themselves, my parents had given me the best bedroom, on the first floor at the front. My mother's bedroom was across the landing from mine and my father's was on the floor above. A curiosity that occasionally caused problems was that the bathroom, which contained the lavatory, could only be reached by walking through my mother's room.

Deborah and I found my mother sitting at the kitchen table reading *Woman's Realm*. It was the weekend and she had a relaxed look; she was wearing a loose pink jumper, knitted for her by her mother, with the sleeves pushed up to her elbows, shiny red beads around her neck and no lipstick. I always thought she looked better without lipstick; it was something she put on to go to work and the carmine red clashed with the cool greys and greens in her eyes. She had an intelligent face with a strong jaw and a bony nose; she had been slim and beautiful in her late twenties when my father had first met her. Now, there were gentle wrinkles, but many people still looked at her twice.

A warmth came into her face as she looked up from the magazine. She and Deborah were good friends, to the extent of sharing jokes about me. She asked if Deborah would like to stay for lunch and, without waiting for a reply, told us it wouldn't be ready for a while because it included baked potatoes.

Upstairs, in my room, Deborah asked why Tom Reynolds

left his home and wife and child, and I told her what Uncle George had said, that he drank too much and upset my grandmother, and that Uncle George and the others had made him go away.

I got out my secrets notebook and wrote out a list of the people who had lived in the house in Dalston. Remembering the conversation I had had with my father in the car, I knew there were nine, including him and two servants; the names quickly came back to me. We were lying on our stomachs on the carpet under the huge map of the British Isles, with the counties coloured in pink, orange, yellow, green and purple, which my father had framed and given to me as a Christmas present. Deborah stared at my list with her chin on one hand. She giggled. 'Who is Rose Porter? And what's this mean?' She hesitated 'La Fras . . . what?'

'She was married to Uncle Ernest,' I pointed to his name, 'and could walk about on her hands while playing the violin with her feet . . . really!' Deborah was laughing and shaking her head from side to side, her hair swinging and brushing the carpet.

'Impossible. How could she?'

'I don't know, but she did. It was her job. She did it in the music halls they had then; you know, an act, like an acrobat but with music.' I found this funny too. 'That's what they say, Uncle George and Dad.'

Still giggling, Deborah stood up, pushed off her shoes and did a hand-stand against the wall. I sat cross-legged watching her. She moved one hand away from the wall and then, more tentatively, the other. She took another step, bent her knees to bring her feet closer together and collapsed on to her back with her feet up the wall. 'See. It's completely impossible.'

I took my shoes off and tried, starting off against the opposite wall. I staggered on my hands and fell in a twisted heap. Deborah picked up my notebook and biro, found my ruler and lay on her front on the carpet again. Very carefully,

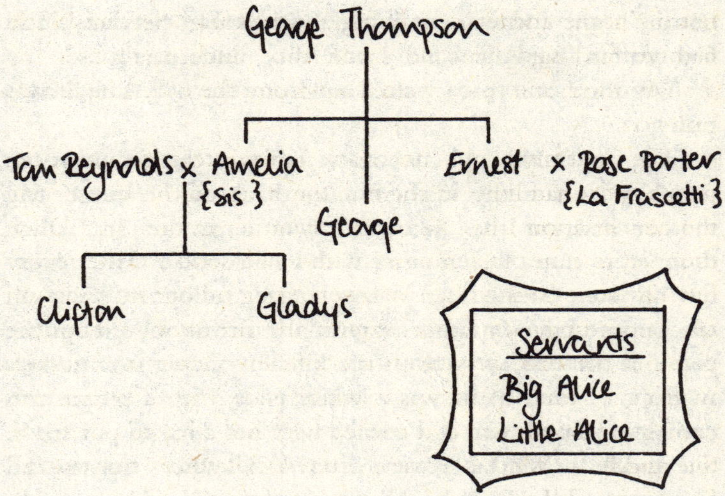

with her nose an inch or two from the paper, she drew a family tree on the page opposite my list, asking me questions to make sure she got it right. It had three generations – my father's grandfather, George Thompson, was alone at the top; there was a long middle line with five people; before she drew the bottom line, I told her my father had had a sister, Gladys, who had died a long time ago.

'So she lived there too. There were ten people living there, then.' I nodded. She muttered to herself, 'Ten people, and two of them were called George and two of them were called Alice.' She used the ruler to draw a horizontal line across the end of the vertical one which led from the 'x' between 'Tom Reynolds' and 'Amelia', and in small, neat writing wrote 'Clifton' and 'Gladys' at the bottom.

'There. Done.' She turned the book round and pushed it over to me. I studied the page carefully. It was all neat and, as far as I knew, accurate. On the middle line, underneath 'Rose Porter', Deborah had written 'La Frascetti' and had framed these words with ornate brackets. She had drawn a box in the bottom right corner containing the heading 'Servants', and had written 'Big Alice' and 'Little Alice' underneath.

My mother's voice wafted up from the hall. Lunch was ready.

We ate at the old mahogany table in the dining-room which led on to the kitchen at the back of the house. My mother had put the *Nutcracker Suite*, a pile of 78s which dropped on top of each other with a click and a clatter every few minutes, on the huge walnut-veneer radiogram. Deborah sat opposite me. My father sat with his back to our old upright piano at the end away from the kitchen, facing my mother. In front of each of us was a white plate with a purple rim containing sliced ham and corned beef and a baked potato. In the middle of the table were a bowl of lettuce, tomato and cucumber salad, a circular, blue-and-white-striped butter dish, a contraption made up of two small bottles with curved necks stuck together which dispensed oil and vinegar, bottles of Heinz salad cream and Colman's mustard, jugs containing orange squash and water, a small wooden pepper-grinder and a glass salt cellar with a silver screw-on top.

We all helped ourselves, passing items around politely; my father poured orange squash for me and Deborah and water for himself and my mother, and made great play of grinding a huge quantity of pepper over everything on his plate. My mother, bright and chirpy whenever my friends were around, talked about summer holidays; we were going to Ilfracombe again, and Deborah was going to Saundersfoot. The merits of different types of caravan were discussed and how both caravan sites had games rooms with ping-pong. My father mentioned the fly-fishing in north Devon, and told us he preferred chess to ping-pong as a rainy-day activity.

When the first course was over, everyone ignored my mother's instruction to stay seated while she fetched the pudding; instead we all stood up and carried everything into the kitchen. The next course was tinned peaches with raspberry-ripple ice cream. While my mother was dishing this out, Deborah asked my father about La Frascetti; was it really true what I had told her, that she could walk about on her hands while playing the violin with her feet?

He smiled and leant across the table towards her. 'I saw her do it many times. She used to practise in our house, in the front room, in the hall, on the stairs. The high point of her act was walking on her hands downstairs while playing a popular tune with her feet. Later I saw her performing at the Hackney Empire, the Britannia in Hoxton and . . .' He paused and stared at the floor, trying hard to remember. At last it came to him, 'Collins's Music Hall in Islington. But she went all over the world, America, Russia, Europe. She was a big act and earned lots of money. My uncle Ernest was her manager for a while, and then became part of the act. I remember seeing him on stage at Collins's, dressed in a top hat and cloak, while she did her acrobatics wearing spangly short dresses and tights like the Television Toppers.'

He took a spoonful of peaches and ice cream. Deborah and I both spoke at once. 'But how did she do it? Hold the violin . . .' 'Could everybody see her bottom?'

My mother laughed. My father ignored me and continued speaking to Deborah. 'She held the bow between her big toe and the next one, and the violin was fastened to her other foot with a strap.'

Deborah put her fingers in her hair and frowned. 'I can't imagine it.'

'Well, she stood on her hands with her knees bent and her feet above her bottom, which you could see, incidentally, although she wore silk knickers with sequins all over them,' he turned quickly to me with a smile and back to Deborah again, 'and somehow managed to push the bow across the strings. It was remarkable to watch.' He took another spoonful. 'Although, when I first saw her at home, I was small and thought nothing of it. I grew up with Rose walking about on her hands in the house, and it didn't seem odd until I got older and my friends started wanting to come round and have a look.'

My mother turned the pile of 78s over and Tchaikovsky came quietly from the corner of the room again. Deborah and I had second helpings of ice cream.

'How did she actually play the notes?' Deborah wrinkled her nose and looked at my father.

This provoked a long discussion involving my mother as well, because my father didn't really know the answer and my mother was the musical one. They decided between them that La Frascetti's violin must have been tuned to four particular notes and that she had probably played the main notes in a popular tune or chorus; even my father admitted that it was unlikely that she could actually hold down the strings with her toes while standing on her hands. As far as my father could remember from the four or so times that he had seen her perform in public, she had always had musical accompaniment; certainly drum rolls and clashing cymbals at the climactic moments; on some occasions he had seen Uncle Ernest playing a xylophone and there had usually been a small orchestra in the pit at the music hall.

My mother had a theory about black notes. She switched off Tchaikovsky and tried various old tunes on the piano to see if any contained just four of them. My father kept whistling something which he said was called 'The Belle of New York'; my mother found this hard to play but got it eventually. It did indeed contain four black notes, and they both got very excited, convinced that these were the very notes that La Frascetti had played all those years ago. My mother played it over and over, hitting the black notes higher up the piano to simulate our long-forgotten ancestor bowing her violin with her feet, while my father drummed on a table mat with two bendy knives.

Eventually my mother went to the kitchen, saying that she didn't need any help with the washing-up. Deborah and I followed her, grabbed tea towels and dried up, and my father came in to put the plates and cutlery away, before going off to the sitting-room for his afternoon nap.

Deborah and I went back up to my room. We stood up for a while, staring down at the family tree on the floor. I said, 'You ought to put "Sis" in brackets underneath "Amelia". That's what they all called her.'

'Did they all call her "La Frascetti"?' She pointed to the words.

'No, stupid. They must have called her Rose.'

'So names in brackets aren't what people were called.'

'Well . . .' This was tiresome. I was about to talk about people having two names for whatever reason, but then she giggled, knelt down and wrote the word with two ornamental brackets.

'What was she like, Sis?'

I thought about it. Uncle George had said that she had given her husband a hard time. She had died in 1942; my mother had known her too, and despite her reluctance to criticise anyone, I knew she had found her bossy and hard to get close to. My father had been very fond of her. After Tom left, and Ernest and George moved away, she had brought him up with the help of her own father; but my father had also found her bossy, a trait he put down to her having had to look after a family from the age of fourteen. He had once told me she was 'beautiful but tough'. Judging by the photo of her that he kept on his desk, I wouldn't have called her beautiful; Sabrina, Diana Dors and Marilyn Monroe, the blondes on my bubble-gum cards, were beautiful. 'Bossy, elegant and tough. Dad thinks she was beautiful.'

'Tough?' No women we knew were tough. A few were beautiful, some were elegant, plenty were bossy.

'That's what Dad said. She took charge of her brothers and the house and the servants after her mum died, when she was fourteen. S'pose that's tough.'

'And what was Old Tom like?'

'Don't know, except he drank too much. My father said he was tall and handsome . . . and he had a long moustache.'

'Have you seen any photographs of him?'

'No. Don't think there are any.'

I sat down on the floor and leaned against the wall – and remembered something I'd forgotten. 'Dad took me to a film ages ago. He wanted to see it because whoever wrote it was someone he liked. It was an old film. It was called "Viva Sonata" or something, and it was all about Mexicans – you know, with big hats and moustaches. Anyway, half-way through, Dad whispered to me that this man, the main man, looked like his father, so on the way out I looked to see what his name was. He was called Marlon something.'

'Marlon!' She wrinkled her nose. 'Funny name. What did he look like?'

'Ordinary. Couldn't see him very well; he had a huge moustache and a hat. He had long, narrow eyes and looked cross all the time, never smiled, not properly.'

'But I bet Old Tom smiled sometimes.' She was lying on her front and staring at the family tree again. I stood up and kicked a tennis ball gently against the skirting board, back and forth.

Suddenly, she said, 'Except for the servants, there were two non-blood relatives living in that house, Old Tom and La Frascetti.' I went on kicking, but thought about it. 'With six blood relatives, including your dad and his sister.'

It seemed strange; it would have been like my father living with my mother's family. My father would have found that impossible. I could tell he didn't even like my grandmother and my aunt, found them snobbish and a bit stupid.

'Two outsiders,' Deborah was leaning on her elbows looking up at me.

The tennis ball went under my bed. Thinking about Tom living with Sis's father and brothers, and even with her brother's wife, I slithered under to fetch it. 'Maybe that's why Tom got drunk so much, got fed up with all the other people in the house?' I rolled out and brushed dust off my sweater.

4

Aristotle's View of History

A WEEK LATER DEBORAH and I were in my room again. We were poring over my grandmother Sis's diary for 1886. My father had lent it to me; he had others, but why didn't I try this one to see if I found it interesting? It was a beige, cloth-bound book, quite worn; stiff brown cardboard showed through at the corners where the cloth had frayed. The endpapers were marbled, navy blue and wine red. The pages were stiff and very white, and crackled when I turned them.

It wasn't a diary in the sense of having dates printed in it. It had nothing printed in it. On the first page, written in large, sloping letters, in black ink, were the words 'Amelia Thompson My Book 1886'. After that there was a page for every day, with the day of the week and the date written at the top. On most days she had written a whole page, and occasionally the day's entry spread over to a second page. The handwriting was quite large, sloped at almost forty-five degrees to the right, with curlicues and flourishes on the capital letters. After we got used to it, Deborah and I found it quite easy to read, although we would frequently get stuck on certain words; Sis's 'e's, 'o's and 'i's were very similar.

The entry for 1 January 1886 described a New Year's Eve party at the house in Norfolk Road, to which more than twenty uncles, aunts and cousins had come. It sounded very jolly, with plenty of food, drink and singing around the piano. Sis seemed to like most of her relatives, but there were one or two whom she described as bores. After a whole page about this, she wrote, 'I will be nineteen this year. It is time for something else to happen.'

Deborah and I read the first ten days of January together, helping each other with the words that were hard to read. Deborah usually finished the page first and waited for me before turning over. Except for Sunday, the days were very similar; her father and two brothers went out, while she and the two servants called Alice looked after the house. Every other morning she went to a grocer's shop in Mare Street, which sounded a bit like Mr Brown's in the High Street, to order food which would be delivered that afternoon. Monday was washing day and the basement area at the front of the house nearly always flooded. Everyone in the family would have a bath in the kitchen in a copper tub that evening. Sis seemed to find her life pleasant but dull.

We wondered where they went to the loo, and at lunch we asked my father. He told us that there was a proper flush lavatory inside the house on the ground floor. 'It was very grand, with a big square mahogany seat, and the bowl was decorated in Wedgwood blue, like plates, with pictures of flowers and birds. In fact it was more comfortable and more convenient than the WC in this house. We were lucky. My grandfather had it installed at great expense; most people in the street had WCs outside in the garden.'

In the afternoon we read through the rest of January, the whole of February and some of March. Nothing much seemed to happen, except that Sis's father went away on business twice for a fortnight and her brother Ernest occasionally brought friends home after school and made a lot of noise. We read about Uncle George, who was seventeen. It seemed extraordinary that this young man – who so long ago didn't seem to do much except go to work at an office, come home, eat, read, sometimes play cards or the piano, and go to bed – was the same man, the one who had just died and whom I had always thought of as very old. On Thursday evenings, he and Sis would usually walk up to a park called Hackney Downs for 'band night'; they would sit on seats outdoors listening to a brass band play popular tunes.

My mother had to work in the shop that afternoon and when she got back we had a late tea in the sitting-room. My father toasted bread with a telescopic toasting fork, holding it against the glowing coals behind the bars of the Cosy Stove. Deborah sat between me and my mother on the sofa, my father sat in his usual armchair, and we watched *Six-Five Special* while my mother knitted and read the *Daily Telegraph*. Irritatingly, my father swivelled his chair so that he could see the television, and I knew what would follow: 'Look at his trousers! He can't walk in trousers like that, surely!' as Joe Brown shook his brush cut into a microphone. 'Why do they have to call women "babies"?' he loudly interrupted Adam Faith, and looked round at me and Deborah as if we would have an answer.

'Don't know, Dad,' I shrugged.

When it was over, he switched the television off with a flourish, turned and said, 'I'm astounded that you two have spent all day reading my mother's diary. What do you make of it?' He took out his tin and started to roll a cigarette. My mother put down her paper.

'It's interesting . . . I liked reading about Uncle George when he was seventeen, but her life seems to go on the same every day.'

'Well. Life can get like that. Most of the world's population do repetitive tasks day after day just to survive.' He glanced at my mother. 'I think at that time she probably was a bit fed up. She had to be a housewife before her time, looking after her father and two brothers instead of a husband and children.' He lit his cigarette, inhaled deeply and blew the smoke towards the ceiling. 'It was a shame, but she coped. She was a tough woman.'

Deborah was staring upwards with her hands behind her

head. 'You don't get much idea of what she thought about. It's mainly one thing happened and then something else happened.' She looked at my father. 'She says whether she likes people, or doesn't, but she doesn't say whether she's happy or unhappy or just going along without thinking about it.'

'Yes. It's more a record of what happened than anything else.' My father leaned forward. 'There are about twenty of those diaries and I read them all years ago, but that's my memory of them. Even when terrible events occurred like my father's drinking and eventually being thrown out, she just records the facts . . . It's almost as though she's not involved.' He sat back and pulled on his cigarette again. 'Do you think you get a good picture of what daily life was like, though?'

It was my turn to answer. 'I can see the routine and the different things they had then and the things they didn't have—'

'You see, the thing is,' my father interrupted, 'she wasn't really a writer. She didn't have the imagination to express things as they really were.'

'But she didn't need imagination. She was there,' I said.

'Perhaps imagination is the wrong word.' He pulled on his cigarette and stared at the ceiling. 'But I think, you see, that good writers, even if they write a made-up story, tell the truth better than someone who just recounts facts . . . and it's probably having a good imagination that helps them to do that.' He then talked about Jane Austen, about whom I knew nothing, Charles Dickens – I had read *A Christmas Carol* at school and seen the *David Copperfield* serial on television – and Robert Louis Stevenson – I had read *Treasure Island*. He seemed to be trying to say that these people told the truth about the world around them.

I couldn't quite see it: Scrooge and Bob Cratchit and Long John Silver seemed like imaginary people to me.

'But they come alive in your mind, don't they?' my father

said. 'And does Uncle George, aged seventeen, come alive to you?'

'No. Not really.'

Deborah shook her head in agreement.

'That's my point. There's something truthful about Scrooge and Bob Cratchit.' He forgot about Long John Silver. 'There were people like them. In fact, there *are* people like them.'

The clacking of my mother's knitting needles stopped and she turned to me and Deborah. 'The best example I can think of is a man called Robert Graves. He wrote two marvellous books about a Roman Emperor called Claudius, but he wrote them as though they were actually written by Claudius.' My father was nodding enthusiastically. 'He imagined what Claudius thought and felt and those books give a better picture of what Claudius and life in ancient Rome were like than anything else. They are better than history books because they seem so real.'

My father lent me two more of Sis's diaries and over the next few weeks I skipped through them, feeling a little guilty about not reading every word. In 1888 Sis fell in love with a doctor; some of her writing about this was rather embarrassing, but for the first time there was a bit of a story and she wrote about how she felt, although it still didn't seem very real.

Months later, because it caught my attention, I pulled *Claudius the God* off the bookshelf in my mother's room and read the first two pages. It was hard to follow, but for a few minutes I was under the illusion that this was actually written by the Emperor Claudius.

Later, I found my father in the sitting-room and asked him how we could know that the book was true and how Robert Graves could know what Claudius thought. He started pulling out volumes of the *Encyclopaedia Britannica* and talking at the same time. 'You see. I've been thinking about this for years. What is truth? It's a question all the philosophers and poets and great writers have concerned themselves with.' I sat down in the middle of the sofa. 'Hundreds and hundreds of years ago, before the birth of Christ, there was a great Greek philosopher called Aristotle and he had a lot to say about truth.' He dumped three volumes on the table and quickly turned the pages of one of them. 'Listen to this.'

He slowly read out passages about the thinking of this Greek from so long ago, poking the air with his forefinger and looking up at me intently from time to time. Some of what he read was very tedious but I got the idea that Aristotle, who my father thought knew what he was talking about, believed that fiction was better than truth. I'd always thought 'fiction' just meant the books in the library that weren't true; but it seemed more complicated than that.

'Aristotle thought that fiction was based on probability, rather than literal truth, and that this made good fiction ultra-real. Fiction distilled the truth. That means that it contains the essence of the truth, whereas, Aristotle thought, people who try to record the literal truth, people who write history – or perhaps diaries like my mother's – convey the truth less well.' He sat back and looked at me. 'Does that make sense to you?'

'I think so,' I said. As he put the books away, I thought about Sis's diaries and how, though she was presumably telling the truth, she somehow wasn't telling the whole story.

~

For me the next year, 1961, was still childhood, still uncomplicated hedonism. My mother worked part-time at the shop she had once owned and my father drove off most mornings in the grey-green A35. I took the bus with Richard and Adam to school in High Wycombe, getting home every day at 4.15; homework fitted in easily, and when the evenings grew lighter, I went, nearly always with Richard, either to hang around the recreation ground behind the station or to trespass in the bird sanctuary by the river beyond the lock.

It was the time of my father's great lawsuit against Sketchley, the dry cleaner. They made a mess of four of his shirts and foolishly failed to admit liability, which he reckoned to be £8, the price of four new shirts. He was an old hand at this, having taken legal action against various parties over the years, although the only other one that I remembered was his action against a shop called Daniel's in the High Street whose manager refused to sell him a football displayed in the window; he was temporarily out of stock and would have had to crawl through a thicket of tents, fishing rods and mannequins in all-weather clothing to oblige. My father won that simply by looking up the relevant acts and case law in the Law Society Library in London and writing a letter quoting subclauses and precedents. The manager sent an assistant round with three free footballs and a note saying, 'All right, you win and I hope we will continue to receive your custom.'

When the Sketchley case looked like actually going to court, my mother encouraged him to drop it, not because she thought he wouldn't win, but because she knew that it would raise his already high emotional temperature. 'Is it really worth it?'

'They tore my shirts. You've seen them, Exhibits A, B, C and D. It's a matter of principle. Why should this greedy chain of capitalists get away with that?' He lowered his voice. 'You may have to be a witness, you know, to prove they weren't torn already.'

She sighed and carried on mashing potatoes. He sauntered out into the garden to look at the budgerigars. I followed.

Reynolds versus Sketchley eventually came up at the County Court in Aylesbury. My mother declined to take a day off work to attend and I had to be at school. My father left wearing his dark suit, which only looked its age from close to, and his Savage Club tie. He returned that evening carrying red roses for my mother and a small transistor radio for me, the thing I wanted more than anything. He had not just won the case, presenting it himself against a fancy London barrister, but had been awarded an astonishing amount of costs. The judge had found in his favour and then enquired what work he did and how much he was paid for it; he must surely have lost some time at work preparing his case. My father told him that he was partly paid in commission. Forty pounds was added to the eight pounds' worth of shirts for that, and then the judge revealed that he knew my father was a writer of some repute.

'When do you fit your writing in, Mr Reynolds?'

Truthfully he answered, 'In the early mornings, milud. I get up at 5 a.m.'

'And how much of your early-morning-writing time has been wasted on this case?'

'Probably four or five days, milud.'

'And how much did you earn from your last book?'

Again truthfully, 'My advance was one thousand pounds, but it sold rather well. I netted six thousand, four hundred pounds milud.' Eyebrows were raised – this was more than twice the judge's own salary – but the Sketchley barrister, presumably accepting that he had lost thoroughly, stayed silent and my father had no need to mention that, despite writing almost every day, he hadn't had a book published since 1949.

The judge fiddled with pencil and paper. 'I award sixty pounds for Mr Reynolds' loss of earnings as a writer. The defendant will pay a total of one hundred pounds in costs.'

This was more than my father earned in a good month, and, as he repeatedly pointed out, it was tax-free. Celebrations continued as the local paper reported 'Local David Slays Dry-Cleaning Goliath', and my father took my mother and me to a department store in Reading where we each spent £10 on new clothes – I bought two pairs of jeans, a sweater and a maroon waterproof jacket called a windcheater, with a collar that turned up over my ears.

On the way home my father lost his temper with a van-driver because he was forced to brake when the van cut in front of us. My father swore at him and drove fast, overtaking other cars in an effort to keep up with him. I was in the passenger seat and could see the anger on his face. From the back my mother called to him to slow down; there was no point in endangering us all.

He turned and looked at her angrily – and drove on in a greater fury, cursing the traffic in his way.

He caught up with the van at some traffic lights, drove alongside it, hooted, pulled down his window, shouted at the man that his driving was a disgrace, and called him a stupid bastard. The van-driver got out, walked round to my father, yelled 'Watch who you call a stupid bastard,' and punched him in the face. He got back in his van and drove off as my father's nose bled all over his shirt. My mother drove home while my father lay on the back seat holding his handkerchief over his face.

~

On an evening in mid-summer Richard called round for me and we decided to go to the bird sanctuary. On the road by the lock we found Dennis leaning against the red-brick gateway outside Uncle George's former home, smoking a cigarette.

Richard was my best friend; he had curly hair and an open, freckly face. A few years before we had played with guns and toy cars and plastic models of red Indians – he had been the Apaches and I the Comanches – on each other's front paths and living-room carpets. Nowadays, we kicked footballs around, looked at girls in the High Street, smoked and worshipped Elvis. Richard was a lasting, dependable friend, a year older than me – he would soon be fourteen – but about the same height.

Lately I had grown to like Dennis, mainly for what I would later be able to define as his dry, lazy humour. He was small and lean, with lank dark hair that flopped into his eyes, and he spoke softly in an Irish accent. I liked to listen to him talk and sometimes found that I was unwittingly mimicking his speech patterns in his presence, and had to stop myself. He liked to tell stories about things that had happened to him, and about Ireland where he had lived until he was eight and where he returned every summer.

He came along with us, holding his cigarette cupped in his hand. It was the middle of July; the evening was still warm; the lock was full of pleasure boats and the riverbank beyond was crowded with fishermen, strolling families and children paddling in murky water. We had to wait until there was no one in sight before vaulting the gate marked 'Bird Sanctuary: No Trespassing'. We stumbled between head-high brambles until we reached a shady clearing under a huge spreading oak. Richard and I had often climbed this tree and that evening, followed by Dennis, we climbed high and then out along a sturdy branch, some thirty feet above the ground. We sat, legs dangling, staring down at the river as the sun began to set behind the white suspension bridge beyond the lock.

Dennis handed out Woodbines that he told us he had removed from his brother's pocket. As we smoked, he spoke about a time, the summer before, when he and his brother had trespassed on a rich man's estate near his grandfather's home in County Waterford. They had been examining some baby pheasants in a wood when a man appeared from behind a tree and threatened them with a gun. He had never run so fast.

He stopped talking, and in the silence we could hear small children shouting as they paddled in the river. There was no wind to rustle the leaves and we caught the throaty rasp of an angry swan; looking down we could see it protecting two mottled brown cygnets from a sailing boat that had gone too close.

'Are you really going to boarding school?' Richard turned to me.

I felt annoyed that he had asked me then, when we were outdoors enjoying ourselves. It was one of my two worries. The thought of either of them sometimes made my shoulders and hands tingle and tremble momentarily – the other, of course, was my father's treatment of my mother.

Soon after I was born, my mother had put my name down for a boys' public school, where her father and uncles had been. Then, when I was seven, an aunt of my mother's, whom I had innocently charmed as a small child, died, leaving money specifically to be spent on my education. My mother wanted me to go to this school because she believed that there I would get the best possible education and that almost any sacrifice, certainly her own, was worth this goal. My father was ambivalent. His political principles shrieked against such a step, but there was an élitist, snobbish side to his character, which I believe he would have liked to subdue but could not. Both of them would miss me, I knew that, but education – which both of them had, in their own opinions and for different reasons, not had enough of – had an allure that transcended personal pleasure and conviction.

When boarding school had been a distant prospect, I had actually looked forward to it. When I was nine or ten, I had read Billy Bunter and Jennings and Darbishire books, and it all seemed like lots of fun away from the restraints of home. It was still nearly a year away. If I was to go, I was to go the following May. We had visited the school and met the man who would be my housemaster; he had been friendly but had seemed old and austere. I was due to take an entrance exam in the autumn.

I stubbed my cigarette carefully on the branch beside me and dropped the butt to the ground. 'I don't know.'

'Don't! You'll hate it . . . No freedom . . . No girls.' Richard stretched, and then wobbled on the branch. He quickly dropped his hands to his sides to steady himself. He was right; what I had thought of as the restraints of home, when I was nine or ten, seemed to have fallen away. Save that I had to go to school and perform a few perfunctory household chores, there were no irksome rules.

'I wouldn't go to a place like that, I'll tell you . . . Don't they beat the boys whenever they get the chance? They do in Ireland. I know.' Dennis squinted against the sun as he peered at me. 'Stay here with us. Marlow's OK, and your school's OK.' He was right as well. I liked the town – the river, the lock, the park, the cinema, the High Street, our house, my friends – and my school was fine, given that I had to go to a school; I was around the top of the class, played football, liked two of the teachers a lot, hated one of them – but everybody hated him.

I knew that, if I said I didn't want to go, I wouldn't have to. My father would take very little persuading, although I would have to give an intelligent reason. That would be easy – I would simply point out that I would be helping to perpetuate the evil class divide by joining what he called 'the upper classes', 'the idle rich', 'the snobs', 'the Tories', 'the toffs'.

With my mother, too, it would be easy to get out of it. But I felt that to do so would be letting her down: in her opinion this type of education was a gift that one should accept gratefully; it would lead to Oxford, as it had for her father and uncles – the school was a few miles from that hallowed city and sending boys there was its speciality. I felt a duty to my mother.

A few weeks before, when I had voiced my worries about the school – the beatings, fagging, bullying and silly rules –

she had hugged me and told me I didn't have to go. But that had made me angry because it had been her idea, not mine; it was because of her, and her father and uncles, whose photograph – three proud men in World War I officers' uniforms – hung in her bedroom, and her aunt – the men's sister, who had left the money – that I was going to this school forty miles away. I hadn't been going to let her down, so why had she suggested I might?

We came down from the tree and tramped on through the woods. Richard knew about birds, which together with the excitement of trespassing was what had first brought us here two years before. He liked woodpeckers in particular. We could hear one and stopped frequently, gazing in silence trying to see it. Eventually, we reached the northern edge of the sanctuary away from the river. Here, beyond the barbed wire, there was an empty field between the woods and the railway line that joined Marlow to Bourne End, Maidenhead and London. Although the sun had almost gone, the air was warm, and the dry, golden grass gave off a sweet smell. Dennis ran ahead of us to the centre of the field and flung himself down on his back with arms outspread; four or five birds which Richard immediately identified as lapwings rose from the ground and circled the field languidly before landing at a safe distance. Dennis lay staring at the sky and we lay down beside him, with me in the middle.

We talked about girls and kissing, and I wondered fleetingly whether my grandmother Sis had kissed boys when she was twelve, and decided that she almost certainly hadn't; there was no mention of such things in her diaries until she met the doctor in 1888 when she was twenty-one. Dennis lit a Woodbine, and we passed it between us. There was a discussion about inhaling which none of us knew how to do. Dennis managed to blow some smoke through his nose and then had a coughing fit. The smell of the smoke blended with the scent of dry grass as the air grew cooler.

When the cigarette was finished, we walked to the end of the field and forced ourselves backwards through a gap in the hawthorn hedge to the field beyond. A group of Friesian cows stared with large eyes as we passed them on our way back to the towpath.

In November I took the entrance exam. There were papers in several subjects and the process went on over three days. I sat in the school's staff dining-room at a polished pine table. One other boy, Nick, a friend but not a close one, was taking the exam and sat opposite me; he was nice but dim and was trying to get into an even posher school than I was, Eton. An elderly man with a rounded back and jutting chin – he had been the school's music master for about fifty years and had retired several years before – sat at the head of the table reading a book through wire-rimmed spectacles with his nose wrinkled and his teeth bared. He had a pocket watch on the table in front of him, told us when to start and when to stop, and beamed genially at us from time to time.

Some way into the first exam, which was Latin, I found that Nick was staring at me and sucking hard on his Parker pen. He glanced at the old man who was absorbed in his book, took his pen out of his mouth, and almost imperceptibly shrugged his shoulders and raised his eyebrows. We had been instructed to write on both sides of the paper. I sat back in my soft-seated dining-room chair, held my paper up perpendicular to the table and read through what I had written. Meanwhile Nick bent over his paper and squinted upwards to read what I had written on the other side.

In this manner, over a period of three days, I consigned Nick to Eton. He was profuse in his thanks and gave me a two-pound slab of Cadbury's Dairy Milk chocolate.

More significantly, I passed with high marks myself. My mother hugged me round the shoulders and kissed my cheek.

My father slapped my back and said, 'Well done, Sunny Jim.' My shoulders and hands tingled as he handed me two shillings.

Soon my parents received a letter from the housemaster saying how pleased he was with my exam results, that I would be in a class with scholarship boys, even though I had not taken scholarship papers, and that he looked forward to seeing me the following May. He enclosed several sheets of paper containing lists: required clothing and sporting equipment; dates and times of terms, half-terms and old boys' weekend; daily and weekly routines, which included chapel every morning at 8.50 except Sundays when mattins would last an hour starting at 10 o'clock; advice about money – he suggested my parents provide me with £3 per term, which he would look after – and something called 'tuck', which meant food; rules – I would be allowed to leave the school grounds only with written permission from a prefect and only on Tuesday, Thursday and Saturday afternoons and on Sundays – parents might visit to take me out every third Sunday after mattins.

The tingling sense of dread reappeared in my shoulders, arms and hands, and moved on into my stomach. But I managed to make it go away. May was still six months away. I didn't have to go. Even though I had passed the exam, I could still get out of it.

5

Dinner in Dalston

On a freezing Saturday, shortly before Christmas, my father and I drove dangerously through ice and sleet to High Wycombe to buy my mother's Christmas present. He was feeling flush.

'I've decided to buy her a gramophone,' he had confided to me that morning during breakfast, while my mother was out of the room.

I was thrilled. At last! 'You mean a record player? One that will play singles and LPs?'

He had to think for a moment. 'Yes . . . although I don't see why it can't be called a gramophone.' He pointed at the pre-war radiogram in the corner of the dining-room. 'It does just the same as that, except it will play records that go round more slowly.'

I didn't argue. Everyone I knew had had a record player for at least two years. 'It's not really a present for Mum, though, is it? We'll all use it, won't we?'

He shrugged. 'She's always playing records. It'll be hers.' I must have looked worried, because he went on. 'All right, we'll buy her something else as well . . . bath salts. What about bath salts?'

Every year cousins and aunts gave my mother bath salts, and every year she gave bath salts to other people, sometimes carefully recycling the previous year's offerings. I could think of nothing more dull than bath salts. 'We ought to buy a record, an LP. Otherwise she'll have a record player and nothing to play on it.'

He smiled. 'You've always been very bright, Sunny Jim, very intelligent.' He grabbed my hand across the table and squeezed it. Then he felt in his pocket and handed me two half-crowns. 'There you are. Five bob. You buy her a record with that, and you can get some bath salts with the change, and I'll buy her one too. We'll need more than one record; otherwise we'll go mad listening to the same one all the time.'

'A single is six and fourpence.' I knew, because I had helped Richard and Adam choose them in Martin's, the electrical shop in Chapel Street. 'She probably won't want a single, because she likes Bach and Beethoven and symphonies. They're on LPs. They cost twenty-one shillings, I think.'

'Good God.' He smiled and looked at me over his glasses as he took back the two half-crowns. 'We'll see what we can do when we get to the shop.'

We got stuck in traffic on the steep hill down into High Wycombe and sat for long minutes with the engine turned off, gradually getting colder and periodically wiping condensation from the windscreen with a duster. He talked about his mother and his father, telling me a lot I didn't know, as he rolled one cigarette after another. He had never been so open with me before – my mother had told me truthfully where babies come from when I had first shown curiosity at the age of five, and she had told me about homosexual men when I was seven, and lesbians when I was eight. Now that I was thirteen and he had something to say, my father mentioned sex for the first time ever as he told me about his parents.

It took us more than an hour to get into Easton Street. We parked and sat in the car as my father continued to talk; his hands gripped the steering wheel as he told me how clearly he remembered the day in 1902 when his father packed two suitcases, said goodbye to him and walked off down the street. The windscreen misted over and my father opened the small, triangular window beside the steering wheel. He flicked his ash through the opening. 'Before he left, he bent down and kissed me quickly on the lips and said, "Goodbye, old chap. Don't worry. I'll see you before long." I was crying. They told me I would see him again soon . . . But I never saw him again.' He reached for his handkerchief, sobbed sharply twice and blew his nose. He pulled hard on his cigarette and tossed the butt through the window. He patted my hand. 'I'm sorry . . . but you did want to know.' He was looking straight ahead at the condensation on the windscreen.

I put my arm round his shoulders.

'He didn't go to Canada until 1906 . . . four years later, but they wouldn't let him see me.' There was a catch, like a small hiccup, in his voice. 'It was cruel, but they did what they thought was right.' He reached down and patted my thigh. 'If Uncle George had been in charge, I think he'd have arranged for him to see me.'

There was a long silence. I continued to lean against him with my arm across the top of his seat, my hand on the warm felt of his overcoat. Then, he turned, kissed me on the forehead and spoke in his normal voice. 'That's the whole story. Let's go shopping.'

We took our time to choose a Dynatron record player. I liked the modern look of its case which was covered in cream and blue plastic material and had a stainless steel strip at the front with three slits in it through which just the tops of three white plastic discs protruded: 'on/off/volume', 'treble', 'bass'. With many mentions of Marconi, my father explained to me and the shopkeeper exactly how it worked. The man, red-faced and with thin black hair stuck sideways across his head with what I guessed was brilliantine, smiled and raised his eyebrows attentively, and managed to maintain this attitude when my father moved on to the transistor, which he informed us had been invented in 1948, 'the year Sunny Jim was born'.

My father placed his hand on my head and I knew what would come next. 'His mother and I had been married for sixteen years.' But for once he carried straight on without pausing for the usual expressions of astonishment. 'Three men were awarded the Nobel Prize for the transistor, but only two of them deserved it. Their boss tried to steal the glory.'

The shopkeeper's lower lip sagged as his eyebrows went up again.

I slipped away to choose a record for my mother. 'Typical of the boss class . . . and you can guess which of them made a fortune.'

'Well, this is it.' The shopkeeper spoke for the first time in several minutes, smiling in agreement once again.

My father joined me by the racks of records. I swiftly picked out a recording of *The Pirates of Penzance* while he took a little longer to decide on Beethoven's Pastoral Symphony.

Although, according to my mother, he was tone deaf, he then sat for twenty minutes in a glassed-in, sound-proof booth humming and waving his hands about as he listened to the slow movements of recordings by Otto Klemperer and Sir Adrian Boult. I fingered the new LPs from Elvis, Billy Fury and the Everly Brothers and wondered what my father would think if I put Brylcreem in my hair.

In the end, ignoring the composer's nationality, my father pronounced that my mother would prefer the English cadences of Boult, especially after what she had been through during the war. The shopkeeper nodded deferentially, as though my mother were a war hero, and told my father that he had made an excellent choice.

After that day, even though he had said that was the whole story, I questioned him often about his childhood, his parents, his numerous other relatives and his friends from the 1890s and 1900s. He told me plenty of funny and colourful stories, and answered serious questions candidly. Over the next three months, he wrote seven chapters of about twelve pages each, detailing as much as he knew of the lives of his forebears and giving an account of his childhood up to the time when he left school, aged sixteen, in 1908. He gave it to me to read chapter by chapter.

That night I heard my father going out to the car after my mother had gone to bed. I knew he was fetching the record player, and heard him carrying it up the two flights of stairs to his room, where we had planned he would hide it in his wardrobe. I was lying in bed reading my grandmother's diary for 1888.

~

Sis celebrated her twenty-first birthday on 1 March 1888, a Saturday. At some expense her brother Ernest booked four seats in the stalls for that evening's variety performance at the Alhambra in Leicester Square. Sis was pleased and looked forward to what her father called her birthday treat; Ernest, her father and her other brother, George, would come – the three men she was most fond of. Although they lived together, they hadn't been out together – just the four of them – ever, at least not since they had all been adults.

Dan Leno and Marie Lloyd were to be the star turns that night; Sis loved to laugh, to hear the latest popular songs and to sing along to her favourite old ones. The other aspects of music hall – the lesser acts, the jugglers, conjurors and acrobats, the drinking and the vulgarity – appealed to her less, but it *was* the Alhambra, probably London's grandest variety theatre, where the seats were in rows and there was a shelf for her glass, and it was her birthday. She knew that she would enjoy herself.

Ernest had bought the tickets, and as soon as they arrived her father bought four glasses of champagne and announced that the rest of the evening was to be at his expense and that the three of them should order whatever they wanted. The elder George Thompson was strong and broad-shouldered with grey hair cut short at the sides, a moustache that flowed downwards and around his lower lip, and a beard that was a continuation of the moustache and covered only his chin; all this straight, strong hair was thoroughly brushed for this, and every, occasion. He was forty-seven years old, imperious with waiters, servants and the craftsmen who built furniture to his design at a factory in Shoreditch, but for the most part benevolent towards his family.

Leno was at his best, Marie Lloyd sang beautifully and with much emotion. The four Thompsons cried together with laughter and sentiment, and continued to drink champagne. But the evening was to become even more memorable for a quite different reason. While Sis was strolling around with Ernest in the first interval, her brother bumped into an acquaintance called Stanley Andrews. On learning that it was Sis's birthday Stanley bought champagne at the bar, toasted her formally and complimented her politely on her appearance. She was wearing a maroon taffeta dress with a fashionably narrow bustle; her hair was up and her long neck was decorated with a new beaded-jet choker with an agate cameo pinned to it, an extravagant birthday present from her father. Stanley told her how beautifully the choker suited her. When it was time for her to return to her seat, he kissed her hand and said that he hoped they would meet again.

They met again, perhaps purposely on both their parts, an hour later, when Sis took her brother George for a walk around the gallery at the back of the auditorium. Sis introduced George and there were smiles and pleasantries; this time Stanley commented on her fan, which was tortoiseshell and fringed with feathers. A little before midnight, as she climbed with her father and brothers into a growler in the rank outside, she glimpsed Stanley smiling and waving at her from the steps.

A week after their first encounter Sis met Stanley again, this time at the Britannia Music Hall in Hoxton, where Ernest worked as an assistant stage manager. Stanley had prevailed on

Ernest to arrange this second meeting and he had readily complied. Though he was only seventeen, Ernest was already a rounded character, an extrovert, handsome dandy with carefully combed dark hair, who believed that he and everyone else should have a good time whenever possible – but he was not irresponsible; it is clear that he cared a lot about his elder sister. No doubt he had noticed that she was struck by this tall, blond, amusing fellow, whom he knew to be a doctor of some kind, and likely he felt that, at the age of twenty-one, she deserved something more than to be housekeeper for her father and her brothers.

Sis only pretended that she needed to be persuaded; Ernest reintroduced her to Stanley in the foyer at the Britannia, and went off to do his night's work.

After that Ernest was no longer needed as a go-between. Stanley would send a note to Sis at her home by messenger, and she would send Little Alice, the servant, who was pledged to tell no one, with a reply. For a few weeks Sis's friendship with Stanley was known only to Ernest, Young George and Little Alice; whenever she went to meet him Sis told her father that she was going to visit a female friend.

Sis fell quickly in love with Stanley Andrews, and he with her. For Sis it was a new and overwhelming sensation. At the end of August she confided in her young aunt, Kate, her father's youngest sister, who was just ten years her elder, a kindly married woman who thought she knew how Sis was feeling. And she probably did; she used the word 'passion' and gave Sis her opinion that it was a form of love that, if all went well, would lead to a still greater form of love. She directed her to a poem by Sappho, lines from which my exhilarated grandmother copied into her diary:

> That man seems to me peer of gods, who sits in thy presence, and hears close to him thy sweet speech and lovely laughter; that indeed makes my heart flutter in my

> bosom. For when I see thee but a little, I have no utterance left, my tongue is broken down, and straightway a subtle fire has run under my skin, with my eyes I have no sight, my ears ring, sweat pours down, and a trembling seizes all my body; I am paler than grass, and seem in my madness little better than one dead. But I must dare all. . .

My father had said that the story of his father was the story of his mother as well. Reading Sis's 1888 diary and reflecting on what my father had written and told me, I began to see what he meant. And over the next few years, I saw that he was right: to make a form of sense of what happened to my grandfather, Tom Reynolds – and why he travelled to Swan River, Manitoba – Sis's story was essential, and the most essential part of it occurred before she met my grandfather.

When she fell in love with Stanley, Sis had been her father's housekeeper for nearly eight years. Her work was not physically arduous – she had the help of the two servants, Big Alice and Little Alice – but her responsibilities were considerable and her freedom limited. She was, as I had told Deborah, bossy, elegant and tough, but she was also deeply attached to her father – more attached than she would have been had her mother been alive – and she hated having a secret from him. She wanted him to know about her fondness for Stanley – she wouldn't use the word 'love' to her father, not yet, anyway – but she dreaded telling him.

In the years between her mother's death and her discovery of Stanley, the only love Sis had felt had been for her father – he had not remarried; he revered the memory of his wife, and remained very close to her two sisters, who were frequent visitors to his home at 59 Norfolk Road, Dalston. He had been the constant beneficiary of Sis's attention in that she cared about what he thought, considered how he felt, wanted him to be happy; she loved him, as far as she could see, in accordance with her Aunt Kate's definition of the love that follows passion; though, of course, she had never felt passion for her father, never before felt the way she felt about Stanley.

To tell her father that she cared about another man was embarrassing, but, worse than that, it seemed disloyal. But she had to tell him and wanted to tell him, and, indeed, wanted him and Stanley to meet. She discussed the matter with Kate, who offered to talk to 'Old George' (as – despite his being only forty-seven – the family referred to him, to distinguish him from 'Young George'). Sis rejected this offer; she would tell him herself.

She spoke to her father late one night in his room on the ground floor across the hall from the drawing-room. As always, when he was at home in the evening, his room was a mass of flickering shadows and yellow candlelight, with ten or twelve lighted candles standing on a variety of surfaces. Old George had grown up in the 1840s, before gas lighting was cheaply available, and, although he permitted and used it in the rest of the house, he preferred candles, lots of them, in his own room. From about 9 p.m., he would lie on his bed, a majestic chunk of rosewood, four feet wide with solid curved ends inlaid with ebony and mother of pearl. As my father said more than once, a lot can be learned about a man from his bed. Old George had bought this one in Paris soon after the death of his wife and it neatly reflected its owner who was strong, well-built, imposing and for the most part unpretentious. Propped up against several pillows, surrounded by newspapers, journals, books and pamphlets, he would read by the light of two three-stemmed candelabra, one to either side of him, but would break off to hold court with any friend or member of his family who cared to call.

That evening, Sis told him that she had a friend she would

like him to meet and that his name was Stanley Andrews. He grunted and smiled with his eyes and through his beard, and asked her why.

She said, 'Because I like him and I am hoping you will like him.'

He went on smiling and told her to ask Stanley to dinner.

An arrangement was made for 18 September, a Friday more than two weeks ahead. In the interim Sis took Young George to meet Stanley at the Britannia, her idea being that, though Ernest could be counted on to talk and be amusing at the all-important dinner, his elder brother, who was bookish and less outgoing, might be less shy if he knew their guest a little better. That evening seemed to go well. Young George was evidently impressed by Stanley's knowledge of his personal obsession, Charles Darwin and his theory of evolution, and afterwards proclaimed him to be 'a splendid chap'.

On 18 September, at around 7 p.m., Sis looked out from the window of her first-floor bedroom and idly watched the lamplighter igniting the gas lamp opposite. It was a warm evening; Stanley was not due for another thirty minutes and he would probably be the polite fifteen minutes late. She had already spent almost an hour dressing and, with Little Alice's help, arranging her hair. She wore a white silk dress, which she had bought at Owles and Beaumont in Oxford Street a week previously; it was cut low at the neck to show off her collar bones and, like all dresses that year, had a narrow bustle; the skirt lifted from the floor and swirled around her ankles as she walked.

Sis was usually confident in her appearance. She knew that, at five feet six inches, she was a tall woman; she thought that her face was striking rather than beautiful, and believed that she could counter the strength of her prominent nose by bringing a mistiness into her grey eyes by defocusing them. That evening, before Stanley arrived, she danced around her room with pleasure; she could feel it physically. She wondered whether she was mad, but decided that she was in love although that was perhaps a form of madness. Other young women had told her that they were in love – and she had dismissed them as scatterbrained. Now she knew what they meant, but was certain that she felt it more deeply than any of them ever had.

She sat down at the small bureau beside the fire and picked up her diary. There was already a lot in it about Stanley: how he spoke to her so intelligently, amusingly and graciously, while gazing directly into her eyes; how handsome he looked with his well-brushed, thick, blond hair, a lock of which often fell forwards over his right eye, so that he frequently had to smooth it back; how strong and beautiful his hands were; how he stroked her hair and put his arms around her; how he had kissed her, and how he had said, 'I love you Sis,' and how she hadn't been able to reply but had merely leaned back with her hands on his shoulders and smiled, before pulling him close and returning the kiss.

On a clean page she wrote the date and a few lines describing her preparations for the coming evening and her great concern that her father should like Stanley. Her brothers liked him, or had said that they did, but it was her father who mattered, who, although a self-proclaimed rationalist, an unbeliever, had taught her that it was important to act on your feelings, as long as no one else suffered as a result.

Sometime before 7.30 Sis put away her diary, picked up her feathered tortoiseshell fan, the one that Stanley had admired the first night she met him, left her room, crossed the landing to her brother George's room and entered, as was her habit, without knocking.

George had not begun to dress for the evening, and his hair was untidy. He was sitting by the window in shirt sleeves and work trousers on a ladder-backed wooden chair designed by his father, reading a book; he had not bothered to light the gas mantles, two pairs of which projected from the walls.

Outside, the sun was low behind a group of old trees at the end of the garden, survivors from the time, thirty years earlier, when Norfolk Road had been a high-hedged lane leading north from Dalston through fields and copses to Shacklewell. The garden was long and wide for a London garden, but was a mess because none of the Thompsons liked gardening and Old George wouldn't pay anyone to look after it.

Young George told his sister that she looked quite magnificent, and, because he usually said what he meant, she believed him; at nineteen, he was already the thoughtful, congenial man who, more than seventy years later, would instruct me to go to Swan River, Manitoba.

Sis left her brother so that he could dress. He and his father and his brother were to wear smoking-jackets that evening. Sis, who loved formality, would have liked them to wear white tie and tails, but her father refused to wear this garb in his own house and would rarely wear it to go out. George and Ernest, as on all such occasions, would follow their father's lead, as would Stanley who had been warned in advance of this minor eccentricity.

Sis went downstairs and entered her father's room. Dressed much like his son in the room above – he had discarded his frock coat, tie and boots on returning from his office – he was lying on his bed, sucking a pipe and reading *The Times*. He gazed with penetrating blue eyes at his daughter, told her she looked 'glorious' and teased her, saying that there must be something exceptional about her friend Stanley.

Sis was embarrassed and went so far as to say that she was fond of Stanley, and implored her father to be nice to him. He kissed her forehead and promised that he would be.

After she had gone, Old George dressed, in his own way, for the occasion: starched white shirt, beige trousers, black waistcoat into which, as always, he carefully fixed his gold chain with pocket watch and seals, a dark silk tie in which he scrupulously crafted a Derby knot. He then spent some minutes brushing his hair and beard, and adjusting his collar, tie, lapels, cuffs, waistcoat and pocket watch while staring into a mahogany-framed mirror shaped like the doorway of a Norman church.

Sis walked down another, narrower, flight of stairs, leading to a dark corridor, at the end of which was the kitchen where a large window overlooked the garden. She wanted to check that all was well and that the Alices knew what they had to do. Little Alice, pretty and large-eyed, was the live-in servant. Until a year before, when Old George had decided to reduce his expenditure, Big Alice had lived in as well and the two of them had shared the small attic room across the landing from Ernest's room, which Little Alice had since had all to herself. Big Alice, a large, red-faced thirty-year-old, continued to come in three days a week to cook and do laundry; in return for one shilling and sixpence she had readily agreed to help out on this special evening and to stay over.

Little Alice, who was nineteen and had worked for the Thompsons for two years, told Sis the next day that the change of routine had made the day almost as much fun as her weekly day off. The three of them had spent all day preparing food, polishing glasses and cutlery, and carrying the dining table upstairs from the breakfast-room to the drawing-room, something that only ever happened at Christmas or for large family parties. Then there had been the carry-on about answering the door and announcing the guest. Sis, whom the Alices had to call 'Miss Amelia', usually got one of them to answer the door, though the three men tended to answer it themselves. No one had ever been announced before. Sis had made Little Alice practise saying 'Doctor Stanley Andrews'; she had repeated the words at least ten times, getting louder each time and trying not to giggle, until the mistress had been satisfied.

She had been flattered to be asked to help with Sis's hair; this, too, had never happened before. She had pinned up the luscious brown locks, so that Sis's ears and neck were revealed in what Alice knew, from secretly perusing her mistress's magazines, was the style made fashionable by Miss Edna May.

When the doorbell eventually rang it almost went all wrong. As Little Alice hurried up the narrow stairs from the kitchen, and before Sis could stop him, Young George strode the short distance from the drawing-room to the front door, opened it and greeted the guest. Crossly, Sis told her brother to go back to the drawing-room and that Alice would announce Stanley. George queried this, saying that surely they all knew who Stanley was, and was brusquely reminded that their father had never met him. George tramped back to the drawing room, grinning and shaking his head.

Meanwhile, a presumably bemused Stanley had handed Alice his top hat and removed his overcoat. In deference to his host, he was dressed down in a double-breasted frock coat, winged collar and tie, and light grey trousers, the uniform that thousands of men wore to go to work. Sis stood on tiptoes to give him a quick kiss on the cheek and walked off to join her father and brothers.

As instructed, Little Alice knocked loudly on the open door of the drawing-room. 'Doctor Stanley Andrews.' She got it right.

Stanley was warmly greeted by the three men. When offered a drink, he asked for a sherry, and then everyone except Ernest sat down. Young George sat beside Stanley on the red velvet sofa facing the fire; Old George sat in his usual wing-backed armchair next to them. Sis took what her father called the French armchair, an elegant, low-backed item, more comfortable than it looked, at the other end of the fireplace; Ernest, a dandy even when dressed down to please his father, remained languidly standing, beside Sis, with one arm on the mantelpiece. After desultory conversation about his journey – from the Borough to Dalston by hansom cab –

Stanley commented on the room, which was high-ceilinged and well-proportioned, and its furniture.

He knew that this was Old George's passion, but it was a natural topic for a stranger to address; despite the less than fashionable location, the furniture in the room was tasteful and looked old and expensive. A Queen Anne mahogany sideboard and the sofa, on which Stanley and Young George were sitting, usually dominated, but on this occasion the dining table and chairs, which were in Adam style, took up the end of the room away from the fire. Old George knew and loved furniture – it was his business – and would not permit any object that he considered ugly anywhere in the house, even in the servant's attic room.

Other rooms contained furniture that had been designed by Old George, but here it was almost all antique, bought in London auction rooms and on travels to northern Europe. There were two exquisite exceptions. The piano had been made by a disciple of William Morris; it was five years old, built from English beech, with carvings of bunches of grapes and trailing vine leaves entwined with ivy. Above the white marble mantelpiece was a chimney glass, one of many designed by Old George and manufactured in Shoreditch by his employers. Huge and intricate, it filled the chimney breast and reached upwards to within a few inches of the picture rail; it was a symmetrical arrangement of mirrors – fourteen small rectangular ones of various sizes set in wood panels around a central upright mirror – painted in white enamel and including shelves, balustrades, carvings, and paintings of flowers and songbirds. It was a beautiful object and Stanley was quick to increase his admiration when Ernest casually indicated that it was the work of 'the pater'.

The walls were papered in a cream, maroon and gold regency-stripe, and this was covered with paintings and prints: two large oils of flowers between the windows; a dramatic painting of the harbour at Cork with stormy waves and sky on the facing wall; prints of showgirls from Paris alongside draughtsman-style drawings of wooden tables and chairs on the wall facing the fire – these were Old George's own work, his designs for items which had been manufactured by the thousand, some of which had won prizes. A pastel portrait of Old George's father hung over the sideboard. Miniatures, sepia photographs and daguerrotypes of family members, dead and alive, stood on most available surfaces and were hung low on either side of the fire.

Sis's tension rose when Stanley asked whether the dark-wood davenport which stood between the windows was made by Sheraton, and Old George explained politely, but at some length, that there was no furniture known to have been made by Sheraton; the item was Chippendale, though unlikely to have been made by the man himself. This led Old George to deliver a short lecture on Chippendale. And the influence of Adam on this doyen of the furniture industry gave Stanley the opportunity to say how much he admired Adam's masterwork, the Adelphi.

Sis, silent and apprehensive at this stage, wondered whether Stanley had prepared for his evening's ordeal by reading up on the great architects and furniture-makers of the previous century; later Stanley told her that he hadn't, that any well-educated man knew about Adam and the rest. When Old George asked him about his job, he answered fully but modestly. He was an orthopaedic surgeon, recently promoted to registrar, which meant he was second in line in his department, deputy to a distinguished consultant, a medical knight. He described his work of setting bones, and improving the mobility of old people, polio victims and children with congenital disorders, adding in just enough anecdote. He took care not to dominate the conversation, listening attentively to Old George's reminiscence of falling off a bus and breaking his arm and of how pleased he had been to receive £26 in compensation just for the brief inconvenience.

Before they sat down to eat, Old George told Big Alice to bring up two bottles of his Gerwürztraminer; he had secretly put this in the wine-cooler earlier, replacing the cheaper stuff that Sis had bought the previous day. Sis squeezed his arm surreptitiously in gratitude and saw this generosity as a sign that her father was on her side. Rare, expensive and hard to find in London, it was his favourite wine and she knew that he had carried these bottles back himself from a recent trip to Antwerp.

Little Alice exhausted herself carrying heavily laden trays up and down the stairs to the kitchen while Big Alice waited at the table; many courses were served; a red wine followed the white; Ernest prattled about theatre and music hall; Young George talked about evolution and why people were getting taller.

At first Sis barely joined in the conversation. She listened intently and kept a nervous watch on the intricate manoeuvres of Big Alice as she served shellfish soup, bread, wine, water, but as she drank the strange-tasting wine, listened to the men and saw her father smiling warmly at Stanley her unease began to disappear.

Old George, who didn't like small talk unless it was about furniture, mentioned home rule for Ireland. The Thompsons were all liberals – admirers of Gladstone, despisers of Disraeli and Salisbury. Stanley had much to say and Sis could see that her father approved. By the time the Alices had cleared away the guinea fowl, which had followed the fish which had followed the soup, and Big Alice was placing the cheese on the table, Sis had relaxed and was talking as much as the men. Her father was smiling and nodding at Stanley's suggestions for improving the lives of London's poor, and Stanley was moving the conversation on to socialism, knowing that he was on broadly safe ground; Old George had reservations, as indeed had Sis, but the conversation remained a discussion without becoming an argument.

When the fruit had been cleared and the port and cigars arrived, Sis, who would usually have left the room, glanced at her father and decided to stay. She felt at ease and talkative, and screeched with horror when Stanley, prompted by Ernest and with Old George's and her own gracious permission, explained in some detail why it was likely that Jack the Ripper was a surgeon.

At midnight, when a hansom cab called for Stanley, they were calmly discussing prostitution and the repeal of the Contagious Diseases Act. Stanley was cheerily seen off at the door by every member of the household except Big Alice. Old George shook his hand heartily and told him he must come again very soon.

Sis picked up her skirts to walk down the steps and saw Stanley into his cab, receiving a brief kiss on the lips. When she returned to the house, she smiled as she passed Little Alice in the hall carrying one more fully laden tray. Pausing outside the drawing-room door, she heard her father's voice, '. . . charming and clever. Perfect for Sis, I am afraid.'

The three men were sitting by the fire sipping port. Her father told her how much he liked Stanley, describing him as very intelligent, and handsome in the same way that Young George was handsome. Sis poured herself a small glass and sat on the arm of her father's chair. She could see what he meant; there was a similarity of colouring and build. Ernest agreed, but Young George snorted and said, 'Tommy-rot.'

Later Sis went to say good-night to her father. He held her face in his hands and said, 'I told you I would like him.' She couldn't remember him telling her that, but didn't care; her greatest wish had been that her father would like the man she loved. She kissed him on the nose and told him that she knew Stanley liked him too.

Before she went to bed Sis wrote several pages in her journal, and then found that she was too excited to sleep.

6

Deborah's Room

On a Saturday in March, almost exactly two years after Uncle George had died, I played seven-a-side football at the recreation ground as I had regularly throughout that winter. There was a league, organised by someone's father, a policeman, who was often our referee. Richard, Adam, Patrick, a friend of Patrick's called Bobby and I were the regulars in Claremont Station, our team – named after the two streets between which we all lived. Bobby was our goalkeeper, and he was good – we were second out of eight in the league – but on this occasion he didn't turn up. The game, against a team from the Baptist Sunday School, was delayed for twenty minutes while Patrick, our captain, went off to look for him.

The sun was out, warming our backs as we kicked the ball around, waiting; it lit up the fields on the curving slopes of Glory Hill, a mile or two to the north. A tractor chugged slowly up and down, transforming a patch of yellow into brown, and a mixed herd of Jerseys and Guernseys, bursts of gold on a dark ground, moved lazily in a field marked by a pair of ancient oaks. Patrick returned with a stand-in goal-keeper, his brother Dennis.

Dennis played wearing jeans and a flat cap, covered himself in mud and let in four goals in the first half; he hated football. Thankfully, Adam, who was small and fast, had scored a hat-trick and I had managed to convert a penalty. By half-time a persistent drizzle had set in, and I noticed that there was a spectator on the touchline, and then that it was my father; he was wearing his new simulated-sheepskin car coat and his old green-brown hat. I wasn't totally surprised; he had a habit of turning up unexpectedly – and sometimes embarrassingly – at my school.

Patrick put himself in goal for the second half and Dennis was sent out to the left wing where he jumped up and down with his hands in his pockets. Adam was moved from the left wing to the right, and Richard moved into Patrick's crucial half-back position. I remained at centre forward, but with little hope of a pass coming in from the left.

Early in the second half I got a strong shot on goal, but the keeper caught it against his midriff and swiftly rolled it out to his captain, an oversized fifteen-year-old with aggressively short hair. The boy set off at speed towards the half-way line. Through the drizzle I could see my father shouting and waving at Dennis, urging him to tackle him. Dennis rushed towards him, but skipped daintily sideways at the crucial moment. The captain of the Baptists charged on and cleverly rounded our left back. Patrick stormed out of goal towards him. As Patrick closed on him, the boy passed neatly to a player running in on his left who booted the ball into an open goal.

Patrick moved his brother into the central, half-back position, and restored Adam and Richard to their normal positions on the wings. The idea was that, even if he couldn't tackle anyone or pass the ball, Dennis should cause some distraction by running around in the middle of the pitch, while the rest of us tried to get an equaliser. The tactic worked. Our right back sent a long pass up to Richard who moved in towards goal, kicking the ball past me to Adam who was coming in fast from the left. Adam scored his fourth, volleying to the goalkeeper's left.

Five-all, and there was less than five minutes to play. From the kick-off the Baptists plunged themselves into attack, leaving only one full-back between me and their goalkeeper, but every time we cleared the ball it was kicked back into our penalty area. Everyone but me was back in defence, and I was in our half of the field.

I thought we would be lucky to draw; there seemed little hope of us getting it into their half, and no chance whatever of us scoring. Then, Dennis, who had been fulfilling his brief by dancing crazily about in front of their players, was kicked on the shin by the Baptists' captain. He fell over and we were awarded a free kick deep in our own half. We ran back up the field and – except for Dennis, who stood in the middle of the Baptists' half gesticulating at the youth who had kicked him – packed into their penalty area as Patrick came out of goal to take the kick.

The whistle blew and he hoofed it towards us. It was high in the air and one of the Baptists headed it straight back up the field. It hit Dennis in the chest and bounced in front of him. He looked up towards the rest of us, kicked the ball ahead of him and ran after it. I ran sideways across the front of the penalty area, shouting to him to pass, but he kept on running and managed to keep the ball at his feet. As a horde of Baptists charged at him, he ignored all our shouts and kicked the ball as hard as he could. It flew past my shoulder and seemed to have a curve on it. I looked round in time to see the keeper rushing across, arms flailing. The ball sailed past him and into the top right corner of the goal.

The whistle blew for full-time. We bunched round Dennis, clapping him long and hard on the back. Patrick rubbed his brother's hair and kept shouting, 'He scored! The little bastard! He scored!' Dennis grinned and shrugged and said, 'No trouble. Any time. Easy.' My father appeared among us and shook our hero, whom he had never met before, interminably by the hand and told him it was the best goal he had seen since a sixty-five-yard dribble by Vivian Woodward at White Hart Lane in 1908. The Baptists drooped away muttering.

The sun came out again and my father joined us as we strolled back from the ground. He walked with Dennis and me, his hat to one side of his head, and told Dennis he would make a great footballer if he could master the sliding tackle, as perfected by the current Spurs centre half, Maurice Norman. When we got to the Marlow Donkey, the brown-painted pub by the railway station, my father went in and bought everyone, including himself, a Coca-Cola and a bag of crisps, ferrying it all out on a tray because we boys weren't allowed inside. We stood in the sun by the side of the road as he told all of us, individually, that we had the makings of great footballers.

We finished our drinks and left. My father went off to call on Wing Commander Hayes – a close friend and the only man in town who knew more about budgerigars than he did. I walked towards home with Dennis and Patrick. It started to rain again. As we parted on the corner of Mill Road, Dennis said, 'Great man, your dad.'

As I walked the fifty yards home I thought about the Saturday football games – how I would miss them. They were already looking for another centre forward; my first day at the new school was just five weeks off.

A little later I left the house and walked slowly around two corners into Institute Road. Warm yellow light came from the library windows, and the streetlights were flickering on as I reached the High Street and crossed towards the fluorescent glow behind the steamy plate glass of the Sugar Bowl Milk Bar. I could hear Little Richard screaming from the juke box. I knew that inside there was chrome, coffee and Coca-Cola, tight T-shirts, black leather and lipstick. The Sugar Bowl was a paradise in which I didn't yet belong. I knew because I had entered it a few weeks earlier with Richard and Adam. Too tentative and too young by a year or two – no Brylcreem and nothing to say to girls with tight sweaters and lacquered hair – we had smoked and sipped

Seven Up in a corner by the door, and were relieved when we returned to the street.

My mother's old shop was just closing, but Deborah's father was still behind his counter in front of the Easter eggs. He was tall and wore rectangular glasses with brass rims and strips of black plastic above each lens. He looked down at me and smiled. 'She's upstairs, with her mother. Go on up.' I pushed aside the curtain at the back of the shop and climbed the narrow stairs with their fitted, wall-to-wall carpet. The living-room was the first-floor front.

Deborah's mother was stitching something on her sewing machine and Deborah was helping, holding the cloth straight as it came out from under the needle. They turned their heads towards me; neither of them could move her hands. Deborah looked at me and frowned. 'Hello. Wasn't expecting to see you.'

Her mother's mouth was full of pins; she tried to smile and managed to raise her eyebrows. I had known her almost as long as I could remember; she always seemed the same, cheerful and chatty, with lipstick, make-up and glossy, dark brown hair, permed into waves. She pulled out the pins, said something about the weather and left the room.

'What's up?' Deborah was looking at me with her eyebrows lowered, a concerned expression that I knew well.

I went on standing in the middle of the carpet and didn't answer immediately. 'Nothing . . . much.' I wasn't sure why I had come.

She took my hand, pulling me towards the door. 'I want to show you something.'

We went to her room at the back of the house. It had been hers since she was born, and I had known it for almost ten years. She rearranged it from time to time – the wallpaper was now delicate and floral in shades of blue – but it always felt familiar, a small, light, low-ceilinged room with a bed in the corner beside the door. Deborah liked white. The bed had a white bedspread, the few pieces of furniture were painted white, and an off-white carpet covered most of the floor. The window looked out on the yard at the back of the shop, where the family car, an old black Austin A40, was surrounded by piles of empty cardboard boxes.

Deborah flopped across the bed with her back against the wall. She looked up at me, grinning. 'What's different?' She glanced quickly around the room.

I sat on the white chair and stared at the wall behind her. There were three familiar pictures and at the end, next to the bookcase by the window, were several photographs of Elvis, cut from magazines and gummed at odd angles to a piece of white-painted hardboard; like all our parents, Deborah's didn't allow anything to be stuck to the walls with Sellotape. I had seen them all before.

I turned around. Above her chest of drawers was a rectangular mirror with about a dozen photographs pushed between the frame and the glass. I got up and looked at them, but they were the same as the last time I'd looked; along with photographs of her family and other friends, there was one of us together by the river, taken by my father the previous summer. Towards the door was a print of Van Gogh's sunflowers, which had been there as long as I could remember, and another piece of hardboard with pictures of men in white T-shirts pasted to it: James Dean and Marlon Brando – the man, unknown to us two years before and who my father had said resembled his father. I raised my hands in a shrug. Deborah giggled and pulled her legs up underneath her.

I scanned the walls again, examined the books and ornaments on her shelves, and looked at the floor and the white ceiling. Then I saw it. Above the head of the bed, beside the door, in an upright frame, was a pencil drawing, about fifteen inches high and ten across. It showed a woman standing on her hands, her skirt falling in folds around her torso, her legs bent; with one foot she was brandishing a violin, with the other a bow. Underneath was written, in sloping capitals, '*LA FRASCETTI*'.

'Brilliant!' I clapped my hands, and leant forward for a closer look.

Deborah got off the bed and stood beside me. 'I did it for school. The teacher loves it. It's going into a county competition. She told me to frame it.'

'Brilliant!' I said again. La Frascetti's hair was hanging straight down around her face, almost touching the floor. Her knickers were striped vertically and reached to her waist. 'That's how I imagined her, but I couldn't see how her legs would be.' I bent closer again. 'They must have been like that. How did you know?'

'Look.' She fetched a doll from the cupboard where she kept her clothes. It was old-fashioned and slim and jointed at the knees and elbows; she had had it for years. It was dressed in a short dress and had short dark hair. She held it upright by the feet, pushed its arms upwards, then turned it upside down on the table with its face towards us. I squatted down to look as Deborah bent its knees forwards and outwards. 'I copied it from this.' She picked up two hair clips and held them against the doll's feet. 'Violin and bow. See?'

I stood up. 'Brilliant. She must have held them like that. It's the only way.' I looked at the picture again. 'Brilliant. Really brilliant.'

She was standing by the table. 'What did you want to say?'

'Nothing really . . . just the boarding-school thing.'

She pushed her hair back behind her ear and looked serious. 'It's a challenge – a kind of test, I suppose.'

'I'm going to miss the football team . . . and not just that, Richard, Adam, you . . . Dennis. I like Dennis.'

She picked up the doll and twisted its limbs around.

'There'll be holidays and we can go on being friends.' She picked up my hand and held it in both of hers. 'Maybe I can come and visit you.' She laughed and I noticed her gums.

'You'd have to come with my mum and dad.'

'That'd be OK.'

She let go of my hand and sat down on the chair, then picked up my hand again. 'You'll be eighteen by the time you leave. I could come and see you by myself before then.'

'God. I hadn't thought of that.' I sat down on the bed. Maybe I wouldn't stay there *that* long. I twisted my hands together; I could feel the familiar tingle of apprehension.

It had grown dark outside. I thought about the town: the lock, the Odeon, the library, the alleyway behind the shops that led to the park and the river. We had lived above the shop for six years. There had been no garden – just a concrete yard like Deborah's, with a car and empty boxes; instead we used to walk down the alleyway to the park, play on the swings, roll down a bank and lie on the grass. When I was very young, my mother had sometimes taken me through a door set into the old brick wall that lined the alleyway. Inside was a garden, beautifully kept, filled with flowers. I could remember the smell of primroses and the drops of water on their petals. There had been blue flowers with butterflies on them; my mother had shown me a peacock and a red admiral. And there was a wooden summerhouse, built of dark planks – but no other building in that garden. It was owned by a rich man who lived alone in a big house in the High Street. He rarely went out and I had never seen him, but my mother had somehow got his permission to take me into his garden. We called him 'the miser'.

Deborah stood up and walked to the window. 'Let's do something, tomorrow. Go up the river to Temple or Hurley. Have a picnic.'

She had never said so, but I knew she liked the river, the birds and boats and locks, and the backdrop of hills and woods, as much as I did. 'OK, as long as it isn't raining.' I stood up to go and peered again at La Frascetti. 'It's so good. You couldn't do another one just like it . . . for me?'

She smiled. 'Maybe. I might.' She raised her eyebrows and shrugged. 'Might not come out right, another time.'

The night was cold and damp. Particles of condensation floated in the air around the streetlights; the headlights of a lorry glowed down by the bridge. I walked past the shops. I was conscious of an unusual sadness, and wasn't sure whether it was within my control, whether I could halt it voluntarily. I was looking at the shops as if I might never see them again: Coster's the tobacconist, with its exotic smells and bowls of pipe tobacco with handwritten labels; Maison George, where I had had my first proper haircut, sitting high up on a special cushion and marvelling at the back of my head repeated endlessly in a tunnel formed by two mirrors; Milward's, the shoe shop where I had put my feet into a machine containing X-rays and seen my toes hazily silhouetted against an eerie green light inside new pairs of Clark's sandals; W. H. Smith and Lloyds Bank, where some of the assistants and clerks recognised me and knew who my parents were. The Home and Colonial Stores, Woolworth's, Keen's the camera shop, Aldridge the greengrocer, Martin's the electrical store, Platt's Garage, the florist called Pinkney's Nursery, the ironmonger around the corner whose name I couldn't recall. It was said to be a market town, and to me much of its identity came from its shops and the people I saw, inside them and in the streets.

I turned into Station Road, my street. It was darker there, and I could see the stars through a thin film of cloud. A constellation that I recognised, but couldn't name, hung above the woods beyond the river at the end of St Peter's Street.

~

I heard my father shouting as I arrived at our gate. I walked silently up the path to the kitchen window. The curtains were open and the lights were on. I could hear my mother's voice, an agitated murmur, as I stood in the shadows close to the window.

The murmur died away and my father shouted again. I could hear nothing for a few moments. Then my father's voice again, louder still. I was frightened. I knew this mood. I knew that there was spit at the sides of his mouth, that his eyeballs were popped forward in their sockets, that he was breathing heavily and glaring at her like a deranged dog. I knew that at any moment he might pick up the nearest object and, just possibly, hit her.

There was more silence. Then an angry bellow – 'You're mad' – followed by words I couldn't catch. Then 'God *strewth*!' More shouting, a stream of words that sounded like one long snarl, and another silence. My mother seemed to be dealing with the onslaught, as she usually did, by saying nothing, but I wasn't sure; she never shouted like he did. 'Paaaah!' The long drawn-out guttural syllable that I detested penetrated the tightly closed window – his unique expression of exasperation that always made me think of an angry snake poised to inflict its venom.

When I was younger I used to cower behind the door, and listen, amazed and terrified. Just once, years before, he had raised his arm to hit me; he had a full milk bottle in his hand. 'Paaaah!' I was five years old and held my arm in front of my face. Just in time he stopped, gazed at the bottle as though he hadn't known it was there, lowered his arm and crept slowly away. Now, I knew, with some certainty, that if I walked in there would be no violence; I was no threat to him physically, but my presence would trigger his shame.

I turned the handle and stepped in. For a few seconds neither of them noticed me. He was standing in the doorway of the dining-room, glowering at my mother, who was sitting at the table with her back to me, head bowed, looking down at her hands. He was shaking, his face red, his eyes and cheeks bulging, his hands held out in front of him, palms upward in a gesture of contemptuous supplication. His voice rose, angry and beseeching, 'God help us!' His mouth was contorted and ugly, his hands clenched into fists. Then he saw me. He shut his mouth and gulped, turned to one side, licked his lips, slowly unbent his hands and put them in his pockets. My mother turned, saw me, stood up, glanced at me and looked down at the floor. My father walked to the sink, filled a glass with water and drank it down. He stared out of the window for a moment, then turned and said in his normal voice, 'Your mother has been wondering whether you really want to go to that school. She—'

'I'm going to the bloody school, so there's nothing to talk about.' I was shivering. I didn't look at either of them. I walked between them into the dining-room, through the hall and up the stairs to my room. I turned on the light and stood in the doorway, listening. The shivering soon stopped, but the tingling, the pulse of fear and anger that must have entered me as I stood listening outside, remained.

Moments later, I heard my father walk across the hall to the living-room and shut the door behind him. He turned the television on, very loud; I could hear Tony Hancock's voice through the floor, followed by the deeper monotone of Sid James. After a minute he turned it down. I wandered into my room and stared unseeingly at the map of Great Britain on the wall. The tingling feeling was subsiding.

I thought about my mother, alone with him after I had gone away to school.

And then the doorbell rang. I heard my father open the front door and say, 'Hello, he's in his room I think.'

Richard came bounding up the stairs. 'You all right? You look a bit funny.' He sprawled on my bed and started turning the pages of Sis's diary for 1888.

I told him about the row I had walked in on. He was sympathetic and called my father a nutter, at which I nodded grimly. He suggested we go for a walk. 'We could even get Adam and try the milk bar again . . . I don't think.' He grinned.

My father was still in the sitting-room watching television with the door closed. My mother was in the dining-room reading the arts page of the *Daily Telegraph* with Louis Armstrong singing 'Mack the Knife' on the record player. I told her we were going out for a while, that I wasn't hungry and would eat later.

We walked towards the High Street. Richard handed me a lit cigarette. I sucked hard on it, blowing the smoke straight back out. It was good to be outside again. We crossed the High Street and went on into the park, taking the lighted path towards the river. Near the towpath, we met a group of boys coming the other way carrying fishing rods. Patrick and Dennis were among them.

'Great goal!' I shouted at Dennis and waved my fist.

'My hero!' called Richard, bowing extravagantly.

'Yeah!' he shouted back. 'Easy! . . . Good bloke, your dad . . . See ya.'

'See ya.'

'See ya.'

I stood by the river with Richard. He picked up a flat stone and spun it out into the darkness. We could hear the plips as it bounced. I stared at the swaying reflections of the lights from the few houses on the other side; through the gloom I could make out a swan standing alone on the further bank. I began to relax. There were always days, and usually weeks or months, between my father's rages; I knew my mother was safe, for a while, anyway.

7

At the Cab Rank in the Strand

ON THE LAST DAY of 1888 thirty-seven people dined, sang and danced at 59 Norfolk Road, Dalston. All but four of them were related to my great-grandfather Old George. Sis had invited Stanley; Ernest had invited his current belle from the music halls, a small, athletic young woman called Violet Henderson; and Old George's oldest friend, a dapper solicitor called Lew Johnson, had come with his statuesque and flirtatious wife, Ada.

As the eldest of eight siblings, Old George had hosted a party every New Year's Eve since 1878, the year he moved into the house. This year both of his late wife's sisters and all seven of his own brothers and sisters – even his rich and arrogant youngest brother, Charlie – were there; and all except spinster aunt Sue had brought spouses and children.

With the exception of Charlie who was a stockbroker and Uncle Coleman, a slow-witted retired policeman who pretended to be more deaf than he really was, all the men of the family, blood relations and in-laws, were small businessmen. They included a bookmaker, a tailor, a watchmaker and jeweller, and Old George's brother Bill who owned a butcher's shop but described himself as a 'general dealer'. Again with the exception of Uncle Charlie who had moved out of London to a large house in Barnet, all of them lived in east London within an arc stretching from Stoke Newington to Hoxton through Hackney and Bethnal Green; and all of them, including Charlie, met up with one another frequently.

The evening provided endless fun, although some – such

as Uncle Coleman and Aunt May Stickalorum, an austere sister-in-law to Old George who came from a family of prosperous undertakers of that astonishing name – had less than others; and one – the alcoholic, and famously smelly, spinster aunt Sue – had more.

When the eating was over and the Alices and the three servants hired for the evening had removed the debris, the piano became the focus and the occasion see-sawed from singsong to knees-up, most of the women and many of the men taking their turns at the keyboard.

Ernest's versatile friend, Violet, thrilled almost everyone. She had even Uncle Coleman in tears with a perfectly timed rendition of 'Take Care Little Mary', and danced solo to Young George's up-tempo version of 'The Belle of New York'. Sis recorded that when Violet's skirts flew up so that those who were sitting down could glimpse her knees, Aunt May Stickalorum's gasps of disapproval caused a wave of hysterical giggling which started with the young cousins surrounding Ernest and rippled around the room and up through the generations until Lew, Old George and the bright-eyed Ada were mopping their faces and slapping their knees.

As midnight approached the children – who had been read to upstairs in Sis's bed – were persuaded to reappear on the promise of 'Four little ducks in a pond' performed by Old George, his two sons, and the urbane Lew Johnson; the smaller children and Aunt Sue then screamed with terror when Uncle Joe turned down the lights and sang the morbid 'True, True Till Death' in an eerie bass with a candle held under his chin.

Whenever Sis played or sang, Stanley stood by admiringly; when she danced waltzes and quicksteps, he was her partner; and when she led the conga around the drawing-room, across the hall and into her father's bedroom, he held her waist and brushed his face against her hair. When midnight struck and glasses were raised, he pulled her behind the drawing-room door and kissed her lips and then her nose; and when Young George played three verses of 'Auld Lang Syne' with increasing ferocity and rococo flourishes, Stanley managed to be opposite Sis in the huge circle of children and adults and made sure that they regularly collided.

Carriages called for the wealthier guests. Others departed in groups on bicycles and on foot; Ernest and Violet undertook the Sisyphean task of moving a hiccuping Aunt Sue the half-mile from Norfolk Road to her rancid bedsit in Mare Street; two families with small children spent the night at the Norfolk Arms on the corner. Sis's favourite aunt, Kate, and her husband, the watchmaker Uncle Gibson (Old George's in-laws were called by their surnames), stayed over, sleeping on camp beds in the breakfast-room with their baby girl.

Stanley was the last to go and made his hansom cab wait while he and Sis took a short stroll in the unkempt garden. Sis held Stanley tight around the waist and laid her head against his shoulder; as they kissed, she was surprised, but not dismayed, to find Stanley's hand covering her breast.

~

The extended Thompson family, except perhaps Aunt May Stickalorum, approved of Stanley, and soon began whispering of marriage. By the time the freezing winter of 1889 ended, some time in March, he was spending most of his evenings at Norfolk Road. He would arrive at about seven o'clock and leave when his cab called soon after eleven. He sat with Sis in the kitchen while she bossed the servants and indulged in her favourite hobby, making clothes from patterns printed in fashion magazines; he played bezique and picquet with her on the big table in the breakfast-room; and in the drawing-room they played duets on the piano, read aloud to each other and sat talking interminably. Stanley never went above the ground floor; decorum did not permit him to enter Sis's bedroom.

However, for a young couple with, as yet, no formal relationship they enjoyed unusual freedom. This was partly because Sis had no mother, but also because Old George was a liberal and, perhaps, a little naïve, and more importantly was away a great deal; Ernest's new job as a booker at the Hoxton Britannia meant he was rarely home before midnight. Young George became an unofficial and informal chaperon, but there was soon an occasion when he too went out, to spend the evening with his new friend, Marie Potts, at her parents' home in Amhurst Road – where, Ernest frequently reminded him, the swells of Dalston lived.

Left alone in the house with just Little Alice, who would appear only if summoned, Sis and Stanley stoked up the fire, sat on the sofa and held hands. Stanley put an arm around Sis's shoulder and her cheek fell against his; gently he kissed her face and lips and hands and hair; less bold, she kissed his hand, his cheek, his forehead. It was by no means the first time they had kissed, but to be at home with her man in front of the fire, instead of standing in a draughty street, was a new and delicious pleasure.

At first, when he was at home, Old George would sit with them, talk and sometimes join in their games; but, with Stanley almost ever present, he reverted to his long-held habit of retiring to his bed surrounded by candles at about nine o'clock – not that he didn't like the man, he did; it was simply that, as Stanley became more familiar, the need to be hospitable and to keep an eye on him and Sis receded.

The door of Old George's room would be left open so that, sitting up in bed wearing a cream cotton nightshirt, he was available to whoever cared to visit, or whomever he cared to invite. The room was large and furnished with armchairs, a sofa and, for nine months of the year, if Old George was at home, a well-stoked coal fire. Friends, as well as relations, knew that the best time to have a chat with Old George was between nine and eleven in the evening as he lay against several pillows, reading and portentously smoking his pipe. Family conferences with his brothers, sisters and children were frequently conducted in this setting.

Stanley would often sit with Sis in the candlelight talking to her recumbent father about science, furniture, politics and murders. Old George was slow to accept new people, but by the summer of 1889 he saw Stanley as a friend and not just as the young man who would soon marry his daughter.

On Friday or Saturday evenings the couple would go to the theatre. Occasionally they would go to the music hall, usually on Ernest's recommendation, even though Sis mildly disapproved of much that went on there; she had a trace of snobbery not present in her father or brothers, and found certain people and activities vulgar. On Sundays, in good weather, they would walk up to Hackney Downs and pay for seats by the bandstand, or take a train with Young George and Marie from Dalston Junction to Epping Forest for a picnic in the woods – Marie's parents had been persuaded, with Old George's help, that mutual chaperoning was acceptable.

It was clear to all that Sis and Stanley were in love and well-suited, but in July Sis began to worry: Stanley had made no attempt to introduce her to his family, though he had mentioned a mother and two sisters living in Hertfordshire, and a brother who was in the navy. In August she recorded that, despite all that had passed between them, he had not made even an oblique reference to marriage. She confided her concerns to her Aunt Kate.

Ernest was the only one to ask her openly about Stanley, teasing her frequently and mercilessly in front of her father and brother. His jokes about questions being popped and his silly suggestions for wedding presents – he promised her his new xylophone on finding her playing it in his attic room – perhaps had a serious intent; he may have wanted to help his sister by bringing the matter into the open. At first his teasing embarrassed rather than worried her. Stanley didn't like to rush things, she felt; but as time passed Sis's happiness became increasingly blemished.

On Thursday 13 September, the day after he received a concerned letter from Kate, Old George returned early from work and persuaded Sis to walk up to Hackney Downs with him – Thursday was early-closing day in Dalston and therefore band night on the Downs. He told her that he had arranged to meet his brother Bill and Aunt Lil Sparrowhawk at the bandstand.

They set out soon after five o'clock; it was a cool evening with a breeze piling the leaves against the high kerb on the east side of Norfolk Road. As they turned into Downs Park Road, Old George put his arm through his daughter's and remarked that it was a shame that Stanley was not coming that evening.

Sis told him that she would be seeing Stanley the next evening and that on Saturday they would be going to the Alexandra where Henry Irving and Ellen Terry were in a play together and, after that, he would be taking her out to supper. Sis was very excited about this and Old George was understandably startled. People of their class – lower-middle – didn't eat out, except perhaps at the music hall, unless they were away from home; they were too cultured to join the lower orders in the pie and fish shops, but – even if they could afford better – were shy of the toffs and swells who filled the smart hotels and restaurants of the West End.

Sis and Stanley hadn't been out to dinner – or to a post-theatre supper – together in the eighteen months they had known each other; Old George was even more astonished when Sis told him that Stanley had reserved a table at Romano's. Neither he nor Sis knew anything of Romano's, except that it was in the Strand, shockingly expensive and one of the fashionable places of the decade.

there, oblivious of the passing of time despite the repeated chiming of the grandfather clock in the hall below, she could think of nothing but Stanley saying, 'Trust me.' Slowly it came to her that from the moment he had said that, as they waited in the queue at the cab rank in the Strand, she had stopped trusting him. She hadn't consciously lied to her father; she had been lying to herself. Looking out at the dark houses opposite, she found she couldn't stop herself crying, deep, exhausting sobs that wouldn't stop even when she lay down and put her head in her pillow.

As the sky began to grow light, she found she could cry no more; she put on a housecoat and went downstairs to the WC across the hall from her father's room. She saw candle-light flickering beneath his door. On her way back she went in. He was lying in bed, hands behind his head, staring at the ceiling with a single candle burning on the table beside him. He sat up when she entered; she sat beside him and told him that she had decided that she did not trust Stanley after all, and asked whether he agreed.

He replied, 'Perhaps,' and told her to try not to worry and that he would investigate the next day. He hugged her and told her that she must sleep. She returned upstairs and spent the rest of the night writing angrily, but lucidly, in her journal.

~

Old George rose early and by 8.30 was walking along the Balls Pond Road towards Highbury Crescent and the home of his lawyer friend, Lew Johnson. Sis got up soon after her father went out, dressed quickly, left the house while her brothers still slept and hurried to Hackney Central station.

Sitting by the window as the train lumbered from the city into the green fields around Dagenham, she thought once again about Stanley standing in the Strand telling her to trust him. She found she was shivering; her temples and upper lip were coated in a cold sweat; her hands tingled as if there were too much blood in her fingers, and the back of her head was throbbing. She hadn't slept and she didn't know what she would tell her Aunt Kate; she just knew she wanted to see her. She loved a man, a charming handsome man, but realised now that there was something wrong, that he seemed to have something to hide, a secret, something shameful. Yet, despite that certainty, she still loved him, wanted him.

At the door she was greeted by Uncle Gibson, short, stout, kindly Uncle Gibson, whom usually she loved to see. Clearly the sight of her, her pallor, her red-rimmed eyes, alarmed him. When Kate appeared, Sis grasped her round the neck and sobbed the slow rhythmical gasps of the previous night, but this time there was no need to stop. The sensitive Gibson removed himself to his workshop, with his two-year-old daughter, Kathleen.

In the cosy Braintree kitchen Kate stood in front of Sis stroking her hair from her cheeks where it was stuck with tears. Sis told her about the theatre, Romano's, the taxi rank in the Strand and the thoughts she had had during the night; Kate listened leaning forward in her chair with her hands on Sis's knees.

Privately, Kate suspected that Sis was right: that the man had a secret which would prevent marriage probably for ever, or at least in the short term. For Sis this was more than a suspicion. It was certainty and she wanted Kate to tell her that it was all right to love a man with a secret. Kate couldn't do that; love had to be founded on total trust; there were no alternatives; all else was unthinkable. She said this gently but unequivocally over and over.

But that day and the next Sis's brain didn't work as it had worked for twenty-two years; the values and safety mechanisms that she had learned as a child and had accepted for so long were suddenly of no use to her, discarded as worthless. That morning Sis was crazy. She said that she feared her father would forbid her to see Stanley and, through her tears, talked of eloping and living with him, unmarried if necessary. Kate quietly pointed to the pitfalls, the loss of self-respect, the loss of family, the loss of her life hitherto.

They talked till near lunch-time, till little Kathleen refused to be parted from her mother any longer. They put her in her pram and walked out to Panfield Woods, familiar to Sis since childhood as her family's favourite picnic place. There, with Kathleen running ahead of her, trying hard but failing to control a hoop that was too big for her, Sis relaxed just a little. She picked up her skirt and ran with her small cousin, told her the names of flowers, birds and trees, and carried her part of the way home on her shoulders.

In the evening, Sis was pleased when Kate insisted on returning to Norfolk Road with her.

When they arrived there was no one at home but Little Alice. Sis went to her room, washed and changed her clothes. Kate joined her and they brushed each other's hair. First Kate fussed over Sis, unhurried and careful; when it was Sis's turn she did her best to reciprocate. Hair in place, they lay side by side on the bed and Sis fell quickly to sleep with her head on her aunt's shoulder. It was seven o'clock.

Soon after eight Old George returned with his friend Lew Johnson. Kate heard their voices and, without waking Sis, got up and went downstairs. There her brother quickly told her his news. What they had all begun to suspect was true: Stanley was already married.

Johnson described how they had gone to Guy's Hospital, and to Stanley's rooms in the Borough, and had eventually found him in a small house in a village called Elmer's End, near Beckenham. The door had been opened by a pale woman, with a baby in her arms and a small child at her side. Stanley had come to the door when she called him but, when he had seen who they were, had tried to close the door on them. Old George had grabbed his arm, held him firmly and demanded to know if the woman was his wife and the children *his* children.

Stanley had stared at the ground and answered, 'Yes.' During the harangue that followed he had held his head in his hands. Old George had told him what decent people thought of married men who preyed on innocent young women and had the cheek to befriend their families, and had rasped his disgust at the way Stanley had deceived everyone, including his own wife and children. Stanley had spoken only once, mumbling, 'I'm sorry. I love Sis.' When the older man had sworn at him and threatened to break all his bones if he went near Sis again, Stanley had tried to jerk himself free – only to have his other arm pinioned by Johnson.

When, eventually, Old George had no more to say, Lew had persuaded him to let go of Stanley and had led him away.

Later, Sis came downstairs and heard the truth from her father and her aunt. She had no interest in any details. She murmured simply that this was what she had expected, left the room and returned to bed. Kate followed and spent the night with her niece lying in her arms moaning and shivering.

~

In the morning, over breakfast, Old George asked Kate and Young George to look after Sis while he went to his office to prepare for a holiday. He would take Sis to a friend's house near Barnstaple in Devon the next day, and he hoped that Kate, and Gibson if he could get away, would join them. Straight away Kate said she would come.

Young George, who had only just learned the truth about Stanley, dared to question the need for him to stay at home guarding his sister – he was already dressed for work in frock coat and starched collar, and was always fastidiously punctual at his office in London Wall. It was a foolish protest and provoked a deep rumble from Old George. His son sent a message to his 'guvnor', saying that owing to a family emergency he would not be able to come to work that day.

At half past eight Sis came downstairs in full outdoor clothing, down to grey kid gloves and a stylish toque hat trimmed with grey ribbons. She took her coat from the hall hat-stand and made for the front door. Young George tried vainly to stop her, but couldn't bring himself to use force. Kate ran after her down the street as far as the Norfolk Arms on the corner. Sis screamed at her to leave her alone. Her brother caught up, ignored her protests and walked behind her in silence to Hackney Downs station.

As they stood on the platform Sis acted as though he wasn't there and, when the train arrived, hit him in the chest and screeched at him to go away. George had to push his way on to the train past a well-meaning porter, who seemed to think he was molesting the smartly dressed young woman; that George was dressed in a frock coat without a hat, collar or tie may have added to the impression that he was some sort of madman.

The train was packed with men on their way to the City – on a normal day George would have travelled the same route less than an hour earlier – and three or four of them leaped up to offer Sis a seat. She graciously accepted one by a window, leaving George standing in the crowded aisle. At the first stop, London Fields, as the train gathered speed to leave the station, Sis stood up, opened the door and jumped out. She caught her foot in the doorway and fell face down on the platform. George could do nothing – by the time he reached the door the train was moving too fast – but, craning from the window, he could see people standing over what appeared to be Sis's inert body. At Cambridge Heath he jumped from the train before it had stopped, sprinted across the footbridge, boarded a waiting train and arrived back at London Fields a few minutes after leaving it. By then Sis had disappeared. George took a cab – to his father's office in Shoreditch.

Old George was angry, but only for a moment. At Hackney Downs Sis had bought a ticket to Liverpool Street which suggested to them both that she intended to get a bus from there across London Bridge to Guy's Hospital. Old George borrowed a hat, collar and tie for his son and they set off by cab.

Neither Sis nor Stanley had been seen at Guy's Hospital or at the rooming house in the Borough. Father and son took another cab to the house in Elmer's End, where they startled the pale woman whom Old George had seen the previous day. Stifling tears, she told them that a young woman had come to the door a little earlier and that Stanley had gone out with her, saying that he didn't know when he would be back; she had no idea where they had gone.

As they returned to the City by train, the two men discussed the possibility that Sis and Stanley had eloped, even though they could not legally marry. They imagined Sis travelling with Stanley to France, Scotland or Ireland and even considered that they might never see Sis again.

Young George – now suitably dressed – went to his office, while his father spent the afternoon at Norfolk Road hoping that Sis would come home or send a message. From there he sent Little Alice with a note to Lew Johnson asking if the law could do anything to prevent Sis's leaving the country.

Johnson returned with Little Alice and explained that there was nothing to be done legally by anyone except Mrs Andrews, who could, if she could afford it, take steps to prevent Stanley from leaving the country until he had made proper provision for her upkeep and that of her children. But he felt that his old friend was being alarmist – a view shared by Kate; that, for her own reasons, Sis wanted to see Stanley, perhaps just one more time. The three of them could do nothing but wait.

Young George came home, as usual, soon after six. A few

minutes later Sis returned, tearful, angry and unwilling to talk to any of them. She had a raw graze on her cheek, but waved Kate away when she tried to look at it. She told Little Alice to bring her a basin of hot water and went to her room.

~

The next day, Tuesday, Sis allowed herself to be taken by her father and Kate to the friend's house near Barnstaple. For many weeks she wrote almost nothing in her diary; the little she did write was angry and vituperative and directed at herself as much as at Stanley. Much of what happened at this time I learned from my father, who as a boy and an adult was close to everyone involved – in particular, he was to discuss these events many years later with his great-aunt Kate, but only after Sis had given Kate permission to speak.

Old George had often stayed at the house with friends; it was the second home of a wealthy London furniture manufacturer whose passion was fly-fishing. Spacious and easy to run – an obliging elderly woman with no teeth came in daily to help Kate – it was on a slope above a road, beyond which were fields at whose further edge ran a bottle-brown stream filled with trout, pike and gudgeon; across the stream dense woods rose steeply to the plateau of Exmoor.

It was late September and their first days there were grey and chill. Sis did little but sob quietly or sit silently staring, her eyes roving but unfocused. On Wednesday Uncle Gibson, having closed his shop until further notice, arrived with little Kathleen. The adults, even Gibson who at first didn't feel that it was his place, tried hard to engage Sis's attention; she would reply in a polite, clipped voice to routine remarks but would look away in silence at any reference to her disappointment. Only the child, Kathleen, could break through. Her innocent admonitions – 'Don't cry, Sis,' 'Why are you sad, Sis?' – produced a faint smile, a stroke of the hair, a cheerless hug.

At first the party spent the time walking by the trout

stream, and, with the exception of Sis, playing chess; she was a good chess-player but declined all offers of a game. And every other afternoon they all walked into Barnstaple to choose food at the High Street grocer. Old George seemed to have a lit pipe with him constantly, and took to taking Kathleen for walks. The child grew attached to him, forever asking for piggy-backs and to be taken to see the horses, a white mare and her near full-grown foal which shared a field above the house with a noisy donkey who made the child scream with laughter.

Gibson had brought his work with him and set himself up with an angle-poise light in a conservatory overlooking the river, while Old George worked at designs for chimney glasses in an upstairs room with a northerly view towards Hartland Point. Kate spent her time with her child and made sure that she was with Sis if no one else was; the two women slept in a large room with twin beds, while the uncomplaining Gibson shared a smaller adjoining room with his daughter.

At least once a day Old George would ask Sis if she would like to return to London or go somewhere else. The answer was always 'No'; it was 'peaceful' or 'quiet' there and she wanted to stay.

A week after their arrival the weather grew warmer, and on the second Saturday the two men went out early to spend the whole day fishing. Sis remained with Kate and Kathleen.

In the warm kitchen, coaxed by Kate and with Kathleen playing around her, hugging her and resting her head in her lap when she cried, Sis gradually began to talk – slowly and incoherently, with snatches of information, angry displays of feelings, tears, opaque silences. She had her aunt's total and devoted attention, as Kate struggled to understand and murmured her sympathy.

Kate was standing by the range making a second pot of

tea when Sis's manner changed abruptly. Clearly and deliberately she said that she wanted to tell her all that had happened, to confess what she saw as the complete, shameful truth. With an intensity that Kate found alarming she demanded that her aunt swear on her daughter's life to tell no one; she would tell her what had happened on the day before they came to Devon and on other days, but she had to be sure that her father, her brothers, Uncle Gibson, no one would know.

When the oath had been solemnly recited, Sis spoke quickly: cursing her own weakness; damning Stanley to hell while repeatedly saying she still loved him; but more than him, continually damning herself. Speaking ever more rapidly, she told Kate that she had sometimes gone alone with Stanley to his room in the Borough. And, yes, she had slept with him. She would never have done that, had she known he was married; she had assumed that *they* would soon be married. She whispered that it had been perfect, but now seemed shabby and shaming. It was his fault; he had deceived her. But it was her fault too; there had been no coercion. They had been in love. They were in love.

Kate was horrified, but was able to hide her shock because Sis barely looked at her as she spoke; she was speaking almost as if Kate was not there. And Sis kept talking. On the Monday, after she had escaped from George, she had gone to the house in the Borough and there she had learned from another doctor – a man she had met before – that Stanley's other home was in Elmer's End. The man didn't know the address. She had got it from the local post-mistress, and had found Stanley with his children and his 'thin, white-faced wife'. She spat these words, but it was clear to Kate that her venom was aimed at Stanley and not the innocents.

She had gone out with Stanley, walked in fields and woods, and had a drink in an empty pub. She had screamed at him, and she had hit him with her fists which she clenched in front of her aunt and banged on the table. She shouted at

Kate that she had hated him, that she still hated him. Then, for the first time in a long while, she faced her aunt, stared at her through her tears and told her, in a whisper that Kate could barely hear, that she had begged him to leave his wife, to be with her.

There was a long silence. The child lay asleep on her mother's lap. Sis spoke loudly again, telling her aunt that Stanley had said he couldn't leave, that he loved her but he couldn't be with her.

The silence resumed and was broken eventually by long, low sobbing. Kate reached across the table and clutched Sis's hand. Sis shouted, 'I am mad!' Looking at her aunt, she then spoke quietly, telling her that she had made love with Stanley that afternoon – on his coat, in a field, behind a hedge. She had known she wouldn't see him again. She hadn't cared that he was married.

Kate pulled her hand away and covered Kathleen's upturned ear. She had nothing to say. Adultery happened in books and occasionally to other people, never to anyone you knew or were related to. She had never heard, or read, of such a scene as Sis had just described. She didn't approve. She would, of course, tell no one. Other than that, she knew only that she wanted time to think.

Her confession over, Sis stood and walked aimlessly about the room. Kate sat silent at the table and the child slept on. Sis turned to her and spoke words that Kate remembered years later, 'Don't judge me. You can't know how it is . . . how it was. No one can, except me.'

8

With the Toffs and Swells

DEBORAH DIDN'T MAKE another drawing of La Frascetti. Instead she gave me the original as a going-away present. On a warm May afternoon, as my parents drank tea with the housemaster, I took it from my trunk and hung it from a coat hook on the green plywood partition that separated my cubicle from the next in a long dormitory with a high, steepled ceiling.

That evening at 9.30 p.m., just before lights out, a red-cheeked prefect told me to take it down: the coat hooks were for clothes only and no decorations were permitted on cubicle walls. I could place framed photographs of members of my family on top of the chest of drawers; that was all. I told him that La Frascetti was a member of my family. He looked at the drawing, turned it upside down so that he could see my great aunt's face the right way up, stared at me with some apprehension and said, 'Are you sure?' I told him that she had been my great uncle's wife, a music-hall artiste. He said he was sorry; it wasn't a photograph. I had no photographs, framed or unframed.

Next day, I discovered that I had a cupboard in which to keep my school books in a room called Hall, where junior boys spent their small portions of spare time and did their prep. There was a nail on the inside of one of the two doors and La Frascetti hung on it for the next four terms.

Polegate was tall and olive-skinned and the only boy in my house who was in the same form as me. Wearing my regulation black gown over my tweed sports jacket and regulation blue tie, I followed him along brown corridors with parquet flooring towards my first lesson, maths. I tried to befriend him by asking sensible questions.

'What's the maths teacher like?'

'They are not teachers. They are dons.' He looked over his shoulder and down at me, and carried on walking.

'What's the don like then?'

He looked back at me and sighed, 'Mr Silversmith. Strange. Funny. You'll see.'

'Are you a wet bob or a dry bob?' Wet bobs rowed. Dry bobs played cricket. I had chosen to be a wet bob simply because I liked rivers.

He spun half round and frowned down at me. 'Wet bob, of course.'

'Do you row in an eight?'

'No, a four.'

'Are you rowing this afternoon? I think I am.'

'Yes. Now stop asking questions.'

He walked on, taking large strides. I hurried along behind him, trying to hold my books against my chest with one hand like he did. We turned a corner and Polegate almost collided with our housemaster, Mr Bird.

'Good morning, sir.'

'Good morning, Polegate.'

'Good morning, sir.'

'Good morning.'

'What's Mr Bird like, would you say?'

'Questions, er . . . Reynolds! Questions! You must stop asking questions. We're in a hurry.'

I followed him in silence as he threaded his way through groups of black-gowned boys coming the other way. To our left were classroom doors, some of them open displaying desks, blackboards and boys sitting and standing about; sun streamed in through tall windows and there was a cacophony of heels on parquet, loud voices and laughter. To our right were more windows. I glanced out at a vast tract of green; mown grass stretched to a distant, blurred horizon and the sky was as blue as it ever is in England. To the left was a cricket pavilion standing high on a grassy mound; red brick with white-painted gables and balconies, it looked like some of the smart villas near the river in Marlow. Beyond it the grass was sullied only by an occasional clump of trees and a few picturesque wooden huts which I was to discover were lesser cricket pavilions and good for smoking in at night. We left the corridor momentarily and crossed some gravel under an arch; to my left I glimpsed a grassy quadrangle with diagonal paths before we entered a replica of the corridor we had just left.

Polegate grabbed the handle of a green-painted door and entered in front of me. The room was full of boys sitting at desks talking loudly and laughing. Polegate turned, sighed and pointed at an empty desk one row from the back; he walked away and sat in the front row by the window.

I sat down and fiddled with my pile of books. A few boys glanced at me curiously and then looked away. A minute later the door was suddenly thrown open and a small, round man with a greying crew cut shot across the front of the room to the window, his gown flying behind him. He glared around the room angrily and then, taking huge steps on very short legs, placed himself behind the teacher's desk in front of the blackboard.

'Welcome back, Set . . . One.' He looked at the far corners of the room and then down at the desk in front of him. 'Adcock.'

'Sir.'

'Addis.'

'Sir.'

'Beauchamp.'

He paused after a boy called Chandler had said 'Sir,' and looked around as though mystified. 'Chandler. Where . . . is Chandler?'

A pale boy to my left put his hand up. 'Here sir.'

'Stand up, Chandler. You're new . . . Scholarship boy. Excellent maths papers. Very good . . . Chandler. Sit down.' He spoke very fast with pauses in unexpected places.

The litany halted again at Partington. 'Where are . . . you Partington?' He was small and sharp-faced and sitting by the door. His cheeks coloured up when he stood up. 'An exhibition. Very high maths mark. Well done.'

'Thank you sir.'

'Are you related to J.P. . . . Partington?'

'My cousin, sir.'

'Hopeless . . . Hopeless . . .' – he spat the word while scratching the back of his head – 'at maths, but . . . excellent wing three-quarter.'

'Yes sir.'

'Sit down, Partington.'

The roll-call continued, and now I knew what to expect. 'Reynolds.'

'Sir.'

He looked around. 'We have three new boys: Chandler, Partington and . . .' He looked down at his desk. 'Reynolds . . . Now where is . . . Reynolds?'

'Here sir.' I put up my hand and began to stand up.

'Did I ask you to stand up?' He glared at me in horror, his mouth wide open.

'No sir.' I sat down amid muffled giggles.

'Stand up, please . . . Reynolds.'

I stood with both hands lightly touching the sides of the desk, looked at Mr Silversmith and tried to smile. 'Stop grinning, please.' There was more giggling. I stared at the back of the boy in front of me. There was silence except for a rustling of paper. I glanced upwards. He had turned his back to the window and was staring at a clipboard. 'Ninety-four per cent in Maths A . . . Eighty-nine in Maths B. I remember your B paper, Reynolds. You rushed a couple of quadratic equations. Over . . . confident I expect. It pays to . . . take it slowly. Otherwise, not bad. Very good. Sit down.' I sat and breathed a long breath out – and had a sudden vision of Nick from my old school; how would he cope in the top maths set at Eton?

'Open your books!' He barked the command. 'At page one . . . hundred.'

I scrabbled through, found the page and looked up.

'And', he drew the word out, 'for-ty.'

I found page 140 and looked up again.

'Seven!' He giggled, and leered at us with small grey teeth. The other boys laughed. The joke was aimed at Chandler, Partington and me.

Page 147 was simultaneous equations. Mr Silversmith spoke, shouted and whispered, and wrote at great speed on the board frequently breaking the chalk. For fifteen minutes we had to solve equations from the book.

One of them had some wavy brackets in it that I had not seen before; I made a guess at what they might mean. As we worked, Mr Silversmith stalked the rows of desks on tiptoes, clutching his gown tight to him as though trying to keep warm. He looked at our work as he passed, but never broke step.

A sudden yell of 'Stop!' broke my concentration. 'Beauchamp, Chandler, Hunt, Partington, Jackson-Smith, Reynolds . . . come here.' He glared around the room. 'The rest of you, carry on. There are . . .' he looked exaggeratedly at his watch, and I noticed that his wrist was white and fleshy, 'nine more minutes.'

We grouped around his desk and he jabbed his finger at

the second equation, staring at us with a hurt expression. 'You don't know what this means, do you?'

Chandler and I both murmured, 'No sir.'

He sighed. 'Does anyone have *any* idea?'

'The sine of what is inside the brackets sir?' Hunt looked down at him hopefully.

There was a silence during which Mr Silversmith put his head in his hands, and then very slowly, without getting up from his chair, pulled the back of his gown up and over his head. Loud laughter came from the rest of the class and someone even banged the lid of his desk. Polegate leaned back in his seat, smirking. With a sudden movement Mr Silversmith stood up, swept his gown back, pushed his face into Hunt's and said with great precision, 'Tan-gent,' splitting the syllables as if the one word were two. He stared round at the six of us. 'Tan-gent, gentlemen. Take the tangent of whatever is within the brackets. Back to your desks. There are . . .' – he looked at his watch again – 'six more minutes.'

~

The next lesson was physics. Polegate was in a different set, so he arranged that Hunt show me where to go. I already felt that I liked Hunt; he was chirpy and freckly and had kept smiling through Mr Silversmith's tangent performance. We walked together through arches and quads, past a clock-tower and along a paved path between old red-brick buildings called fives courts.

We reached a flat-roofed, concrete building and entered a room where boys were sitting on tall stools at benches with sinks and taps. I had done no physics before so I was in the bottom set with Hunt, Chandler and a lot of seemingly older boys, many of whom had lumpy names; Upjohn, Ormrod, Bracegirdle and Hincks were hairy and broad-shouldered, and sat in that order in the back row where they whispered and started small fires from time to time.

~

That afternoon, among a stream of boys, Hunt and I bicycled the three miles to the boathouses on the Thames. The river was a sea of sleek boats – eights, fours and single skulls – moving at different speeds in all directions. Coxes in peaked caps shouted and banged the sides of boats with their fists, and coaches rode bicycles along the towpath bellowing in competition with each other.

I had my first lesson in a heavy, wide, wooden boat called a tub. It was hard, but after a while I began to relax, pull strongly on my oar and even enjoy the experience. Suddenly I felt a great thwack in my solar plexus; my oar seemed to have got stuck in the water. I was winded and pushed off my seat into the arms of the boy behind me. The boat rocked and spun and water cascaded all over me.

Our coach, a prefect called Richards, found it funny as he told me that I had caught a crab because my strokes were too long; I should lift my blade out of the water sooner; I was trying too hard. This was contrary to my father's advice about getting the most out of life, but I was prepared to do anything to avoid being hit in the stomach by a heavy piece of wood. So I tried less hard, and rowed better.

I had to wait for Hunt, so I wandered a little way up the towpath and looked around. I remembered the dark majesty of Quarry Wood rising behind the lock in Marlow. These bleak fields were no substitute. The countryside was flat and the river here, south of Oxford, was narrow. As I stood there, looking at the horizon and trying to shut out the shouting, sweating oarsmen in the foreground, a line of swans came round a wide bend, a quarter of a mile to the east.

Hunt came up and told me that, if I liked gazing at swans, I should join the fishing club.

~

My parents visited every third Sunday which was as often as they were allowed. Because it was so small, the A35 attracted attention beside the Bentleys, Jaguars and Rovers on the gravel under the horse chestnuts by the pavilion. My father attracted attention because of his age, his hat, his trousers which were a little too short, his new hearing aid with its wire dangling from his ear to a brass microphone clipped to his breast pocket, and his outspokenness. My mother, despite clothes that didn't come from Harrods or Peter Jones, blended in – her father and uncles had been at the school after all.

On their first visit they brought photographs of themselves. My father's was a studio portrait taken in 1947 – he had cut it out of a copy of his autobiography; my mother's was more up to date – a fixed-smile polyphoto from a set taken for my grandmother. Facing each other in a new, brown leather frame which opened like a book and stood on my chest of drawers beside my hair brushes, they looked like a conventional couple of similar age – my father frowning and exuding *gravitas* in a dark jacket and puffed-out tie, my mother showing a little teeth with hair newly shampooed and set and a piece of costume jewellery holding her blouse together – and not at all like the real thing, an elderly seed salesman and his middle-aged wife who worked in a shop, or, as I still liked to see them, the cleverest, funniest man and the most loving, unselfish woman in the world.

On their third visit, a hot Sunday in late June, they brought Deborah with them. I took her to see my cupboard in Hall, so that she would know that La Frascetti was displayed in the only place possible. I found that boys were staring at her and making faces at me, and for the first time I glimpsed her through other males' eyes. She was slim, as she had always been, and wore her dark hair neck-length and parted a little to one side, as she always had. In blue jeans and a white T-shirt – the kind of clothes she wore to the library and the Odeon in Marlow – she wasn't overdressed, unlike many of the boys' sisters who hung around on the gravel on Sunday mornings in hats, silk blouses and pearls. Like me, she was thirteen, approaching fourteen, and I came to see – as other boys raised their eyebrows knowingly at me behind her back – that she was a teenager, not a girl – Audrey Hepburn, not Hayley Mills.

Deborah's looks and her habit of holding my hand gained me some kudos among my peers. On that first visit, she seized my hand and swung it as we dithered on the gravel by the A35 waiting for my parents to extricate themselves from drinks with the housemaster. Several boys were nearby watching us and others were peering from windows. I was embarrassed, but pleased to find when I returned in the evening that my new friends – and some who had not been so friendly – were keen to know all about her.

Was she my girlfriend? Had I snogged with her? Had she got a sister? Did she write me letters? Had I got a photograph of her? There were cruder questions than these which I pretended not to hear, but I grabbed at the opportunity to boost my status, playing up my relationship with Deborah as far as I reasonably could, implying that we were boyfriend and girlfriend who snogged at every opportunity – and I wrote asking her to send a photograph.

The truth was that we had walked around a pub garden talking while my father snoozed and my mother read the *Observer*. I had loved being with her; seeing her climbing out of the A35 had reminded me of the freedom I had lost – something that was constantly on my mind anyway – but talking to her had clarified my conviction that I would regain it – once I had done my duty. She kept telling me that I wouldn't be at this school for ever, that there would be years afterwards when I could do exactly what I liked.

As I lay awake that night in my drab cubicle in the high-ceilinged dormitory, I remembered what Deborah had said and decided that when I left I would get a job, any job, and enjoy the freedom that earning my own money would bring.

Hunt and Chandler and a boy in my house called Connolly, who had wavy blond hair and played the guitar, became my closest friends. But I was generally accepted by the crowd, and I had no enemies – beyond those prefects who used their power to torment us fags with laborious and unnecessary tasks.

There was a boy, who joined my house in the term I did, who had no friends. His name was Jessop. He was tall and awkward in his movements and, when I met him – on my first day at school – a little supercilious and pleased with himself; he certainly wanted me to know that he had won a scholarship. The group soon decided that he was stuck-up and homosexual – which was ironic, since the majority of the boys were homosexual to a degree during their schooldays.

On Sunday mornings there was a queue for chapel; we all had to stand in our allotted places, wearing white surplices, so that we could enter the chapel in two parallel white columns. The audience for this spectacle was made up of dons and any visiting parents who were sufficiently interested to attend the hour-long weekly mattins. My place in the queue was immediately behind Jessop.

One Sunday, another boy tapped me on the shoulder, handed me a needle and indicated that I should jab it into Jessop's bottom. I wasn't keen; I had some sympathy for Jessop and there were prefects standing about making sure that we behaved properly. However, when I hesitated, I found there was a group of six or seven behind me, giggling and egging me on. I made sure no prefects were near, and stuck the needle in. Jessop shrieked and jumped in the air holding his bottom. The giggles behind me turned to howls of laughter. Jessop turned on me with a scowl, but at that moment we had to start walking in our parallel lines.

As we knelt and sat and stood and sang hymns, I regretted what I had done and thought about my father telling me never to conform, never to follow the herd. I had slipstreamed the herd, meekly, without thinking.

~

Despite the camaraderie of Hunt, Chandler, Connolly and others, and although I had new things to do like fishing, playing snooker and breaking bounds, I continued, as the terms went by, to dislike my new way of life. I missed my parents, my old friends and my freedom, and felt stifled by rules and timetables, silly traditions, casual insults and inane brutality.

I affected an air of unconcern; I had a need to pretend – to my parents as well as my peers – that everything was all right, that the indignities did not disturb me. I thought from time to time of my father's rant against capitalism – 'I will not suffer from a system I despise' – and broke rules as and when it suited me. I was beaten by prefects, the housemaster and the headmaster with tedious regularity, but I made certain that I did nothing that could get me expelled. I fitted in to the extent of doing my schoolwork to a reasonable level and playing a role in certain sports, but I greatly disappointed Mr Bird who told me that I didn't try hard enough, that I was capable of excellence and should not waste so much energy flouting authority.

Chandler and Connolly, whom I soon came to call by their Christian names, Pat and Peter, were my main accomplices. We weren't evil; we just smoked and drank, and spent time in coffee bars, betting shops, pubs and cinemas. And, of course, I put a photo of Deborah on my chest of drawers and told the prefects that she was my sister.

Towards the end of my second term I was beaten by Henderson, the head of house, for the third time for no particular crime – just for an accumulation of small misdemeanours racked up by the prefects on a points system. After the ritual – six strokes delivered in the presence of a witness, the deputy head of house – Henderson asked me to come to his study.

He told me to sit down on a sofa next to a table with a kettle and instant coffee on it. 'I don't like beating you all the time. In fact, I don't like beating anyone. It's a bore.'

I said that I was sorry. I'd try not to break the rules.

He picked up a packet of biscuits and offered me one. They were chocolate digestives. I took one, he sat down and we munched silently together; his hands dangled between his knees and he stared at the carpet. 'You're brainy aren't you? You're in the fifth form already.'

I nodded and said, 'I suppose so.' I knew that Henderson was taking a scholarship to an Oxford college.

He looked at me for a few seconds, then looked down at the carpet, then at me again. He handed me another biscuit and bit into one himself. 'It can be hard being brainy in a school like this . . . probably in any school . . . if I say so myself.' He smiled. 'Try to belong, Reynolds. Do you know what I mean?'

'Belong . . . here?'

'Yes. There are some good things. Find them.' He gave me another biscuit. 'Just ignore the rest.'

~

I wasn't sure what the good things were, though I guessed that they didn't include smoking in a hollow tree with Pat Chandler or bicycling to Oxford and trying to talk to girls in Woolworth's with Peter Connolly.

Over breakfast at home on the first day of the holidays, I told my parents what Henderson had said about belonging and how I didn't feel that I did and why should it matter anyway. My father lowered the *Guardian*, his paper since the *News Chronicle* went out of business, looked at my mother, and said, 'Try to belong. "Only connect." Wise chap, your friend Henderson.'

My mother put down the *Daily Telegraph*, reached across the table, picked up my empty cereal bowl and placed it inside her own with the two spoons on top.

'For God's sake, Mary! David wants to know about belonging . . . what the boy, the prefect, meant . . . and all you can do is collect the dishes.' My father's voice rose. 'Lord deliver us!'

My mother looked at me as if my father wasn't there. 'He means you should try to feel part of the school, the community, and take the opportunities on offer, like you do here in Marlow. Don't fight against it. Learn what you can. There will be good teachers and not so good teachers. He means take advantage of the good ones, enjoy the good things, enjoy yourself . . . He probably also means: don't waste time breaking rules.' She smiled and touched my hand. My report had referred to my being 'a little unruly'.

My father licked a Rizla paper and spoke again, in his normal voice. 'He could also mean: respect the institution. It's been there a long time. Just that very fact gives it some value.' This seemed an odd thing for him to say – he who wanted to remove the idle rich and give power to the workers – but I didn't argue. I just buttered some toast as he went on. 'There is value in ritual and tradition and, yes, your friend Henderson is absolutely right, it is worth belonging to an institution like that . . . I mean allowing yourself to feel that you belong . . . as long as you don't swallow it all hook, line and sinker. Take the bits that seem good to you.' I found this confusing. What my mother had said made more sense.

9

My Hat!

SIS SPENT TWO and a half months away from London, returning just before Christmas. The party stayed at the house in Devon for three weeks during which Old George arranged an extensive and leisurely sales trip, beginning with visits to old friends in the furniture trade.

After a few days in a newly-built, red-brick mansion in Prestwick, where Sis played interminable games of cards with the wife and daughters of a red-faced upholstery magnate, dubbed by her father 'the King of Kapok', father and daughter moved on to a luxurious old house in the Warwickshire countryside as the guests of a religious and hospitable family called Taylor. Here Sis was allowed more time alone and passed the days outdoors, shrouded in a thick black cloak borrowed from Mrs Taylor. For long hours she sat under a giant cedar at the northern edge of an impeccable lawn; when she tired of sitting she wandered beside a canal which had been diverted from a nearby stream, lined with red brick and filled with goldfish for the pleasure of the Taylor family.

At the Taylors' Sis and her father were joined for a weekend by Young George, who had barely spoken to his sister since she jumped from the train at London Fields. Sis was touched that he had come – touched sufficiently to make a short entry in her journal. Clearly he had travelled to see *her*; he had little in common with the Taylors beyond a generosity of spirit. They hugged and cried together in his dark-panelled bedroom, and he gently urged her to embrace the future and abandon the past.

She brushed her face against his tickly tweed jacket to remove her tears. Though she saw the good sense of his advice, she knew she couldn't act on it – not then, perhaps never. She told her brother that he was lucky to be a man, and he replied that he would never behave as Stanley had done. Of course he wouldn't, but the irony was plain. Her innocent brother had no conception of what Stanley had really done; except for Kate no one ever would.

He noticed that she had lost weight. He touched her chin and felt her upper arm through her sleeve. He urged her to eat properly. She knew she should, but told him truthfully that she never felt hungry.

Sis and Old George went next to the large ramshackle home of a family called Inglesant outside Leicester; here they regularly sat down to eat with a noisy group of eight children, and the huge, maternal Mrs Inglesant urged Sis, whom she considered unhealthily thin, to eat at least as much as her four-year-old.

Sis became a passive bystander in her own life. She didn't object to following her father about or to being mothered and bossed by Mrs Inglesant or anyone else; the only thing she objected to was the three-hole earth closet at the end of the Inglesants' garden. Old George had business to do with his old friends, but father and daughter spent hours and days together, playing chess and talking – although Stanley was never mentioned.

After Leicester they spent some days in Dublin, and at the beginning of December passed through London en route for Paris, staying at Norfolk Road overnight. It was Sis's first trip to France and she was, as her father had intended, distracted by the newness and strangeness; she was amazed by Old George's ability to speak what sounded like fluent French and by the fact that he had close friends there, too.

They travelled to Brussels and then to Antwerp, where in a hotel room by the harbour, with trams ringing and rattling in the street below, she stared into a mirror and realised that she was caring about something again; she found that she missed her home, her brothers – funny Ernest and kind, sweet George – and Little Alice, to whom she felt almost like a mother – and Kate; she would love to see Kate. She knew she had upset her and longed to explain, to try to make her understand; then Kate would forgive her. She was not a scarlet woman. She was just Sis, an ordinary woman who had fallen in love. It was just bad luck that the man had been . . . no good? A villain? A deceitful fool? He was those things, but he was also good-looking and clever, and she remembered how he had made her happy. She still loved him, imagined that she always would, but knew that she could not see him again.

In Antwerp she began to write normally, lengthily, in her journal again, for the first time since the horrible night after the dinner at Romano's. She wrote no more about Stanley, but filled two pages with observations of her father.

She had always loved him, of course, but now she felt a new admiration: for his easy-going ways, his strong sense of morality and the calm, competent way that he dealt with life. She wondered what he would have done if he had discovered the full truth about her passion for Stanley, and decided that for once he would have been nonplussed – torn down the middle between his moral values and his love for her. She wrote about his wit, his jokes, his twinkly eyes; the affection and respect that he had received from so many people of different kinds in different places as they had travelled. She praised his work, his furniture designs which he was constantly engaged in selling and to which she had seldom given a thought.

This is not to say that in a hotel in Antwerp, Sis suddenly regained her spirit. When they returned to London three days before Christmas, something she both dreaded and looked forward to, she felt awkward, as though she was an outsider; she found it impossible to respond to the cheerfulness, and especially to Ernest who had a noisy new lady friend. When he spoke to her seriously and said how sorry he was, she was pleased and they hugged, but otherwise his natural banter, with which she had lived happily for twenty years, depressed her. With all of them she became withdrawn and, when asked her opinion on household matters, an arena she had formerly ruled, she simply agreed to anything that anyone suggested.

On Christmas Eve, Kate came with Kathleen and they had a long talk in Sis's bedroom while Little Alice minded the child. Kate told her how hard it had been for her to understand, that she had thought for days about what Sis had told her, but that she had had a flash of understanding; she too had once felt passion – for her husband, Henry, Sis's Uncle Gibson. 'Don't laugh,' she said.

Sis didn't laugh. She understood and was struck by the humdrum nature of her position. She had simply fallen in love with the wrong man. That was all. Many women, like her aunt, seemed to find the right man; some found no man at all; a few, like her, made mistakes.

Kate told her that she was still shocked by the thought of the room in the Borough and of Stanley's raincoat. But she smiled as Sis blushed – and confirmed Sis's own opinion that she was not 'a bad woman or a sinner'.

The family had a quiet Christmas, apart from the frequent presence of Ernest's new lady friend, a young woman from the East End with a Cockney accent who performed in the music halls. The New Year party of course had to happen, but was a sombre affair compared with the previous year's. Sis spent the time quietly telling Kate and the sympathetic Lew and Ada Johnson about Dublin and Paris and Antwerp. When the supposedly deaf retired policeman, Uncle Coleman, told her that he'd heard that she had had 'a bit of trouble', she sparked up and retorted that she was surprised that he had heard anything.

Sis took up her former routines, without enthusiasm but now without resentment; her role was to make her father happy, and she no longer looked for anything else. He, in turn, began taking her to dinners and parties; he was invited to many and he now made sure that she was invited too.

According to my father, Kate encouraged this while Young George protested, thinking, probably rightly, that his father was hoping that Sis would find another, more appropriate, man; there was something undignified, her brother thought, about her being put on show in the hope of finding an admirer when she was still so hurt and vulnerable.

But she enjoyed being her father's constant companion. She dressed well, behaved politely, her wit gradually returned, and she knew that he felt good as he entered rooms – grand and not so grand – with her on his arm.

At the end of April Ernest married Rose Porter in a church in Bethnal Green. The aunts, uncles and cousins, down to the smallest Sparrowhawk, were there. Young George was best man; Old George, for once resplendent in formal dress, walked down the aisle beaming with the bride's mother on his arm; Sis caught the bride's bouquet outside the church and giggled with Kate.

On a still, humid evening early that summer of 1890, Sis and her father dined at the Johnsons'. The french windows in the dining-room were open to a rose-filled garden where five men and five women loitered over pre-dinner drinks. Sis and Old George knew everyone present except a handsome man of medium height whom Ada Johnson introduced as 'a sort of brother-in-law'. He was the brother of Ada's much younger sister's husband. His name was Tom Reynolds.

He seemed uncomfortable in the company; as he stood awkwardly beside his brother and his host, sipping whisky and listening to them discuss whether Gladstone could become prime minister again, Sis guessed he would rather have been anywhere but there. When he took his place at the table, he still seemed ill at ease even though the two people he knew well – his brother and his sister-in-law – were sitting close to him.

Tom Reynolds was a thirty-one-year-old bachelor, with the type of good looks that can make men or women forgettable because they have no memorable features. He had a rakish, brown moustache – more fashionable than distinctive – swept sideways from the corners of his mouth. My father said of him that, like many handsome men, he was shy and frequently diffident; women had been drawn to him, but he had backed off, seeming to push them away as if to say, 'Why me? I'm no one special.' He was a good listener, enjoyed one-to-one conversations, but became tongue-tied in a group. He was the eldest of seven children; his brother Bill, who was facing him across the table, was five years younger and an ebullient, non-stop talker.

Sis was sitting on his left and sensed his awkwardness; he was fiddling with his fork and seemed to be pretending to listen to his brother who was still talking loudly about Gladstone. Sis leant towards him and asked him why she hadn't seen him there before.

He explained himself, his relationship to Bill and – through Bill's wife Sarah – to Ada Johnson; and she explained herself, her father's long friendship with Lew Johnson.

He told her about his work, at the Welsbach Incandescent Light Company in Westminster, and about the intriguing Baron von Welsbach who had invented the dazzlingly bright, almost everlasting gas mantle. Sis discovered that he travelled to Germany and Belgium from time to time, and that he knew Antwerp well – it was his favourite city. They talked enthusiastically about the port, about Notre-Dame Cathedral and its famous Rubens, 'Descent from the Cross', and about other works of Rubens in the Royal Museum. Sis noted that he had two pet expressions, 'Tommy-rot' and 'My hat' – the way he said 'My hat', in particular, made her smile. When she mentioned the printer Plantin, his house and the museum of his work in Vrijdagmarkt, Tom became ecstatic in his praise for the man whom he described, with many 'My hat's, as a genius.

The food came and went, glasses were refilled, and they talked on. She liked talking to him, appreciated his dry, self-deprecating humour, and she noticed that fine lines radiated from the corners of his eyes and vertical furrows appeared in his cheeks when he smiled. One of his stories made her laugh out loud, and she saw him begin to relax.

Dropping his voice and leaning closer to her – he seemed almost to have forgotten that there were others at the table – he told her about his family, his eccentric, portrait-painter father, dead more than ten years, and his mother who ran a small boarding house in Bournemouth and who still had three children at home. With good-humoured derision, he spoke of his 'crazy' sister Emily who was constantly unwell but believed that God would, one day, make everything all right. It was clear that he had little time for God-botherers.

Sis found herself talking about her mother's death, the effect it had had on her and her brothers, and then, quietly, about her father: what a good, upright man he was; how he had cared for her and her brothers while building his reputation as a furniture designer. Tom listened attentively, and she was sorry when the port arrived and she had to follow the other women from the room.

~

A week later Old George received a letter from Tom asking permission to call on him and Sis at their home. Sis told her father that she liked Tom, but had no desire to encourage him. However, it was decided that it would be rude not to entertain him, that Sis could make it clear that she had nothing to offer except friendship, and that she would not be left alone with him. Old George sent a note inviting Tom to call for drinks after dinner, at 8.30 p.m. the following Friday.

Tom arrived on time carrying an extravagant bunch of white chrysanthemums mixed with deep-red roses, and was shown into the drawing-room by Little Alice. Greeted warmly by Old George and introduced to Young George, whose first impression was that he liked this man, he handed the flowers to Sis who blushed and thanked him.

The flowers were taken away by Little Alice – to be returned later in a blue glass vase for final arranging by Sis on the sideboard – and drinks were poured: sherry for Sis, port for Tom and Young George, whisky for Old George. There was the usual discussion among relative strangers about where he lived – lodgings, which meant a room with breakfast and evening meal provided, in a new terrace near the Angel – and how he had travelled to Dalston – by tram up Essex Road and then a walk along the Balls Pond Road.

After some talk about the furniture, Old George stood up, nodded to the three of them, told them to come and see him later on, picked up his whisky and walked from the room.

Tom looked bemused at this and Sis explained that her father always went to his room at nine o'clock. She suggested that the three of them play dummy bridge.

Decorum and their former agreement dictated that Young George must stay with Sis and Tom, but after a rubber of bridge – in which Tom partnered Sis, and George beat them playing with the dummy – to Sis's irritation he excused himself and left the room.

Sis and Tom faced each other across the baize-covered card table in front of the sideboard. There was a silence before Sis remarked on the beauty of the flowers he had brought. She stood up and smelled them.

He told her how good it was to see her again and how he had enjoyed the evening at the Johnsons'.

She said that she had enjoyed it too.

Then, with the correct amount of deference, he asked if he could visit her again.

'Of course.' The response somehow slipped out, without her thinking about it.

Tom smiled as George returned. They cut for partners for another rubber; Sis drew the dummy.

She thought later how she could have politely discouraged him; women knew how to do that and did it often; she had done it on occasion; there was an etiquette for these situations. For some reason – she didn't know why – she had just said it, 'Of course.' Was it that she was tired of nuance, didn't care about all that any more, and had simply answered his question literally? 'Of course' he could come again. He was a nice man. She liked him. Why not? But, if that was her attitude, wasn't she being terribly modern! She didn't think of herself as modern. She was an ordinary woman with ordinary morals – she had thought about her ordinariness, her cleaving to convention, over and over, and had convinced Kate of it, with sincerity. Anyway, he would come again and she would see whether she wanted to be modern.

Sis lost the rubber, and they crossed the hall to see Old George.

'The holy of holies,' Sis heard her brother mutter to Tom as they entered.

Tom hesitated by the door, seemingly transfixed by the flickering light of a dozen candles. Old George invited him to sit down. He took a padded, armless chair at the end of the bed, and – as he said later – felt as though he had arrived in the premises of an arcane religious sect.

Old George smiled and acknowledged that gaslight was Tom's living, and told him that he valued it and used plenty of it, but that he liked to celebrate flame, the first source of light.

Sis wondered why her father was being so pompous, but

Tom simply looked startled and said, 'My hat! You certainly have a lot of candles in here, sir.' Sis and Young George suppressed their giggles.

There was a noise at the front door and the sounds of a man and a woman talking. A moment later Ernest walked in, greeted everyone loudly and introduced himself to Tom.

Ernest knew Tom's brother Bill, and was soon telling Tom that he must come and see his wife Rose's new act. It was still being rehearsed, but would be a scorcher; one impresario wanted them both – he had become her manager and played a small part in the act – to perform in St Petersburg, and another wanted them in New York. Tom should come to the first public performance at the Britannia. He would get him good seats.

As he spoke, a thudding noise came from the stairs, followed by the screeching of a violin.

Tom stood and looked through the open door to the hall. Old George stayed in bed smiling, and the others remained in their chairs. The sound grew louder and closer, and Tom could hear an approximation of the tune of 'Daisy'. Then, into his line of vision, came a woman walking on her hands; her legs were encased in silver sequinned tights and her short black skirt fell around her torso. She stepped off the bottom stair and proceeded across the carpeted floor of the hall. She was playing the violin with her feet.

'My hat!'

'My wife, Rose. Stage name, La Frascetti.'

10

The Large-eyed Beauty

IN THE SPRING of 1963 my parents sold our home in Marlow, put the furniture in store and went to live in a caravan among other caravans in a flat, sparsely grassed field near Taunton. The seed company had promoted my father and posted him to Somerset, where their business was flagging. The caravan was to be a temporary arrangement while they looked for a permanent home.

During my Easter holiday I slept on what served as a seat in the daytime, with my father snoring two feet away on the facing seat. My mother had a fold-down bed over which we had to climb if we wanted to go out at night for a pee on the grass or, worse, to walk fifty yards for a shit in a breeze-block cubicle. My mother, whose Edwardian childhood had been spent in a large house in South Kensington with plentiful servants, looked unhappy for much of this school holiday but, when I asked her how she could put up with it, she smiled and said that it was fun for a short time and that it wouldn't be for long.

I had no friends there and my days were spent either with the Ordnance Survey map on my lap directing my father to farms, or travelling to Taunton by bus with my mother where we shopped and played golf on a municipal nine-hole course near the centre of the town. We were poor golfers – I had never played golf before and, as far as I know, nor had my mother – but there was nothing else to do, and we found that we enjoyed walking about among trees and bunkers while hitting a little ball and chatting.

Marlow was more than one hundred miles away. I hadn't had a chance to say goodbye to Richard, Deborah or any friends. I wrote instead and Deborah wrote back. She said she missed me. I missed her too and when I went back to school we went on exchanging letters.

When I next came home, for the summer holidays, my parents had moved into a furnished first-floor flat in a tree-lined street near the middle of Taunton. This was still to be temporary, my mother told me; they just hadn't been able to find a suitable house.

It was a hot dry summer. At the beginning of August my father took some days off and the three of us made excursions to Minehead, picnicking and swimming from the beach. The swimming costumes that they had worn every summer for as long as I could remember were on show once again: my father's navy blue and woolly; my mother's a turquoise one-piece with ribs and seams in the bosom region and narrow shoulder straps. They seemed unusually happy and surprised me by holding hands in the waves and splashing each other. I sat on the sand watching them from a distance; they seemed strong and much younger than they were. Yet they were old – seventy-one and fifty-seven.

On a hot afternoon later in the month, I returned to the house after a trip to the record shop in Corporation Street. As I let myself in, I could hear my father's voice. He was shouting. I stood downstairs in the hall listening. There was a silence. Then, my mother screamed, 'Don't! Don't! Put it down!' I ran up the stairs and found them in the kitchen. He was standing over her. His arm was raised; there was a heavy frying pan in his hand. His face was red and damp with sweat, and his whole body was shaking. My mother's back was towards me. One hand was in front of her face, the other was on the floor. She was trying to get underneath a small Formica table.

My father turned and glared at me. Still crouching, my

mother ran from the room, pulling me after her by the arm. She half ran, half fell down the stairs and along the narrow hall to the front door. I followed, brushing past the old woman who lived underneath us. Out in the street my mother seized my hand and ran to the end of the road. She stopped at the corner and looked back. My father wasn't following us. Her face was white and she shuddered rhythmically as she drew in deep draughts of air. She was still gripping my hand. I put my free arm around her shoulder. She glanced briefly up at me. She looked sad, almost heartbroken, rather than frightened.

She kept hold of my hand and we hurried across the main road, past a parade of shops and into a side street. There she stopped and sat down on a low wall. She pulled a handkerchief from her sleeve, wiped her forehead and blew her nose. I stood beside her and kicked the wall with both feet as though dribbling a football, gently at first and then with increasing ferocity. I stopped when the pain shot from the big toe of my right foot up into my calf. I put my arms round her and hugged her tightly. She didn't move. I held her like that for a few moments with my chin resting on the top of her head. Then I let go and sat down beside her.

I was holding a paper bag and pulled out the record I had bought fifteen minutes earlier. I looked at it: the Beatles' 'From Me To You'. My mother took it from me. 'Oh good . . . I like that. We must go home and play it . . . soon.' The corners of her mouth flickered as she tried to smile. She looked very tired. Strands of hair were hanging loose on either side of her face.

I leaned my head against her cheek. 'We shouldn't go home yet.'

'No. I'd like a cup of tea with sugar in it.' She was still a little breathless. She didn't usually take sugar. 'You can have a Coke.' She felt in the pockets of her thin cotton skirt. 'Damn!'

She shrugged and looked sad again. 'I've no money. We'll just have . . .'

'I've got money.' I showed her three shillings and eightpence, and pointed at the record. 'The change from buying that.'

~

It was a proper tea shop, with table mats and doilies and willow-pattern china. When the waitress brought the tea we both ordered a scone with cream and strawberry jam.

My hand trembled as I spread the cream. I put the knife down and swallowed hard. I was sweating and felt nauseous. I didn't want her to notice.

'David! What's the matter? You look very pale.' She came around the table and held her palm on my forehead for a moment. 'Put your head between your knees . . . and you must have some tea with lots of sugar too. Go on! No one will notice.'

There weren't many people in the tea shop, and none of them was near us. I turned sideways in my seat and bent forward, and stayed like that while my mother went to order more tea. I heard the waitress bring it and my mother tell her that I was feeling a little faint. The waitress remarked on the closeness of the weather and opened another window.

The nausea began to pass. I sat back upright, drank the sweet tea fast, poured another cup and dropped a handful of sugar lumps into it. I began to feel more normal.

My mother picked up a napkin, leaned across the table and wiped my forehead and nose and cheeks. 'Do you feel better? You look a bit better.'

'I think so.' I gulped more tea.

'I think you've suffered mild shock.' I looked at her, unsure what she meant. 'A shock, or a fright, can affect you physically.' She looked down at her plate. 'I think your father gave you a fright . . . He certainly gave me one, but I feel better now.'

'He could have killed you.' Suddenly I felt furious.

'No . . . I don't think he would have actually hit me, even if you hadn't come in . . . though I am so glad you did.' She smiled and looked away. 'He's never hit me with anything except his hand, and he hasn't done that for a long time. When he picks something up, he always puts it down at the last second . . . sometimes it seems like the very last second. Then I walk away . . . and he does, too, in the opposite direction.'

'I think you should leave him.' I blurted it out. I had had the thought a few times over the last year or two, and I had voiced it once before. I didn't know anyone whose parents were separated, but I had read about it in the papers.

She looked at me without smiling, and bit into her scone. 'You'd miss him, wouldn't you?'

'I wouldn't stop seeing him.'

'Yes . . . but you'd see him less, if we . . . lived separately.' She was staring into my eyes, as though trying to understand my deepest thoughts. 'You wouldn't like that . . . would you?'

'I wouldn't mind . . . I feel as though I wouldn't mind if I never saw him again ever, because of the way he treats you . . . but I suppose I would want to after a while.' She was still gazing hard at me. It seemed that she was actually contemplating leaving him – and I felt pleased.

She looked away. 'Can we afford another pot of tea?'

We could, just.

~

The next afternoon I helped her to hang out washing in the garden we shared with the old lady from downstairs. My father was out selling seeds.

I had asked her before why she had married my father all those years ago, and she had seemed to answer as completely as she could: she had seen him as glamorous and clever, and intriguing because he was so unlike her parents, unlike anyone she had known before. They had first seen each other at a meeting of something called the Federation of Progressive Societies in London – my father was leader of the Federation's Economics Group. The year was 1933. She was twenty-six and he was forty-one.

Both of my mother's grandfathers had been millionaires – one an English banker, the other an American wholesale chemist called George Washington van Duzer who lived, during my mother's childhood, at the Dorchester Hotel in Park Lane. Both these men had several children, most of whom, including my mother's parents, lived off their inheritances. As my mother grew older, though she was fond of her family, she became increasingly desperate to escape from the complacent and comfortable enclosure in which she was expected to do nothing beyond marry a wealthy man of the same class. She had been brought up at home by nursery nurses and governesses until, when she was fourteen, she was sent to a smart girls' boarding school. She enjoyed that, but was taken away at the age of sixteen because she was a girl and in her parents' world girls didn't need education.

In her twenties she became determined to educate herself. The quest led her from her parents' home in South Kensington to the draughty hall in Clerkenwell that housed the Federation of Progressive Societies; at the same time, and to the dismay of her parents, she bought some independence by getting herself a job – in the film industry as a continuity girl.

In a book written fourteen years after he met my mother and two years before I was born, my father described how in the spring of 1933 he had sat in the audience at a meeting of the Progressive Societies at the Memorial Hall in Farringdon Street, where 'my eyes wandered about the hall, idly seeking the best-looking girl they could find'. He saw my mother sitting above him in the gallery and remarked to a male friend sitting next to him, 'That one up there . . . about the best looker I have seen in this set-up.'

The friend knew her slightly and told him that she was rather shy, but 'a cut above the average here. Been very well brought up: a perfect lady and all that.' And he told my father her name, Mary Miller.

They didn't meet that evening; but she noticed him eyeing her up, and took a good look at him when she was sure that he was looking the other way. She knew who he was – the leader of the Economics Group and the author of a book on economics – and had been struck by his passion and humour when he had spoken from the platform at a previous meeting.

Later in the year, the Federation of Progressive Societies held a summer school in the Quaker village of Jordans in Buckinghamshire; the venue had been suggested by my father because he lived there with his four-year-old daughter, my half-sister Ann. My mother stayed with other members in an old timbered hostel run by Quakers, and most of the Federation's lectures and discussion groups were held in a meeting house nearby. But one group met regularly at my father's cottage and among its members was 'the stately, simple, large-eyed beauty, Mary Miller'.

My father invited my mother 'to volunteer for the unpaid, thankless task' of secretary for his Economics Group. Another member, concerned on his behalf, told him to be careful because my mother might already be engaged, to a tall handsome man in the Education Group. My father retorted, 'I want someone to send out the messages to my blessed group. I'm not looking for a wife.'

But then, 'On Midsummer night we went for a drive in my car. It was a still, breathless evening. The world was filled with the scent of blossom riding the heady air of the year's zenith. You could feel its effect upon your senses.' During the drive he stopped the car because a rabbit was sitting in the middle of the road. They sat talking long after the rabbit had gone. He told her about his daughter Ann and how, two years before, his world had been destroyed when his wife and baby, Ann's sister, had died within ten days of each other. He saw 'the glitter of tears in her lovely eyes. She was very gentle. She let me kiss her. I did it in a spirit of awe and reverence. We were engaged.'

My father called at the hostel early the next morning. 'I had had a sleepless night wondering about my sudden and unexpected decision. "Were you really serious?" I asked her. She was. She came to me with the same quiet understanding smile, speaking in a low soft whisper. "Did *you* really mean it?" She too had lain awake.'

As I stood in the garden with her, thirty years later, handing her clothes pegs so that she could clip my father's shirts and underpants to the washing line, I asked her whether the attraction she had felt for him was completely gone. She stared at me through a gap in the damp washing. She seemed to be wondering how truthful she could be. 'You can tell me the truth. I want to know it.'

She looked down at the ground and then up at me from beneath her eyebrows. Her eyes seemed large and her face small. 'Almost . . . Almost gone.'

She pulled some clothes pegs from my shirt pocket, moved to an empty space on the washing line and reached up to fasten some socks.

I followed her. 'I hate him for the way he treats you . . . but I love him as well I suppose.'

'That's good. You should love him . . . I want you to love him.'

11

Wise Old Men

ON 1 DECEMBER 1963, nine days before my father's seventy-second birthday and two weeks before the end of my term, my mother packed a suitcase, wrote a note to my father, took a train to London and went to live with her uncle in Chelsea. My father was out calling on farmers.

She had planned her flight. Uncle Godfrey had already moved into a larger flat, and a letter from a lawyer reached my father the following morning telling him that my mother was divorcing him on grounds of cruelty, and suggesting an informal arrangement whereby they would both see me during my school holidays. The lawyer asked my father not to visit me at school during the remaining days of term to avoid adding to my presumed distress.

My mother sounded cheerful, but concerned for me as she told me all this on the telephone in Bird's office – while Bird and Mrs Bird hovered in their sitting-room next door. The next morning I received a letter from my father, abusing both my mother who, he said, was mad and had always been seriously unstable – he hinted that there were many things I didn't know – and Uncle Godfrey, a wicked philanderer who, by turning on his own niece, was now guilty of incest. My father thought it better that I live with him and proposed to take me to America – even though, before my mother left, he had found a new place to live, which he described as part of a stately home in beautiful countryside. The letter began and ended with well-worded declarations of his love for me.

I read it standing up in the study I shared with my guitar-playing friend Pete Connolly and an obliging character called Paul Snape. I sat down feeling weak, helpless, thinking that I would have to fight my father to get my way – to stay in England and continue to see my mother. If Connolly and Snape hadn't been there, collecting their books together for the morning's classes, I might have cried – something I hadn't done for a few years.

I gazed across at Deborah's drawing of La Frascetti which Snape thoughtfully polished from time to time. My sense of fear came more from the thought of disappearing to America with my father, never to see my mother again, than from the insinuation that terrible proof of my mother's insanity had been hidden from me – although that disturbed me too. But the allegations about Uncle Godfrey were not believable, so perhaps my father, in his fury, was also imagining that my mother was mad.

I spent much of the day hanging about with Bird while he and I talked, and spoke on the telephone to my mother. By late afternoon my mother's solicitor had made me a ward of court. First my mother on the telephone, and then Bird in his sitting-room, explained what this meant: the court – and not my parents – was now my legal guardian; I couldn't go abroad without its permission; it would decide when and where I would see my parents, and where and with whom I would spend my school holidays. I had a vision of my life being ruled by an empty panelled room filled with high-backed chairs and a picture of the Queen, until my mother explained that 'the court' meant 'a judge in chambers' and that that meant a wise old man sitting in an armchair by a fire.

The next day my mother arrived driving a rented white mini and I was given special leave to spend the afternoon with her. She had had her hair done in a looser wave and was wearing a close-fitting grey jacket that I hadn't seen before. Though she frowned a lot as we talked, she seemed happier – as well as smarter – than I could remember. She seemed to want my approval of what she had done and I tried to communicate that I was pleased, but worried about what my father might do.

As we drove north through Kennington and North Hinksey she said I shouldn't worry and that she would explain something important later. First she wanted to talk about Uncle Godfrey and what I thought about living with him – I would have my own room in his new flat. And he had made her a proposition: 'He says that if I will drive him occasionally in his car – he can hardly drive any more because of his eyes – and help him with paperwork such as paying his bills, we can live with him for free.'

I really wanted to talk about my father and the important thing that she had said she would tell me later, but I forced myself to think about Uncle Godfrey. I liked him – he reminded me of Wilfrid Hyde White. A few years before, after eating a strawberry mousse provided by him, I had been sick all over his carpet – and *he* had apologised to *me* for giving me a bad mousse and had insisted on clearing up the mess himself. Afterwards, my father – who often said that he couldn't bear Uncle Godfrey because he was idle and rich – had declared that the way he had dealt with the strawberry vomit had been the behaviour of a perfect gentleman and that I should learn from it.

He was eighty-two years old, the younger brother of my mother's father and the lone survivor of six brothers and sisters. He had attended the school I was at, had been to Oxford and, like his two brothers, had been an artillery officer in World War I. He had acted in minor parts in British films in the twenties and thirties – and that was all the work he had ever done. A long time ago he had been married and had had one child, a daughter close to my mother's age who had died when she was sixteen.

The idea of living with him appealed to me – he was always jovial but didn't pay too much attention to me – and he was very fond of my mother, and she of him. I also thought I would like his local shopping street, the King's Road, Chelsea; like the High Street in Marlow, it had a grocer, a greengrocer, a butcher, a fishmonger and a bakery, but it had three cafés with chairs and tables outside and some of the people who sat at them, I had been told, were artists. Uncle Godfrey's proposition seemed very fair to me, but my mother had a reservation. 'It's very kind of him, but I'm not sure. I don't want to be dependent on him.'

'You won't be dependent. You'll be helping him with the driving and other things.'

'I know, but I could get a job and pay proper rent.' She frowned. 'I want to be *in*dependent, you see.'

I did see. I had the same aim myself.

We had tea in a hotel, in an airy room with a view of fields and leafless trees, and sat beside each other on a chintz-covered sofa. A waitress put tea, scones and cakes on a low table in front of us. After she left, the only sound was of other people talking quietly several feet away. As my mother reached for the teapot, I said, 'What did Dad mean about you being mad?'

She forgot the teapot and sat back in the corner of the sofa. I waited, and thought that perhaps I shouldn't have asked – but I badly wanted to know that she wasn't mad, and never had been.

'I had a nervous breakdown during the war. It wasn't that serious. I was depressed and spent a few days in a hospital – a mental hospital – having treatment.' She looked at me from under her eyebrows. I noticed that she was wearing her pale blue eye shadow, something she wore very rarely – on formal occasions.

'So that's all he's talking about?'

'Yes . . . He often brings it up and calls me a madwoman when he's angry.'

'I didn't think you were mad.'

She smiled. 'Good.'

I asked what she had been depressed about, and she hinted that it might have been to do with her failure to have children for so many years. She smiled more broadly, and for a moment I felt smug – just by being born I had saved my mother from depression.

'You'll have to see your father,' she said, 'but maybe not for a bit, not till he calms down.'

'Of course I'll see him. I *like* seeing him—'

'Perhaps you can take friends with you. I'm worried about you being alone with him.'

I pushed a small cube of sponge coated in yellow icing into my mouth, and swallowed it quickly. 'I *like* being alone with him. He's one of the best people to be alone with.'

I slid down on the sofa and rested my head against it. I was worried about the next time I saw him because he might try to take me to America – he was quite capable of ignoring what an old man in an armchair might say. And he would make vile remarks about my mother. But I had no fear of being alone with him.

I imagined sitting beside him in the A35 – and remembered guiding him miles down a narrow lane that turned into an almost impassable track, because the map showed there was a building at the end. If it was a farm I would receive two shillings – my father had increased my usual commission twice as the track grew rougher and his scepticism grew – and if the first person we saw was a man in a flat cap I would receive another sixpence. Instead of a farm and a farmer there was a bare-headed, tall, bearded man, a little younger than my father, living frugally in a tiny cottage with no electricity and thousands of books. He didn't want any seeds, but he gave us tea and cake he had made himself, and my father and he talked all afternoon about philosophy, politics and religion. After a while I took his border collie for a long walk. On the way home my father gave me five shillings 'for finding the most interesting man in Somerset'.

Recently my father and I had talked more than ever. We sometimes argued, and occasionally – when I refused to agree with a view that he put forward with what he thought to be flawless logic – he lost his temper in the familiar red-faced, bulging-eyeballed way, repeated his argument more loudly than before and ended the conversation by bellowing his standard refrain: 'If you can argue against that, God help you!' I had found this upsetting years ago, but nowadays I just shrugged and there was a short silence, and he would start talking in a normal voice about something else.

I looked at my mother. She was staring out at the trees, with her chin raised high; she seemed extraordinarily relaxed and confident. I felt proud of the stand she had taken, her seizing of independence. My anger had gone; I sat up and told her that the only thing that worried me was my father's idea of taking me to America.

She said that is was unlikely that he would mention that again. She pulled an envelope out of her bag and took out a small pink card. 'But you have to have this . . . just in case. It's just a safeguard – nothing to worry about.' Printed on the card were the words 'HOME OFFICE: CHILD WELFARE DEPARTMENT' and a telephone number. 'If anything happens – if Dad did try to take you somewhere, I don't think he will – you ring this number from any telephone. You don't have to put money in if it's a telephone box. You say where you are . . . and someone will quickly arrive to help.'

'Blimey! Who?'

She took my hand. 'Look, I don't think this will happen, but he just might try to take you to an airport . . . or to somewhere like Dover, to take you abroad. I really don't think he will; he knows that he'd be breaking the law if he did. But that's what this is for. If you ring the number, a policeman or woman will arrive very quickly . . . or, if you see a policeman, you can show him the card and he'll look after you.'

My hands tingled. I felt like smoking a cigarette, but I didn't do that in front of my mother. I put the card down on the table and took a large bite out of a scone. 'I could always just run away. I can run faster than him.'

'Yes, but you might not know where to go then . . . or you might not have any money. You can go into a police station and show this card.' She took my hand again, and frowned as she looked into my eyes. 'I really don't think it'll happen. Just keep it with you when you're with Dad. Hide it in your wallet.'

'OK.' I looked at her and shrugged, feigning a bravado I didn't feel. 'Quite exciting, really.' I put the card in my wallet, wrapping it inside a letter from Deborah.

Later my mother gave me two five-pound notes, to be spent only if my father created an emergency.

That evening, I showed the pink card to Connolly and Snape, and told them I might have to sprint through London airport, find a telephone and then hide until the police arrived.

'*Very* James Bond.' Connolly looked at the card, turned it over and passed it to Snape. 'You be careful, my son.' He took my hand and held it against La Frascetti's chest – Connolly, Snape and others had turned that part of my great aunt into a talisman.

Biting his lower lip, Snape handed the card back. 'Not much fun, Dave, really.'

I left them and went outside through a door at the bottom of the stairs. It was dark, with a little light coming from the moon behind clouds. I had been wanting a cigarette since tea-time. I crossed a quadrangle and a stretch of mown grass, walked between some buildings and tapped on a mullioned window. Pat Chandler's face appeared inside the glass; he was shading his eyes with his hand. A minute later we were inside the hollow tree, blowing smoke upwards, away from our clothes towards the sky, and whispering to each other for fear of being caught. I told him about the tea with my mother and the pink card. He asked to see the card and studied it in the light of a match.

'Chroist!' – he had begun to adopt what he thought was a Cockney accent – 'but probably nothing'll happen. Your old man can't be as mad as that.'

I pulled on my cigarette and flicked the ash on to the ground. 'He can be pretty mad sometimes.'

Pat usually spent time in London during the holidays – his father had a flat there, though his main home was in Dorset. I told him about my new home with Uncle Godfrey and we made plans to meet. Apart from my mother's elderly relations, he would be the only person I knew.

'What do you do in London?' I had a vision of endless streets filled with red buses and people I didn't know.

'Go to the pictures . . . coffee bars . . . shop in the King's Road. Portobello market is . . .'

I had a sudden memory of walking beside the river in Marlow with Deborah and, without meaning to, I stopped listening to Pat. There was a swan near the further bank and we were talking about Uncle George and my grandfather who went to Canada.

'. . . and I often eat out with my old man . . . and he takes me to his club, late drinking and gambling.'

The only place in London where I had ever eaten out was the Kenco Coffee House in the King's Road. My mother and I had sometimes had lunch there with my grandmother and my aunt. I always had a brunchburger – a hamburger with a fried egg on top – while the three women had something unpleasant-looking and -sounding called *oeufs florentine.*

Pat and I left the tree, moved stealthily between some buildings and headed out across the huge expanse of grass that, at that time of the year, was divided into rugby pitches. We reached the western edge where there was a thin line of trees and a barbed wire fence separating the playing fields from farmland. With our coats buttoned against the cold, we walked side by side in the shelter of the trees until we reached a small sports pavilion; there we sat down, gazed out at the clouds running across the moon and shared another cigarette, cupping the glowing tip in our palms. The lights in the school buildings were at least half a mile away. We regularly made this seemingly senseless trek, probably because it was the closest we could get to freedom.

~

The judge in chambers announced that I was to spend half of my school holidays with each of my parents, but my father continued to insist that I should live with him – because my mother was mad and Uncle Godfrey was degenerate. At the end of term my mother was afraid that my father might ignore the court, meet the school train at Paddington and try to take me away somewhere. To pre-empt this, she collected me in the new Morris Minor Traveller that Uncle Godfrey had bought for her to drive him around in.

As we drove towards London, we debated whether to stay at Uncle Godfrey's that night or find a hotel; my mother was concerned that, if my father *did* go to Paddington, he might turn up at the flat and create a scene; there was Uncle Godfrey to consider as well as ourselves. I was keen to go to the flat to see my new home, and in the end my mother convinced herself that her fears were a little far-fetched. It was a small risk and we would take it.

We arrived after dark, in the late afternoon. Uncle Godfrey was out. It was an elegant old building, with marble steps to a front door flanked by pillars, and the flat was in fact a three-floor maisonette – though Uncle Godfrey didn't like that word.

We had the top floor to ourselves, two bedrooms and a

bathroom. My room had been newly decorated in colours chosen by my mother, the walls light grey and some new wood furniture a darker grey. There were some bookshelves with no books on them – most of my possessions were in Somerset – but there was a small new record player and some familiar singles in a new wire rack; my mother had brought ten or twelve of my favourites in her suitcase from Taunton. The carpet and curtains were pastel blue; a new bedside lamp had a blue shade; and there was a print of Venice by Raoul Dufy with several blues in it. The room looked startlingly modern and co-ordinated – unlike anything I had ever known. My mother looked relieved when I showed that I liked it.

I put on 'Jailhouse Rock' and began to unpack my school trunk. My mother was two floors below making tea. As the record stopped I heard the doorbell. I thought nothing of it and was putting on another record when my mother came in. She put her finger to her lips and switched the light off.

'It could be Dad . . . I'm not expecting anybody.' She was whispering.

The bell rang again, a long blast followed by a short one.

'Well, if it is him, he won't get through the door from the street. Do we *have* to turn the lights out?'

'Someone from another flat might let him in on the buzzer. Then he'll be just outside the door downstairs.'

I remembered that the door to the maisonette contained panes of frosted glass with wire mesh embedded in them. The bell rang again and whoever was ringing it left their finger on the button for several seconds.

'It *is* him. Anyone else would have gone away by now.' My mother took a deep breath as the ringing started again. 'God, I hope he doesn't get through that outside door.'

'Even if he does, he can't get through the inside one . . . can he?'

She looked at me, her eyes wide and her mouth hanging open. 'Stay here. I'm going to double-lock the door and put the chain on. Don't make any noise.'

I went to the top of the stairs and watched as she disappeared soundlessly into the darkness. The bell cut into the silence again and stopped abruptly. I heard a click and a faint chink of metal. My mother reappeared. 'Double-locked and chained.' We stood together in the gloom as the bell started once more. 'If only we'd gone to a hotel. I'm such a fool.'

'It isn't definitely him.'

'It must be . . . who else would—'

'He'll have to give up soon.'

A faint glow appeared from the landing below and moments later we could hear voices. 'Someone's let him in.' My mother started to creep down the stairs. I followed.

As we reached the first floor landing, I heard my father's voice clearly. 'This is Godfrey Miller's flat? . . . Thank you.'

A female voice answered, and then a different bell, louder, rang very close to us.

'My wife and her uncle are in there. They've kidnapped my son. They're dangerous. I want him back.' His voice was raised.

Again, the female voice said something I couldn't hear.

The bell rang again. Then he knocked loudly with his fist. 'Mary, Godfrey, David. I know you're there.' He was shouting angrily now. 'I want to see David.'

The female voice became audible. 'I don't think there is anyone in. There is no point in shouting like that.'

'Oh yes there is! They've kidnapped my son. Left me standing on Paddington Station. No sign of him. Then a teacher tells me he was collected by his mother in a car.' The bell rang again and the letter box rattled. 'They're in there. My wife who's deserted me after thirty years and her uncle who's seduced her away – seduced her with money, the bloody old rascal—'

'Really! You shouldn't speak like that . . . You're causing a disturbance.'

'Well go away and let me cause it by myself, you old trout!' The door rattled and the letter box opened. 'Mary! Godfrey! David! I know you're there. Come out. I'm not going to hurt you. I just want to see David and talk to him.' I stepped back, almost involuntarily. He was just a few feet away on the floor below. His voice was slow, clear and loud. 'I'm not leaving until you come out. I'll stay all bloody night if I have to.'

My mother moved towards the doorway of Uncle Godfrey's bedroom – a faint light was coming from the window. She looked at her watch and put her mouth to my ear. 'Stay here. I'm going to phone Aunt Susan.'

'What can she do?' She was my mother's younger sister, a small, brusque woman who since her divorce years before had lived with my grandmother a few streets away.

'I don't know – get the police or something.' She went into Uncle Godfrey's bedroom and silently closed the door.

My father went on shouting through the letter box – and then there was another voice. 'I do think you should stop that. There's no one—'

'And who the hell are you?'

It was a cultured male voice. 'I live just here and you are disturbing me.'

'Well, I'm sorry about that, but my son has been kidnapped.'

'Then you should call the police.'

My mother returned. 'Susan's calling the police. Let's hope they come quickly.' She gripped my forearm. 'Let's sit down.'

We sat on Uncle Godfrey's bed and heard my father tell

the man outside that he would be quieter, but that he was going to stay where he was. 'Even if they are not in there, they have to come back some time.'

There was a luminous clock beside the bed. The minutes went slowly by. My mother sat beside me with her hand on my arm. I could see things in the room in dim outline: a chest of drawers, a mirror, paintings on the walls and an object that I found out later was a trouser press. Sporadically my father rang the bell and from time to time it sounded as if he was looking through the letter box. The man with the posh voice seemed to have gone away. After fifteen minutes I stood up and tiptoed towards the window. My mother pulled me back. 'Don't touch the curtains. He could be out in the street, watching . . . The police will be here soon.' We went on sitting in the dark; three or four times she apologised for getting us into such a crazy mess and each time I whispered that it wasn't her fault.

A policeman arrived just after half past seven – and, surprisingly, Aunt Susan arrived with him.

My father started shouting again. 'Ah! At least one member of the family will speak to me. I suppose you know that Mary and Godfrey have kidnapped David. They have no right. He's my son and I want to see him.'

Aunt Susan pretended that she had been telephoned by one of Uncle Godfrey's neighbours. She spoke calmly. 'Clifton, you really must leave. Mary and David are not here – and, if they were, they wouldn't want to see you in this mood.'

My father appealed to the policeman, who listened politely to his tale of kidnapping, seduction and incest and suggested he come to the station to make an official complaint. The policeman politely asked Aunt Susan to wait outside. Gradually, talking to my father almost like a friend, he calmed him down. And after a few minutes they left.

My mother hugged me; suddenly I was trembling. 'It's all

right. It's all over. It won't happen again. You were marvellous.' We waited a minute or two, then went down to the kitchen, taking the chain off the door on the way. We turned the light on and blinked at each other. She quickly poured some whisky into a glass, added water and handed it to me. 'Sip a little of that.'

I sipped and swallowed and shuddered with the heat of the spirit in my throat. She took the glass, drank the rest and shook her head. There was a sound at the door, the light in the hall went on, and Uncle Godfrey walked in wearing a grey overcoat and an Anthony Eden hat. 'I gather there's been a spot of bother in the Balkans.' He beamed and shook his head. 'All over now, Susan tells me.' He seemed even more jovial than usual – alerted by Aunt Susan, he had spent the last hour in the pub around the corner. 'Give the boy a drink, Mary. It sounds as if he's earned it.'

12

Free Will and the Rabbit

THE SIEGE OF 81 Cadogan Gardens – as Uncle Godfrey would refer to it with a smile – was perhaps necessary in the sense that, if it hadn't happened, something else enabling a display of emotions – perhaps yet more alarming – would have happened instead. Later I came to think of it as a funerary ritual marking the end of a relationship. My father was chief mourner; my mother and I, secondary, less upset, silent ones; the old trout and the man with the posh voice were the congregation, present only to listen and make appropriate responses; Aunt Susan, who had short hair shaved at the back, sang solo treble in the choir; and at the end of the service the unknown policeman uttered the last rites. Uncle Godfrey may only have provided the premises and provisions for the ill-attended wake, but for a little while he seemed to be the benign godhead confirming that everything in the world was still all right.

The siege occurred on 15 December; on 20 December I was on a train heading for Taunton, looking forward to spending the days before Christmas with my father. After telephone conversations with my mother's lawyer and one with me, during which he was at his most warm and jocular, he proposed that we all accept the ruling of the judge in chambers: I was to spend half my holidays with him and half with my mother.

Pat was in Dorset until after Christmas, so I spent the days in London reading, playing records, shopping with my mother and visiting old ladies – of whom, within walking distance, there were five related to me, whose ages ranged from seventy-five to one hundred and four.

In the evenings we had drinks with Uncle Godfrey and helped him to do *The Times* crossword – he did it every day and found it hard to go to bed if he hadn't finished it. I didn't understand the clues, but I liked his calm way of doing things; he would read out a clue, push his glasses up to his forehead, lean his head against the back of his chair, close his eyes and throw out suggestions to me and my mother while sipping whisky and blowing smoke at the ceiling.

Dinner was timed to fit in with Uncle Godfrey's favourite television programmes – *Highway Patrol*, *Wagon Train*, *Rawhide*, *Bonanza* and *Seventy-seven Sunset Strip* – and was cooked earlier in the day by his daily woman, whom he called 'the Jorkin'. He told me about her the first evening, not long after the siege. 'The Jorkin, Mrs Jorkins, has been in the family a long, long time. All her life, in fact. I remember when she was born – not long before the war.' He looked at me over his glasses. 'The first war, that is . . . Her mother, Dearnley, was my mother's lady's maid and her father, Plumridge, was the groom – then he was my brother Roland's batman all through the war.' He rubbed his eyebrows. 'Marvellous couple. Still alive. Live in Hastings. I get a Christmas card from them every year.'

Later my mother told me that Uncle Godfrey regularly sent money, like a pension, to Mrs Jorkins' parents – and that he took a lot of interest in her many children.

The night before I left for Taunton we had to stay upstairs because Uncle Godfrey had a friend coming round. I asked who the friend was, and was amazed when my mother told me in a whisper that he had a girlfriend. I asked how old she was.

'Young, somewhere in her twenties, I would think. I've only met her once, very briefly.'

'*How* old is Uncle Godfrey?' I thought I knew the answer, but I had to check.

'Eighty-two.' She smiled. 'I think she might be what they call a gold-digger, after Uncle Godfrey's money, but never say I said that. It would upset him terribly.'

Later, standing motionless in the dark on the stairs, I glimpsed blonde hair, a red coat and a stocking with a seam at the back.

~

I had a compartment to myself and sat by the window with a picnic provided by Mrs Jorkins – smoked-salmon sandwiches, crisps and a fat slice of her home-made chocolate cake. As the train crossed the Thames at Maidenhead and shot on through the Berkshire countryside, I thought about my friends, not far away in Marlow. It would soon be a year since I had seen them, and Deborah was the only one who had written. At school, Pat Chandler, Pete Connolly and Dave Hunt were good new friends – I had known them for more than eighteen months – but Richard and Adam, Dennis and Deborah were still somehow my real friends. How would it be, if we met now? Would they have grown up and somehow be different? I was unsure even about Deborah. I shut my eyes and imagined her face. She was sitting on the bed in her white room. The vision of walking with her by the Thames came to me again; she was beside me to my left and the swan was across the river to my right. I could smell the grass and the mud, and hear children shouting and the plop of a fisherman's float. I longed to be there – by the river, at the lock, in the woods, in the town where I had grown up.

I had owed Deborah a letter for a few months now; I decided that I would write to her from my father's new home.

~

It was dark when the train reached Taunton. A cold drizzle blew into my face as I walked along the platform. I could see my father standing under a dim, yellow light by the exit; he was wearing an off-white, belted raincoat which I hadn't seen before. I smiled at him as I queued to hand in my ticket. He grinned back at me, gave me two thumbs up and raised his hat.

I held his shoulder and he took my bag as we kissed. 'You're on time. Well done! I've left dinner in the oven, so we'd better be quick.' I could see his breath in the night air; his lips were cold and his shoulder damp. Perhaps he had been standing there a long time. The A35 was parked on a slope outside and hadn't changed: I felt oddly reassured by the indentations in the cracked plastic of the passenger seat, the twisted red strap that pulled the door shut, the small stones and the ash on the floor and the smell of stale tobacco smoke.

'It's twenty minutes from here. I hope you'll like it, but it looks best in daylight.' He pushed his hat back and let off the hand-brake.

'When did you move in?' I knew the answer, but couldn't think of anything else to say.

He told me it had been two weeks ago; the place still needed some sorting out, but he liked it because there was plenty of space and beautiful surroundings. He had got the furniture out of store and said that he had done his best with my room; he had hung up the big map of the British Isles and my posters of Elvis and the Beatles. But it was my room; I should move things around, do whatever I liked. He wanted me to see his new flat as my home.

I still liked Elvis, but I wasn't sure that I wanted the poster of him any more; it had been on my wall in the old house for so long that I had stopped noticing it. Jean Shrimpton and Leslie Caron were my pin-ups now; I had pictures of them on a pinboard at Uncle Godfrey's.

My father drove quickly and neither of us said much. We turned through a white-painted five-bar gate on to a tarmac drive that wound among rhododendrons before becoming gravel as it crossed a broad stretch of mown grass. An old-fashioned streetlight shone down on some cars and cast its glow on a wide pink-painted building with gables and a stone portico with steps and pillars.

'Looks pretty posh!'

He turned and smiled. 'Well, it is. The front part is divided in two. Nice families. One of them's got a son about your age. Our flat's at the back.' He drove along the side of the house and into a cobbled courtyard lit by an old lamp fixed high on a wall, and parked beside two other cars. The walls here were old red brick. 'There are four flats. Ours is on the ground floor, just there.' He leaned across me and pointed.

He unlocked a white-painted, tongue-and-groove door which stuck a little as he opened it. There was a smell of something cooking. He opened another door, and we were in a long room with tall windows.

A fire glowed and a yellowish light came from a standard lamp that I recognised. The walls were hung with familiar pictures and the furniture and rugs came from our old house, but there were long red curtains that I hadn't seen before. The old sofa and my father's big, upholstered armchair were in front of the fire, and the television, which he had acquired when he worked as a TV repairman, was on the small table with castors that it had always been on. He explained that, when the house had belonged to the lord of the manor and been home to just one family and their servants, which wasn't very long ago, this room had been the kitchen. My room had been what they called the still room, his had been the laundry, and our kitchen had been their scullery.

He took me to my room and stood by the door while I walked around. It had a low sloping ceiling and was larger than any room in our old house, but not overwhelming. 'I don't know if you still like those curtains. Perhaps they're just for children. We could soon get something else.'

They were from my room in Marlow – little coloured houses on a grey background; my mother had made them when I was about seven. They hung down too far and didn't quite meet in the middle – the window was long and low – but they looked all right. It was strange, but good, to see them again, and I told him that I still liked them.

The Beatles laughing in grey round-necked suits were next to the big framed map of the British Isles facing the bed, and Elvis in white T-shirt and black leather was on the wall facing the window. I walked around touching furniture that I had known all my life, but hadn't seen for a year: a wardrobe that my father had made from hardboard and two-by-one; a chest of drawers that my mother had painted primrose yellow; a pottery lamp with 'David' written on it that had been given to me as a small child.

On the dark-stained floorboards he had laid an old Persian rug that had been in the dining-room at our old house – its colours faded by years of sunlight. Its complex geometric patterns had fascinated me probably for longer than I could remember, and I had used its outer border as a road for my Dinky toys. He had taken trouble to arrange everything as he thought I'd like it. The bed was made, with blankets, eiderdown and pillow neatly in place, and there was a small armchair with a cushion precisely placed to make a diamond shape.

'It's great.' I waved my arms in the air and smiled. I liked it and was grateful.

He put his hand round my shoulder and I could sense him swallowing his emotions. 'Good. Well, you can change it, however you like.'

We ate at one end of the living-room, *coq au vin* with potatoes, peas and carrots. It was hot and delicious and I told him so. He smiled and told me he could follow a recipe as competently as anyone. He offered me a glass of the Spanish red wine that he had bought for cooking and surprisingly had one himself. He asked about school and what it was like in London, and I told him, without mentioning my mother or

Uncle Godfrey. He listened as he ate and made none of the derisory comments that I expected. We spooned out more chicken and shared the remaining wine, half a glass each.

He told me to stay where I was while he fetched the next course; he was holding back a smile. He returned carrying an oval plate and with mock ceremony placed it in the middle of the table. On it was an Arctic Roll, something I often ordered when we ate in cheap restaurants on days out from school. He knew I liked it and grinned as he cut us each a thick slice.

'I didn't know you could buy this in a shop. Fantastic—' He had gone before I finished speaking.

Still grinning, he came back with a bottle of cherry brandy, tore the paper seal, pulled out the cork, plonked it on the table and suggested I pour some on. For a moment I thought that he was joking, but he laughed and said, 'Go on. It'll taste good.'

Throughout my childhood there had always been a bottle of cherry brandy in a cupboard in the kitchen – possibly the same bottle – and my father had allowed himself a small glass at Christmas and New Year. The only other alcohol in the house had been a bottle of sherry which was occasionally offered to visitors and from which my mother had a glass about once a month before lunch on a Sunday.

This was a new bottle of cherry brandy. He splashed some on to his Arctic Roll and passed me the bottle. 'Go on.'

I watched the red liquid running over his ice cream and seeping into the surrounding sponge cake. I poured a little on to my slice and then a little more. It *was* good and I told him so.

'I may not have any capital – your mother owned the house, you probably know – but I've got a salary, lots of commission and I don't have to support her any more – so we can spend a bit and enjoy ourselves.' He started to cut two more slices of Arctic Roll.

'But you don't want to go on working for ever.' He had recently had his seventy-second birthday.

'I'm all right. I enjoy it . . . But I'll stop one day.'

Later we sat by the fire with cups of instant coffee. He turned the television on, and off again – there was a party political broadcast on behalf of the Conservative party on both channels.

He smiled at me as he rolled a cigarette and said, 'So how do you feel now about free will and determinism?'

I sipped my coffee and wondered what was on television next. It was a subject he brought up from time to time. I had once made him very angry by suggesting that it wasn't worth discussing; whatever the answer, people just went on living. He had shouted then – about freedom and responsibility. Did I not care whether the likes of Hitler and Mussolini, and Heath, 'the acid bath murderer', were accountable for their crimes – because they *weren't*, if everything was determined? Since then I had tried to take the matter more seriously, but I hoped this was going to be a chat rather than a lecture with readings from the *Encylopaedia Britannica*.

'I don't suppose you've thought about it lately?'

I smiled and shook my head. 'No. No time for that kind of thing, Dad.'

'Too worried about girls, I suppose.' He laughed and lit his cigarette. Then he put it in an ashtray and stood up. 'Let's have a *glass* of cherry brandy. What do you think?' He started walking towards the kitchen.

'OK. If you're sure.'

He seemed very happy – and I wondered whether he intended to get drunk. I had rarely seen him drink and had never seen him drunk. I had heard from my mother about him being drunk on some occasion before I was born. It hadn't sounded very pleasant, not because he was violent but because he was sick all over the place and lay in bed groaning as he recovered.

He came back with two small glasses of cherry brandy, sat down, raised his glass and said, 'Your health.'

I raised mine and repeated the toast. I sipped the cherry brandy, the first time I had tasted it undiluted by ice cream. It was sweet and fiery. I took a larger gulp and swilled it round my mouth. My tongue and the inside of my cheeks burned.

'You realise that you owe your existence to a rabbit.' He was looking at me and smiling; I could see the deep creases at the sides of his eyes. I was startled and stared back blankly. He relit his cigarette. 'I don't mean anything to do with Darwin.' He went on smiling. 'I mean the rabbit that sat in the middle of the road, on a night when I took your mother for a drive . . . thirty years ago now.'

I saw the connection: the Progressive Societies' summer school, midsummer night, 1933. 'I think I know what you mean . . . I read your book. Remember?' I sipped at the cherry brandy and wondered at the way his mind worked.

He leaned forward. There was going to be a lecture, but it looked like being an unusual one. 'That rabbit *caused* you to be born. And, in a way, that rabbit established that there is free will *and* determinism.'

I leaned back in my chair cupping my glass in both hands as he continued.

'Did the rabbit sit in the middle of the road, cleaning his whiskers, of his own free will? Or did the chemicals and the synapses in his brain determine that he sit there? Or did a higher power, God, for example – another form of determinism – make him sit there? And was it pure chance that I drove down the road with your mother at the moment that the rabbit chose, or perhaps was programmed, to sit in the middle of it?' He tapped the low table between us with his forefinger. 'I had no control over the matter of the rabbit being there – from my point of view that was determined – call it my fate.

But, I think I exercised my free will when I decided not to run the rabbit over.'

I started to smile. I found this very funny, but I wasn't sure if I was meant to.

He returned my smile, but went on. 'I *could* have run the rabbit over. Your mother would have been horrified – and you wouldn't exist. The question is: did I stop the car because I am chemically programmed not to run over rabbits – no, man is a hunter-gatherer, but that's not the point – *or* because I *chose* not to run it over? Newtonian physics and the enlightenment philosophers – Bacon, Locke and so on – would say that my decision can be explained by science, somehow, ultimately. I used to believe that – I was brought up to believe it and that if we could understand how science works we could make a better world – but I've begun to question it lately – look at the atom bomb.' He quickly poked the fire and pulled on his cigarette. 'Think about it this way: I had nothing to gain by either running over the rabbit or not running it over – except that your mother would have disapproved if I had deliberately killed it, but then, if I had been alone, I would have made the same decision. Accrediting all actions to science and chemicals suggests that what follows an action can, theoretically, be predicted; I couldn't predict that I was going to fall in love with your mother fifteen minutes later, and she with me. An action determined by chemicals has to have a predictable result. I'm inclined to think that I *decided* – of my *own free will* – not to run the rabbit over, and that no scientist, or omnipotent God, could have predicted the result. Therefore, there *is* free will.' He sat back with a contented smile and asked whether I agreed with what he had just said – whether it made sense.

I told him it did, and I meant it. I liked to think that I and everyone else had free will – even if, but for him, I would never have thought about it. And I liked it when he spoke quickly and clearly about what he thought were important matters. I had a suspicion that some professional philosopher would refute what he had just said, but I didn't care. I loved him, and what he had said made sense to me.

He stretched and seemed pleased, and then talked about what he had, in fact, gained from using his free will to stop the car to oblige the rabbit: me and my mother; he dropped his voice and stared into the fire when he mentioned her. And I wondered whether his interest in free will and the rabbit had arisen because what had begun that night in 1933 had now ended.

Later he talked about the sixteen years and the 'trillions and billions of sperm' that it had taken to conceive me. I didn't like thinking about his sperm and wondered if he was getting a little drunk. And, though I didn't want to, I couldn't help contemplating the places where his sperm had fetched up and the five children it had helped to create – I had seen photographs of his first two wives.

'Now that *was* chemically explainable, *determined* you might say. Your mother's womb—'

I managed to stop him by saying that I knew all about that – and turned the conversation on to Spurs and the dreadful news that Dave Mackay had broken his leg at Old Trafford the previous Saturday. As we speculated about who could possibly replace him, a man both of us admired and spoke of as though he were a friend, I began to feel tired – and wondered whether cherry brandy was very alcoholic.

~

I woke early and opened the curtains. There was a mist hovering above an expanse of lawn. Fifty yards away a line of leafless trees, with a spattering of rooks' nests, rose behind dull green bushes. I could hear the clacking of my father's typewriter. I turned on the fire and put on my dressing gown.

Beside the window there was a set of bookshelves, about

six feet high and three feet wide, one of many similar structures that had been dotted around our old house, built hurriedly by my father from unplaned wood. It was filled with books, but I had only glanced at it the night before.

Two shelves contained my old books, an assortment that included *Treasure Island*, *Eagle* and *Tiger* annuals, *The Catcher in the Rye*, *The Carpetbaggers*, *Peyton Place* and some Agatha Christies. On the other shelves were books that belonged to my father, although it seemed that he had put them there with me in mind. He had once written a list for me of what he considered to be 'essential reading for anyone who wishes to call themselves educated'. It named about thirty books, most of which seemed to be on the shelves in front of me – including a six–volume Everyman edition of *The Decline and Fall of the Roman Empire*, three volumes of *War and Peace* and Prescott's *Conquest of Peru*.

The top shelf was full of paperbacks, mostly orange and white striped Penguins, with a few green ones – Margery Allingham, Ngaio Marsh, Raymond Chandler – at one end. On the bottom shelf, next to several light blue cloth-bound volumes by Daniel Defoe, was a row of books with beige cloth spines. Though I had seen only a few of them before, I knew that they were my grandmother Sis's diaries.

I pulled out the *Tiger Annual* for 1957 and read the cartoon strip that had been my favourite six years earlier, 'Dodger Caine and the Amazing Hoop-la Wheeze'. It was disappointing – an absurd story with clear-cut heroes and villains – and I wondered why I had been so entranced by it; perhaps because it was set in a boys' boarding school, a location that at the time had seemed exotic and exciting. I tried the 'Rockfist Rogan' strip; the pictures – of handsome British fighter pilots and angry-looking Germans – were still good to look at, but the story was silly.

I put the *Annual* back and ran my finger along the spines of my grandmother's diaries, counting them; there were sixteen. I pulled out the one at the right-hand end to check the year; it was 1901. Next to it was 1900 and at the other end of the row was 1886. My father had put them in order. I had read the first four. I picked the fifth one, 1890, opened it and soon remembered that I had read some of this one as well, but not all of it. I wanted to read more, but I wanted to concentrate, not just skim through. Perhaps when I came back in January I would take time and read.

13

Two Turkeys

On Christmas Eve, swaddled in overcoats, scarves and gloves, my father and I drove up the A4 – which my father called 'the Bath Road' – towards Buckinghamshire. The sky was a clear light blue, snow was forecast and the heater in the A35 struggled to keep the windscreen clear of our condensed breath. As we sat in a queue of slow-moving traffic on the edge of Marlborough, my father asked me whether I had thought any more about original sin.

'No. Not really, Dad.' I had never liked the sound of original sin. It was a peculiar expression for what seemed to mean taking a dim view of babies, although from previous discussions and readings out loud from the *Encyclopaedia Britannica* I knew that it meant more than that.

'Well I have.' He wiped condensation from the window beside him and passed me the damp duster. 'Give the back window a wipe. There's a good chap.' I stood on my seat and stretched across to the back. 'I've come to the conclusion that it is an optimistic, rather than a pessimistic, doctrine, because it carries within it the notion of the perfectibility of man. I think that is what St Augustine and St Thomas Aquinas were getting at . . .' – the back of the seat was digging into my stomach, and however hard I tried I couldn't reach the corners of the window – 'not to mention Plato.' I twisted round and sat back in the seat. He looked at me as he inched the car forward. 'Could you give that a wipe?' He gestured at the window beside me.

'I'm actually beginning to think that Voltaire was wrong.

He called St Augustine a debauched African, you know. He could have been right about that . . . but I think he may have been wrong to insist that children are born sweet and innocent. Obviously, original sin isn't inherited from Adam and Eve' – he blew his nose loudly and thoroughly – 'but it could be inherited from your parents. What do you think?' He turned and looked at me. The car was stationary. A small girl was looking at us from the back window of a black Ford V8. 'I mean . . . take that little girl. Do you think she's sinful?'

'How would I know?'

He turned sharply. 'I'm just using her as a symbol . . . blast it! For all children.' He slapped his hands down on the steering wheel.

I tried to think of something intelligent to say. I thought about the time when Deborah's father had found us in the bathroom looking at each other's privates. We were four years old. That wasn't sinful; my father had said it was natural curiosity. Then I remembered sticking the needle in Jessop's bottom. 'I think . . . probably . . . all humans are capable of bad behaviour . . . even babies . . . and therefore, yes, that little girl is sinful – though that seems a rather strong way to put it.'

'That's what I think, though for years I agreed with Voltaire . . . and Rousseau . . . until I started thinking about it again, recently. The good thing is . . .' He passed me his tobacco tin. 'Roll us one will you? . . . that that ought to mean that everyone has the potential to improve from birth onwards. With the right nurturing and education, that little girl could become a saint.'

'And with the wrong nurturing she could become a Nazi I suppose.'

'Yes, but not necessarily. She might have something within herself, from her genes – perhaps a gene from a saintly ancestor – that would make her rebel against her Nazi parents.' He peered through the windscreen at the little girl and waved at her. She stuck her tongue out. I finished rolling and handed him the cigarette. 'There you are! Sinful! But hopefully not a Nazi.' He waved again. The little girl turned away and spoke to someone. A woman in a headscarf appeared beside her in the window and frowned at us.

'She looks like a Nazi.'

He picked up the duster and wiped the windscreen. 'She looks like Mrs Larkins to me – Peggy Mount, you know?' He dabbed again at the damp glass. 'Don't you think? Can you see properly?' He handed me the duster.

The woman was still looking in our direction. She *did* look like Peggy Mount. 'Well . . . it could be.'

'I think it is . . . Do you want to get her autograph?'

'No Dad.'

'I bet she wouldn't mind. She's probably very nice, in real life.'

'I'm *not* going to get out of the car and go and ask that woman if she's Peggy Mount . . .' I started to laugh to myself at the thought. 'She might not be . . .' I was giggling and my voice was becoming uncontrollably high-pitched. 'What would happen then?' He turned towards me. He was laughing silently too. '*You* go and ask her.' I pushed him on the arm.

'Nothing would happen. She'd just say, "I'm not Peggy Mount, but thank you for asking."' He made an involuntary farting noise with his lips. His face broke into a broad smile and his eyes turned down at the corners – he looked as though he might be going to cry. He leaned forward with his face on the steering wheel, stretched out his arm, pushed me and squeaked, 'I'm not going to go . . .' He was holding his stomach and didn't seem able to speak. 'There might be a man in the front. I could get punched.' For a few seconds his whole body shook and, again, he couldn't speak. 'On the nose.' He rocked up and down in his seat and started howling. 'Oh dear! Oh God! Peggy Mount!' He pulled out his handkerchief. There were tears on his cheeks. 'Suppose it wasn't her . . .' I was stuck firm in silent giggling – my stomach ached and no sound would come out. Laughter was coming from him in huge rhythmic whoops. Peggy Mount and the small girl were six feet away, frowning at us. My face was covered in sweat. I put my head on the windscreen and wound down the window. My father was saying, 'But *you* wouldn't . . . get punched. Go on! . . . Go and see if that's Peggy Mount. Mr Mount wouldn't punch a child.'

I felt sick and stuck my head out of the window. At last the ability to make sounds returned. 'I'm not a child . . .' I pulled my head in and lay back wiping my face on my sleeve. 'I'm a rebellious teenager. They'd hit me before you.'

Peggy Mount turned away as the V8 suddenly moved forward. My father started the engine and said, 'Where do you think Peggy's going for Christmas?' He picked up his cigarette from the floor. I was too exhausted to answer. The small girl went on staring at us, all the way to Newbury.

~

Ann is my father's daughter from his second marriage – the one whose mother and baby sister had died within a week of each other, and whom my mother and father had discussed in front of a rabbit on midsummer night 1933, a few minutes before they decided to get married. She was twenty when I was born.

My father also had two children from his first marriage, both of whom had children who were a little older than me. Ann had a husband, a son who was six years younger than me and two aunts, sisters of her dead mother, both of whom had husbands and children. Most of these people were crammed into Ann's house for Christmas.

On Christmas morning I found Ann alone in her kitchen and asked her what she knew about my mother's nervous breakdown during the war – Ann had been a teenager then, living with my parents and going to a local school. She remembered: my mother had been taken away in a car; it hadn't been serious. It had likely been caused by the way my father treated her; for one thing he had undermined my mother's attempts to get close to her, Ann, but there were other things – she hinted that he had been interested in another woman.

Some of the adults had a few drinks before lunch, though my father didn't – he sat in an armchair by the fire smoking and playing games with his grandchildren – and younger people like me had Coke and lemonade. Lunch was the usual thing – turkey, flaming Christmas pudding with sixpences, crackers and paper hats.

As we sat looking at the debris, the husband of one of Ann's aunts, who was called Uncle George, realised that we had forgotten to watch the Queen's speech. Borrowing his wife's shawl, hat and handbag, he made up for the omission. He was an excellent mimic. He talked about the problems of having lots of corgis, Sir Alec Douglas-Home's peculiar lips, how to cope with an elderly mother and his encounter with the King of Tonga. Group hysteria took hold, and my father removed his false teeth – in case he swallowed them, he explained later. Uncle George ended by telling us how much he disliked his loyal subjects and his three children – especially baby Andrew.

I had to eat turkey again in the evening at my grandmother's flat. There were no young people. Old ladies predominated and – despite the presence of my mother, Uncle Godfrey and a spirited, eighty-four-year-old great-aunt, known as Auntie Toto – the celebrations were more formal. When the crackers had been pulled and my grandmother and three other elderly women had put their paper hats on, I told them about the highlight of my Christmas – Uncle George and the Queen's speech – and did an imitation of his imitation of the Queen, deliberately leaving out the bit about the elderly mother.

When I had finished Uncle Godfrey said 'Bravo' quietly and patted me gently on the back. The old women stared at me unsmiling. My mother wiped her mouth with a white table napkin and looked at the floor. I was disappointed; obviously I wasn't as good a mimic as Uncle George.

Later my mother and I walked home with Uncle Godfrey. It was cold and we linked arms with my mother in the middle. They both tittered as my mother explained that she had found my performance very funny but hadn't dared to show it; my grandmother and the other old ladies didn't think it was proper to make fun of the Queen.

Uncle Godfrey let go of my mother's arm, reached behind her and patted me on the back. 'It was a very good Queen, David, very good Queen.' His titter grew into a laugh. 'I particularly liked the bit about the King of Tonga. It wasn't just you and me, Mary. Toto was in hysterics! Did you see her? She was in agony, biting her lip.' My mother was nodding but didn't speak. 'I tried to catch Toto's eye, but she wouldn't have it.' My mother made a series of sounds, like wrong notes on a violin, and Uncle Godfrey's laugh boomed off the walls of Cadogan Street. 'It was almost as funny as David . . . you and me and Toto pretending not to be amused.'

Late that night I lay in bed in my grey room and thought about Uncle Godfrey and Auntie Toto and wondered why some old people could relax and enjoy themselves while others couldn't. I decided it might depend on whether they had had happy lives or not. Auntie Toto was the one who, because she couldn't get divorced from her husband, had lived with a man for many years without being married. As I turned off the light I looked across at my pin-ups of Jean Shrimpton and Leslie Caron and remembered that I hadn't yet written to Deborah.

Three days later I went to meet Pat outside Peter Jones. He was leaning against the 19 and 22 bus stop smoking a black cigarette. It was Saturday morning, and later that afternoon we were taking a train to Goring for a party at Pete Connolly's home. Pat wanted to buy some clothes to wear that night, and he thought I should too. He offered me one of his cigarettes – Sobranie Black Russian in a box with a lid, like Uncle Godfrey's du Mauriers. As well as looking strange – rolled in black paper with a glossy gold strip around the tip – it tasted odd – mild and aromatic – but not unpleasant. Someone had given this box to his mother for Christmas and he had pinched it.

There were three men's clothes shops not far up the King's Road: Sydney Smith, Cecil Gee and Smart Weston. I wasn't sure what we were looking for. The main thing was not to wear anything we wore at school, but I already had a pair of black Chelsea boots, a black corduroy jacket, some khaki needlecord jeans and a black T-shirt with a white anchor on it, all of which I thought were pretty snazzy. Pat was talking about getting a matelot shirt – of the type worn by Frenchmen with berets and strings of garlic.

We sauntered into Sydney Smith and peered down into the glass cases of shirts, sweaters, socks and underwear. An assistant asked if he could help us and Pat mentioned matelot shirts. The man led us across the shop, produced a pile of them in Pat's size and laid them out on a glass counter; all were dark blue and white, but there were different materials, different sleeves, stripes of different widths; some had anchors stitched or printed on and some didn't. Pat scrutinised them for about ten minutes, feeling them and holding them against himself, and decided that none of them was quite right.

In the window of Cecil Gee there was a bronze male mannequin wearing a matelot shirt identical to one we had just seen. Pat glanced at it and said, 'Cecil bloody Gee. Let's go to the Picasso. Have a coffee.' The Picasso was further up the King's Road, further than I had ever been. We passed the Chelsea Potter and Pat said it was a good pub, but that they probably wouldn't let us in.

Inside the Picasso a man in a beret was playing draughts with a young blonde woman. Pat ordered hot chocolate and I asked for a cappuccino – I had never had one before, but I had seen my mother drink them in the Kenco Coffee House and heard my grandmother describe them as 'a lot of froth'. We sat against the wall and looked at the blonde woman. 'Good legs,' Pat said quietly. She was wearing a short tight skirt and socks instead of stockings. Her legs were bare and we could see the tops of her knees. She looked at us and smiled. I looked away quickly and wondered if she'd seen me looking at her knees. She seemed Bohemian and exciting.

My cappuccino came and I sipped it right away, covering my lip with froth and burning my tongue. Pat nudged me and whispered, 'I think she fancies you,' and chuckled loudly.

I glanced up at her again. She had lit a cigarette and was talking intently to the man in the beret. 'Get stuffed.'

I thought about Pete Connolly's party that evening and began to feel nervous. I hadn't been to a teenagers' party before. I knew from Pat and from talk at school that there would be lots of girls and dancing – and that I was expected to find a girl and snog later in the evening when the lights would be turned down. I had never kissed a girl except Deborah when we were very young, and I hadn't danced since my mother sent me to a dancing class in Marlow where I had done waltzes and quicksteps – also with Deborah.

I woke on Pete Connolly's floor with a headache and another pain which Pat condescendingly explained in detail, and called 'ball-ache'. But the pains didn't matter; nothing mattered because my skin was glowing and warm and my brain was idling with a sensation that one day I would call euphoria. I had danced for several hours, but the catalyst had been snogging in the dark, unaware of time or place, with a girl who, Pat, Pete and others confirmed, was 'a complete bombshell'.

14

A Hot Proposal

ON A NIGHT IN January I sat close to the two-bar fire back in my room at my father's home, and wrote a long letter to Deborah. I told her that I missed her, gave her both my new addresses and described all that had happened in the six months since I had last written. Before going to bed, I smoked a cigarette and scanned the bookshelves. An old green cardboard folder was sticking out from the bottom shelf against the upright next to my grandmother's diaries; it hadn't been there on my previous visit. I opened it, although I knew what was there – the chapters my father had written for me two years before, about his childhood in the 1890s. I had read them then and given them back to him.

That week my father seemed calm and content – he had bought another bottle of cherry brandy – and I wondered whether he enjoyed living alone, without my mother who had always seemed to irritate him. Most nights I sat up late reading my father's chapters again and my grandmother's diaries. Sometimes I flipped from his text to hers to see if she wrote at the time about an event that he had remembered sixty years later. The many mentions of my grandfather Tom reminded me of Swan River, Manitoba. I hadn't thought about the place or the old man who had told me to go there for a long time. Would I go, one day? I decided I would, and hoped that it would be with Deborah.

Tom brought Sis a bowl of fuchsias and seemed to enjoy his second visit. Ernest and Rose were there, music predominated and he showed that he could sing – in a mellow baritone that Sis admired. Twice, while the others were grouped around the piano, Sis and Tom spoke to each other for several minutes almost in private, much as they had over dinner at the Johnsons'. She noticed his eyes again and the lines that came from them when he smiled, and she saw that he had bad teeth under his huge moustache – but she was reminded of the warmth beneath his shyness and of how easily she could talk to him.

When he visited a third time, her brothers and Rose went out for the evening, and Old George gave Tom permission to be alone with Sis – then and in the future if they wished – a clear sign that he approved of him. Tom gave Sis a brooch, a small gold fox with tiny rubies for eyes, and told her that as soon as he saw it he knew it would suit her. He was right; she thought it beautiful – and she realised how expensive it was.

They sat on the red velvet sofa where she had sat many times with Stanley and, with some prompting, he talked about his childhood and youth and how his father had died twelve years before. As the eldest of seven children, he had felt responsible for his mother and his younger brothers and sisters, the youngest of whom had been a baby. He had worked hard to keep the family together and to gain qualifications at night school and had joined the Welsbach Incandescent Light Company as a junior accountant. There he had been promoted several times; he said this modestly, but Sis could sense his pride. By working hard, he and his brother Bill and his sister Emily, who worked as a housemaid, had enabled his mother to raise the younger children; otherwise he feared they would have ended in the workhouse.

Sis was surprised to learn that his family home had been nearby at the further end of Greenwood Street near London

Fields; he told her diffidently that a few years earlier he had played in the same rugby team as her brother George – George hadn't recognised him so he hadn't mentioned it. Now, they had left Greenwood Street, and he and Bill had found his mother a larger house in Bournemouth where she could take lodgers and live with her younger children.

Sis told him about her mother's death and how she, too, had felt responsible for a parent and younger siblings. They talked about duty and the satisfactions and frustrations that came from it – and about their fathers. Tom's had been artistic and had worked as an engraver; Sis thought he sounded not unlike her father – creative and kind, but forceful. That night she recorded that she liked Tom 'a great deal' and she thought it significant that his father had died in the same year as her mother. She noted again that he was handsome, and she thought that his pipe might account for his bad teeth.

For a few weeks Sis and Tom met frequently at Norfolk Road, and he took her to theatres and the smarter music halls, for strolls on Hackney Downs and long walks across Hackney Marshes; they visited Kate in Braintree and Tom's mother – whom Sis found 'warm and quiet, like her son' – in Bournemouth. From small things Tom said and from questions he asked, Sis began to realise that he would soon propose marriage. She was unsure how she would answer. He had become 'a great friend and companion', but she didn't think that she loved him.

She remembered the passion she had felt for Stanley and told Kate that she didn't feel at all the same about Tom. Kate said that a marriage without love couldn't work. She shouldn't accept a proposal from Tom – not yet anyway. If she didn't want to turn him away, she should tell him the truth about what she felt and then a long, unofficial engagement might be appropriate. She might grow to love him; Kate told her how she had come to love Uncle Gibson more and more as time had passed and that their child had made them even closer than before.

Tom perspired in the heat of a hot August evening in the drawing-room at Norfolk Road, and waited until Sis had sat down. 'I have never done this before. I hope I do it properly.' He knelt on one knee, took her hand and frowned with formality. 'Will you marry me?'

She hugged him around the neck. 'Yes.'

She hadn't known what she would say; she had decided in an instant. They stood up and kissed for the first time – a brief kiss. He drew away and handed her a small leather box. He had chosen it – a gold ring with a single ruby – because it matched the brooch that she liked; she could change it if she would prefer silver or a diamond. She told him sincerely not to be silly – it was beautiful. She put it on her finger. It was a little big, but she didn't say so. She kissed him again – for longer this time – and held him for a moment when he tried to move away.

A few minutes later Tom asked Old George's permission to marry his daughter. Old George was in his shirt sleeves and told him to take his jacket off – he looked hot – and, of course, he could marry his daughter.

That night Sis wrote that in that moment, as he knelt down, she knew that she wanted to be married to him. She liked him, almost loved him; in time she would love him – especially when they had children. Kate was too cautious and, before long, would see that she, Sis, had done the right thing.

Sis wanted to be married as soon as sensibly possible. Tom's only concern was that they needed to find a home – his lodgings were too small for them both – but it was quickly agreed that he could live at Norfolk Road while they took their time to find the right place. Old George would give them a bed as a wedding present and it would be put in Sis's room.

They were married at noon on 11 October, 1890, at St Mark's Church around the corner from Norfolk Road. Sis enjoyed herself. Her cream satin dress from Gamages in Holborn was much admired; the three bridesmaids, among them her little cousin Kathleen, looked exquisite; at the reception, at a smart hotel near Highbury Corner, her father made an affectionate and amusing speech; and everyone behaved properly – except Aunt Sue, but that was to be expected. All that is known about the honeymoon is that they stayed in a hotel in Hastings and that Sis discovered that Tom ground his teeth while he slept.

When they returned to Norfolk Road, Tom was anxious to find them a home. Before they were married Sis had shared his vision of life together in a house with a garden in Islington, Highbury, Hackney or Dalston. But she had been preoccupied by her wedding, and now she found that she wasn't quite ready to move away from her home and her family.

She hid her feelings from Tom, but discussed them with her father. He reminded her that Tom was eight years older than her, had worked his way up to a well-paid position in an internationally famous firm and earned more than he did. Though it was commonplace for married couples to live with their parents – some of the houses in Norfolk Road and all over East London were crammed with people of all ages – it was natural for a man of Tom's age and income to want his own house.

But Sis felt, privately, that 59 Norfolk Road had room for everyone and that, before long, when her brothers had their own homes – as she was sure they would – it would be the perfect place for her and Tom and the children she hoped to have, and she could continue to live with and care for her father. What would happen to him if she and her brothers all moved away?

On a Saturday in November Tom took her to see a terrace of ten new houses in a street south of Dalston Lane, and timed how long it took them to walk there – six minutes. The houses were two-storey, built of yellow brick, with angled bays, slate roofs and white-painted mouldings and windows. There were two rooms downstairs with a kitchen and scullery at the back, and three rooms upstairs. The small garden was dug and ready for planting, and there was a flush lavatory in a lean-to just outside the kitchen door. The asking price was £275 which could be paid in instalments; Tom had the first instalment waiting in the bank and money to buy furniture, carpets, curtains, everything that was necessary.

Sis wandered around with her arm through Tom's. She liked the house but found it a little small; she'd like to think about it. The builder suggested that they should make up their minds soon; six of the ten had been sold already.

On the walk back to Norfolk Road Tom explained that the house might be small but it was big enough for the time being and that it was as large as he could sensibly afford – given that she wanted to be close to her father and brothers. Apologetically, Sis confessed, for the first time, that she was finding it hard to think about leaving her father, but that she would try. Tom let go of her arm and walked faster. It was a minute or two before he replied. He told her that when her father got old, which would be a long time yet, of course he could live with them; he, Tom, would be rich and they would have moved to a larger house by then.

What began as a discussion, while they walked, became an argument on the corner outside the church where they had been married, and then a row in the breakfast-room when they reached home. Sis argued that they would be better off staying at Norfolk Road; it was large and spacious and filled with beautiful furniture – while the new house was small and depressing – and one day they might have number 59 all to themselves. Tom asked if she expected him to wait for ever to get his own home – her father was blooming with health and in his early fifties – and said he hadn't realised he had married him as well as her. Sis told him he was lucky to have married anyone. He retorted that he wouldn't have bothered if he had known she was such a nag and a Daddy's girl.

Sis ran to her room in tears. She saw that Little Alice was in the kitchen and must have heard all they had said. That evening Tom went to the Norfolk Arms after dinner and returned at 12.30 banging doors and stumbling up the stairs.

The following Tuesday evening they hugged and kissed and apologised. Sis told Tom that she had been silly and that she did want to move to the new house. Tom said that he had thought it over and, if she really wanted to stay with her father a bit longer, he would 'adjust his expectations' – there was the advantage that he would be able to save up more money; it was just that she hadn't told him that that was what she wanted before. She confessed, tearfully, that she didn't really know what she wanted and they agreed to leave things as they were for the time being.

In May, the next year, 1891, Sis discovered that she was pregnant. She was excited, if a little fearful; Tom was euphoric and the house filled with flowers that he bought for her every evening as he passed through Liverpool Street Station.

In September – to avoid the crowds – they had a week's holiday in Margate, where Tom had often been as a child when his father was alive. They stayed in a guest house facing the beach and spent the days walking, talking and sitting in tea rooms; in the evenings they played chess and Tom read *Tristram Shandy* aloud while Sis lay on the bed. She decided that her love for him was growing; she felt more at ease than she had on their honeymoon almost a year before. And she liked being on holiday. In London the running of the house and the men's constant need of meals and clean clothes were tiresome, even though – funded by Tom – they now had Big Alice coming in more often to cook. She thought again about living with Tom and her child in a smaller house, and remembered that he had said that they could afford a live-in servant; perhaps it would be better? But she said nothing.

15

Looking over the Bristol Channel

My father was born at 7 a.m. on 10 December 1891 in Sis's bedroom on the brass bed that Old George had bought as a wedding present. It was a Wednesday and he had not been expected until the following weekend. Doctor White, the family's doctor for more than twenty years, delivered him with the help of a local nurse.

Sis's labour had begun at six o'clock the previous evening. Tom and Old George spent most of the night awake in Old George's room playing chess by candlelight. Young George slept on the drawing-room sofa, so as to be away from the inevitable noise and disturbance; Ernest and La Frascetti were away performing in St Petersburg. Little Alice stayed up all night, keeping the cooking range and the fires alight and carrying towels and bowls of water up and down stairs; she was even admitted to the labour room – she kept her eyes averted and rushed away as soon as she could.

A few minutes after seven Tom was called to Sis's bedroom where Doctor White handed him his son wrapped in a cream shawl. Sis lay smiling, propped on several pillows; Little Alice had already brushed her hair. The doctor and the nurse left, and Tom held my father, stared at him and saw that he had dark hair and blue eyes just like his. He stroked his cheek and whispered 'My son' and 'My hat' several times before sitting on the bed next to Sis where they admired him together. My father ignored them and went to sleep.

The new family had a few minutes alone before the two

Georges came in to congratulate them and examine the baby. My father woke up as his grandfather held him on his knee and rubbed his nose gently with his own before passing him to his uncle. Young George held him at arm's length in such a way that Sis feared that either he would drop him or her son's head would fall off. With Sis's permission, Tom handed my father to Little Alice who rocked him in both arms in a manner much approved of by Sis. Throughout this ordeal my father, who was less than an hour old, gazed around wildly but made no sound.

Kate had been summoned by telegram and arrived with Kathleen in the afternoon – it had been planned that she would stay for two weeks and run the household so that Sis could rest and concentrate on her baby. Kate thought her great-nephew was 'a true Thompson' with 'his grandfather's piercing blue eyes' but also liked his mouth which was 'wide and firm like Tom's'. She spent time alone with her niece, discussing the details of the birth and giving advice, particularly that Sis mustn't forget Tom; men often felt ignored when a baby arrived and this could lead to trouble. He was a good, dutiful husband and she must make him, as well as the baby, feel loved.

The following Sunday Ernest and Rose returned, after a three-day journey from St Petersburg, and suggested that there should be a party to celebrate the birth, especially as – in accordance with the family's radical views, which originated with Old George – there was to be no christening. Sis and Tom liked the idea, but Kate counselled against; there should be no upheavals until mother and baby were thoroughly settled. Ernest and Rose were disappointed but set up their xylophone on the landing outside Sis's bedroom door. While Ernest struck the keys and sang a music-hall ditty called 'There's a Baby in Our House', Rose cartwheeled and somersaulted in and out of the room. From his cot next to the bed on Sis's side, my father waved his arms and made a few noises and then went silent during the lullaby 'Sleep Pretty Baby, Sleep', played as a xylophone duet.

For several days the family discussed names. Tom wanted to call him Thomas Clifton, his own names and those of his father; Clifton was an old family name of the Reynolds. Sis liked Thomas and she liked Clifton even more – it was unusual and sounded distinguished – but insisted on George; the eldest males in the Thompson family were always called George. A suggestion that he should have three names was quickly dismissed; only girls and toffs and swells had more than two. Thomas George and George Thomas were considered, but Sis had decided that she liked Clifton, which meant that either Thomas or George had to go. In return for Clifton, Tom agreed to drop Thomas on the understanding that their second son be given his name. With two Georges already in the house, they decided to address their son as Clifton and put it first; it soon got shortened to Cliff or Cliffie.

He was a small child surrounded by adults – the second son did not appear – and he noticed things when he was very young that he remembered decades later, including his grandfather in the mellow light of candles resembling the painting of God that he saw in a Bible, his Uncle George always reading, the servant Alice being kind and very pretty and, of course, his aunt Rose walking around the house on her hands. He learned that his mother sniffed when she was annoyed and that his father sometimes came home drunk and had to be left alone while he slept on the sofa in the breakfast-room.

While he was too young to be allowed out in the street on his own, Cliffie often played in the garden. One afternoon he heard a voice singing a song about someone called Sweet Rosy O'Grady. A curly-haired boy was standing on the wall at the end of the garden. When a voice from the back of the boy's house shouted, 'Stop that blasted noise,' he sang even louder, ran along the wall and began to jump up and down on the corrugated iron roof of a neighbour's hen house causing the hens to add to the din. The boy's name was Toppy Wheeler and he and Cliffie became close friends, although Sis disapproved because Toppy was 'common' and an 'urchin'.

Occasionally Cliffie went to Toppy's home and he was always shocked at how different it was from his own. A rusty bookbinding machine covered in dust and cobwebs took up a large part of the basement kitchen, which was also the living-room; Toppy told him that his grandfather who now worked in a factory used to make his living from it. The rest of the room was filled by a big table which was always covered in gin bottles, unwashed crockery and empty tins, most of which had once contained condensed milk. There was a sour smell, like vomit. Along the passage, where the WC, whose door wouldn't shut, opened off the scullery, the smell was worse; it was caused, Toppy said, by something that was wrong with his own bowels.

Toppy's mother – he had never known his father – always dressed in black and generally sat without moving in front of a fireplace overflowing with cold cinders. Toppy said that she had 'bad legs' and she told Cliffie that she suffered from dropsy. She usually had a bottle of gin within reach and Toppy often fetched beer for her from the Norfolk Arms. Toppy had an adult brother, who slept in the front basement room and kept the back garden well tended. Unlike Cliffie's own garden which backed on to it, it was a paradise of flowers and blossom in which he loved to play.

When he was still quite young, Cliffie decided that his family was unusual; his grown-ups were always reading, or having serious discussions about people and things that sounded important – they hated two men called Salisbury and

Joe Chamberlain and they liked a man called Gladstone. Cliffie knew that they were in favour of something called the rights of man and that that was also the name of a book, and that they wanted people to be nicer to a creature called the bottom dog; his uncle Ernest, in particular, talked a lot about this dog.

By the time he was five, he understood who the bottom dogs were and saw that his friend Toppy was one of them – and he became confused by the attitudes of adults. His mother was on the side of the underdog, and especially the bottom dog, but she didn't want him to be friendly with Toppy because he was a common urchin.

The adults were also confusing about God and religion. His mother made him kneel down every night and pray to 'Gentle Jesus, meek and mild', but he heard the grown-ups saying that they didn't believe in God and his mother telling a man on the doorstep that God was a lot of nonsense because, if he existed, he would help the poor. She told the man to stop bothering her and to go away and look after the underdogs. Afterwards she said, with a sniff, that he was a silly man who had come from the church.

His mother had an opinion about everything and argued a lot with other people, and with his father more than anyone. With him, Cliffie, she was very loving – always smiling, lifting him up and kissing him – and she was always polite and friendly to his grandfather, but with other people she sniffed a lot and was often cross. His father was different; he was friendly towards everyone and, though he had opinions, was less argumentative and hardly ever got cross. His mother was always there, but she was often busy with food or making clothes or talking to other people or bossing Little Alice; when his father wasn't at work or out at the pub, he was always ready to talk or play games. As Cliffie grew up, he asked lots of questions and found that his father, more than anyone, would answer them properly – and, if he didn't know the answer, he would get out a book called *Whitaker's Almanack* and read bits out loud.

As time went on his mother seemed to get more cross with his father and to tell him off more often. Cliffie was worried one night when he heard his mother shouting and his father murmuring apologetically. A few weeks later he heard his mother shouting again and caught the words 'You drunken sot!' His father walked out of the house slamming the basement door. He knew that his father sometimes got drunk, but then lots of people did, especially men; he often saw them in the streets and he and his friends imitated the way they wobbled as they walked and spoke without leaving gaps between words. It was something men did; he hadn't realised that there was anything wrong about it.

Then Cliffie noticed that his father was drunk more often, on Sundays as well as Saturdays, and that a routine had developed. At lunch-time on Saturday his father would go out to the pub. In the afternoon, when Cliffie heard his key in the door, he knew that he would be drunk and would sleep on the breakfast-room sofa until dinner-time. Then he would go to the fried fish shop on the Balls Pond Road and come back with fish or saveloys, and pease pudding for dinner. After dinner he would go out to the pub again and return when it shut at 12.30, often sleeping the night on the breakfast-room sofa.

On Sunday mornings Cliffie and his father would go for long walks together – on which for a time Cliffie regularly wore his highwayman's outfit with a cape and a triangular hat. They would call at several pubs on the way and at each one his father would order 'three fingers of Johnny Walker' and buy a cake for Cliffie to eat while he waited outside, which was never for more than a minute or so. When they got home Sunday lunch was usually ready. Though drunk, his father would manage to carve the joint and, after it was eaten, do the washing-up with the help of the Alices.

Soon after he had heard his mother call his father a drunken sot, his father gave him a cake outside a pub on a Sunday morning and told him not to tell his mother, when she asked him, as she always did, how many pubs they had visited. Cliffie realised that there *was* something wrong about getting drunk. But he loved his father and from then on enjoyed the secret side of their outings, and soon became a good liar.

~

While I was reading his account of this, Cliffie had been snoring in the room next door. Suddenly he was standing in the doorway in front of me wearing a brown-and-red-checked dressing gown and sky-blue pyjamas. His hair was sticking up at the back. 'I saw the light on. Are you all right, old chap?'

'Fine. Just reading about your childhood.' I looked at my watch. It was a quarter past one.

'Oh!' He smiled and rubbed his cheeks with his palms. 'I just put that there because it seemed to belong with my mother's diaries . . . How is it the second time?'

'Great. I *love* Toppy Wheeler.'

He grinned. 'So did I.' He looked at the carpet while nodding his head. 'Long ago. Long, long ago.' He looked up. 'I went to Spurs for the first time with Toppy.'

'I know. I just read about it.' I stood up.

'Well . . . don't stay up *too* late.' He went out and shut the door carefully. The door opened again, and he put his head in. 'And don't smoke too much, or you'll end up coughing like me.' His head disappeared before I could say anything.

By the time I went back to school I had read my grandmother's diaries as far as 1897. After 1892 she wrote progressively less – there were many days and, in the later diaries, weeks – when she wrote nothing. In 1897 she wrote more fully, probably because she had something to write about.

~

For two years or so after the birth of her son, Sis felt that she had come to love Tom. He was kind and attentive and proud of her and Cliffie. She liked the way that he put one arm around her waist while pushing Cliffie's pram with the other when they went walking in fine weather on Hackney Downs. And she was charmed when he bought a camera and set up a dark-room under the stairs, because he wasn't satisfied with the posed portraits of her and Cliffie taken at the studio in Kingsland High Street.

Occasionally he mentioned his dream of owning his own house and living in it with just her and Cliffie and a maid – and the rest of their children, who, annoyingly, had not yet begun to arrive. She deflected him by saying that Cliffie was too young for such an upheaval, but the truth was that she didn't want to spend most of her time alone with a child and a maid-servant – Tom had only Saturday afternoons and Sundays away from work; she had grown used to a home where many people, especially her father, came and went.

Eventually, in the heat and humidity of the summer of 1894, Tom's resentment surfaced. He said again that he hadn't expected to be married to her father as well as her – and this time he added in her brothers and her sister-in-law. There was a row, and a week later another, and then another, and he began to attack her character – calling her an opinionated bully and telling her how exasperating he found her unwavering belief that she was always right. And, always an enthusiastic drinker at social occasions, he started to drink at other times and to come home from work late and tipsy; there were words over late, re-heated dinners and afterwards he would retreat from her to the Norfolk Arms, returning after midnight properly drunk, singing, staggering and, sometimes a little abusive.

Many times he told the Georges and Ernest of his frustrations – especially of his inability to be master of his own home – and they sympathised; they knew that Sis could be difficult and knew what he didn't: that she had been near-destroyed by a man. And they thought Tom was a good man – he had an important job, earned more than any of them and, above all, tried hard to make Sis happy – but they, even Old George, couldn't tell Sis how to behave. She was an adult and a mother – and, more than that, their daughter and their sister; their loyalty was instinctive and lay far deeper than their reason.

Only he could persuade her and he tried many times, but he always failed. Once she reminded him that, a few years ago, soon after they were married, he had said that he would adjust his expectations. He couldn't remember saying that, but, in the end – sometime in 1895 – he did adjust them; he stopped suggesting that they live elsewhere – and his acceptance of defeat was probably more palatable because, long ago, he had begun to replace his dreams with drink.

His work – a place where he was respected and prized – was another consolation, and he made sure, for a while yet, that there the drink didn't hurt his reputation for diligence and good sense. His third consolation was his son, whom he loved as much as he loved Sis and who returned his love without question.

Sis's Aunt Kate gave him more than sympathy; she had always liked him and continued to stick up for him – he never drank excessively when he visited Braintree. On 25 April 1896 Sis and Kate talked in Kate's kitchen while Cliffie played with his cousin Kathleen. Sis moaned about Tom and his drinking.

'Why Sis, you don't know how to manage him,' Kate said.

'How can I love a drunken sot?'

'But he wouldn't *be* one if you really loved him.'

On a cold morning as we trudged across a field, damp with melting frost, I asked my father if he really remembered the actual words spoken by his mother and Kate on 25 April 1896; Sis had mentioned the conversation in her diary, but he had written the words down just two years ago, early in 1962.

'Completely. I do. I was standing outside the kitchen door in Braintree. I was playing hide-and-seek with Kathleen and two of her friends and I was seeking. I was going to go through the kitchen to the garden, but I stopped by the door and listened.' He walked a few more steps and stopped. 'I would have been five.'

'I reckon you were four. It was April 1896 according to your mum's diary.'

He looked at me. 'Maybe . . . but it's remarkable how clear the memory is.' He went on walking and said over his shoulder, 'Can't remember what happened last week, of course.'

Half an hour later we were sitting on a wet log on top of a hill looking at the Bristol Channel three miles away. My father was wearing an old honey-coloured duffel coat and smoking a roll-up. 'Are you reading her diaries pretty thoroughly? A lot of it's very dull.'

'Every word so far. But she didn't write so much after you were born.'

'She didn't have so much time.' He pushed his hat back, put his hands on the log behind him, stretched out his legs and gazed at the view. 'Beautiful. I knew there'd be a view from up here.' There was a line of small puffy clouds on the horizon and above them the sky was pale and streaked with white. Over our heads it was a rich blue and cloudless. The sea was dark and sparkling and to our right a river looped across flat fields.

He yawned and turned to me. 'You know, I think I always blamed my father for the things that went wrong when I was a child. He was weak, relative to my mother . . . but it was hard for him – he loved her, but she didn't really love him . . . She shouldn't have married him; she only did it on the rebound from that accursed Stanley Andrews. He's to blame . . . for whatever there is to blame anyone for. I don't blame my mother. I never did.' He looked away and down at the river below. 'But now I feel that I don't blame my father either; I always have done. I grew up blaming him . . . because he wasn't there. But I see now. That was unfair.' He looked round at me and smiled. 'But it's a good thing they did marry. Otherwise we wouldn't be here.'

He took my hand, and neither of us spoke for a while. He was looking across the fields to the sea, with his chin up and his hat still pushed to the back of his head. It was a strong profile, a high forehead and a prominent, curving nose. He pointed at a large bird circling over a wood, a buzzard he said.

Before we left, he made me stand in a patch of gorse and gaze resolutely at the horizon, so that he could take my photograph.

~

In June 1896 Sis discovered that she was pregnant. She was pleased, but cautious until August when she felt a movement inside her. Tom bought her a gold brooch – three long-stemmed flowers with rubies at their centres in the *art nouveau* style – and regularly came home early bringing flowers and chocolates. He went to the Norfolk Arms less often and for shorter periods, and the number of pubs he visited on Sunday mornings with Cliffie was reduced to two.

~

In the early hours of the morning of 13 February 1897, Cliffie was woken in his bed in his parents' room by his father. His mother wasn't feeling well and Little Alice was going to help to look after her; he was to go to bed in Little Alice's bed. His father carried him. It was warm where Little Alice had been lying and Cliffie soon fell back to sleep.

In the morning he was taken to neighbours and spent the day playing with their children. They were taking turns on the rocking horse in the late afternoon when he saw his father watching at the door. He looked tired but happy; Cliffie noticed the familiar creases on his temples. When he ran to him, he lifted him into his arms, took his pipe from his mouth and brushed Cliffie's face with his big moustache. 'Time to go home, old chap. There's a present waiting for you.'

Cliffie was excited. He had forgotten his mother was ill. He wanted to know what the present was. He badly wanted a set of garden tools, so he could make his garden like Toppy's. As he walked along the wet pavement holding his father's hand in the failing winter light, his father said, 'It's a little sister.'

'A baby! Only a baby!'

16

Milkshake at the Sugar Bowl

A MAN IN A BROWN suit came to collect the A35 at the end of July 1964. It hadn't been cleaned for a while but my father and I patted it lovingly on the bonnet; we had been many miles and discussed many important matters in it, and in the Easter holidays it had taken us to John o'Groats and back without breaking down. Parked beside it was my father's new car, a black, twelve-year-old Vauxhall Cresta with chrome strips on the bonnet and red leather seats. It had a pre-war look, tall and rounded. My father thought it was beautiful; I liked it for lots of reasons – it was spacious and filled with walnut and chrome, and, with his hat at a certain angle, it made my father look like James Cagney.

My father had retired. He had still been enjoying the job, but his legs were getting stiff, his deafness had worsened and he was annoyed with the management for their frequent raising of the thresholds at which he was awarded bonuses. He was seventy-two, had been working since he was sixteen and wanted to get away from 'those bloody capitalists at head office'. He had earned a rest, he said, and would give more time to reading and writing.

He and I had toasted his retirement with cherry brandy the previous evening. The man in the brown suit driving off between the rhododendrons provided the only other ritual.

His request to keep the A35 had been turned down, but the firm paid him £500 to thank him for putting them ahead of their competitors in three counties. He used some of it to buy the Cresta, and soon drove it back to Buckinghamshire where he found a new home: part of a Georgian house in the old part of Beaconsfield, not far from Marlow. There I had a small room on the first floor next to his, with the same curtains and books, and a view of apple trees in a walled garden. The living-room, the kitchen and an ancient willow-pattern lavatory were downstairs. We shared a bathroom with a woman and her son who lived in the rest of the house, but we washed and I cleaned my teeth in the kitchen sink.

My mother also began a new life that summer of 1964. She hadn't intended to live with Uncle Godfrey permanently. She got herself a clerical job at London University, and gained her longed-for independence, at the age of fifty-eight, by moving to her own flat, in a newly built block in the Fulham Road near the Forum cinema. She was anxious about it because it had only one bedroom and I would have to sleep in the living-room; she couldn't afford anything larger and remain in Chelsea where she had grown up and where so many of her relations still lived. I reassured her truthfully that this didn't worry me; after all, I lived in two other places and would only be there for a few weeks in a year.

After she moved, she began to join clubs and societies, notably a club for divorced people of both genders and an art group where, to judge from the strange images that soon covered the walls of the flat, she progressed rapidly from impressionism to pop art. She also joined the Overseas League, a stuffy club off St James's, because, she said, she liked the people and she could stop off there when she was in the West End, which she was frequently, visiting art galleries and going to the theatre with other divorced people.

I asked her – while trying to sound amused and unconcerned, which I was until she answered – whether she brought any of the divorced men home while I was at school or at my father's. She gave me a coy look and replied ambiguously at first, but she warmed to the topic and informed me casually that it was normal for women in their late fifties to be interested in sex and, more disturbingly, that, despite his defects and the appearance given by their sleeping in separate rooms, my father had been an excellent lover – she had had her own bedroom all my life only because my father began to snore during the war. She even told me that when I was around, they had used a code: 'I think I'll go to bed early tonight.'

Her candour was embarrassing but appreciated, and gave me a vision of the lives of adults; they just said something in code and someone who was sitting in an armchair reading the *Daily Telegraph* would go to bed with them. It seemed very worldly and for ever beyond my reach.

That autumn, after much argument on my father's part, a divorce settlement was reached whereby he benefited from a new law that required relatively wealthy ex-wives to pay alimony to hard-up ex-husbands. He had calculated that he could live off the state old-age pension, supplemented by a little social security to which, as someone with minimal savings and no income, he would be entitled. He therefore turned down regular monthly payments from my mother, accepted £3000 as a lump sum and spent it fast, on a luxurious fortnight alone in Paris and a two-month cruise as a passenger on a tramp steamer to the West Indies, from which he returned brown, grinning and with a thousand stories just in time for Christmas.

On the first Saturday in January 1965 I persuaded him to drive me the five miles from his new home to Marlow. I told him I wanted to see the town again. But more than that I wanted to see Deborah.

I was nervous as we set out in the Cresta. I hadn't seen her for two years and she hadn't replied to my letters. She was probably caught up with people – particularly boys – whom I didn't know, and I would be an awkward arrival from the past, but I wanted to see her; there was a chance that she would be the same, with the same easy empathy that I had always liked, and that our friendship could be resumed. I thought about entering the familiar shop. Her father would be standing behind the counter and would greet me in his restrained, friendly way, and her mother would be upstairs and effusive, but I couldn't imagine how Deborah might be. She was sixteen now.

My father was talking about the cheapness of salmons' heads at the fishmonger in Beaconsfield, unaware that I was clenching and unclenching my calf muscles to ease my tension. He had arranged to see his old friend and fellow budgerigar-fancier Wing Commander Hayes, and I planned to leave him to that and meet him later.

~

I walked slowly up the High Street, past the Sugar Bowl café, the florist, Mr Brown's grocery and my mother's old shop. I could see Mr Neame, the Brylcreemed manager my mother had taken on years before, standing in the back. Nothing had changed and, two doors up, the sweetshop looked the same.

I wasn't ready to go in. I walked quickly past, half-imagining that Deborah would run out, grab my hand and suggest a walk. I glanced at the window. It was filled with pastel-coloured lights, tinsel and boxes of chocolates. The panes were decorated with wispy triangles of cotton wool. I glimpsed warm yellow light and someone moving inside.

I crossed the road further up and walked back on the other side. A woman in a purple coat carrying a shopping bag came out, but the door with its advertisements for ice cream and cigarettes shut quickly behind her. The light was on upstairs and I could see the back of an upright chair. I walked on until I was opposite the Sugar Bowl, crossed the road again and walked back up as far the florist. I stared vacantly at the flowers on the pavement and thought about walking the other way and forgetting about Deborah.

I wondered why I was so apprehensive. I took my hands out of my pockets and walked quickly up the street. I stopped outside the sweetshop, turned up the collar of my donkey jacket and pushed on the door. A pudgy man with short hair looked up from behind the counter. There were no other customers. I looked towards the door that led to the stairs hoping that someone I knew would come through it.

'Is Deborah around?'

He looked puzzled. 'Deborah? No. No Deborahs.'

I walked towards him and rested my hand on the counter. 'Deborah Baylis? Don't the Baylises own this shop any more . . .?'

His frown became a smile. 'The Baylises! No. They went . . . ooh . . . eighteen months ago. We took it on a year ago September.'

'Where did they go to?'

'Just a minute.' Two small girls had come in and were holding up their money for packets of bubblegum.

'Well . . . Someone told me they went to somewhere in Wiltshire.' He pulled at the back of his neck. 'I never met them myself. Old man had a heart problem? Or something? The group bought the business. I'm just the manager.'

I thanked him and left, and walked towards the river. She could have written and told me her new address. I reached the end of the High Street and stood on the corner looking at the church and the bridge, and across at our old street with Burger's tea shop on the corner. I couldn't think where to go next. It was much too soon to meet my father.

I started walking through the park towards the river. In my vision of this day I didn't visit Richard – he hadn't answered my letter and wouldn't be interested in me any longer; I was going to spend time with Deborah. But now he seemed better than no one, and he might know where Deborah had gone. I turned back.

As I walked through the streets, I remembered that I had Deborah's last letter – from two summers ago – in my wallet. I took it out and looked at it as I walked. Though it didn't say much, I had been pleased to get it. It was mostly about how much she liked drawing and how she couldn't imagine me and my parents living in a caravan – she had drawn one with three people leaning out of the windows – and she said she hoped I'd come back to Marlow.

I had come back – too late. 'How *stupid*.' I spoke out loud as I walked past the library. The letter ended 'love Deborah' with a single kiss, as usual. I had taken more than six months to reply to it – and by then they had moved to Wiltshire. 'How *bloody stupid*!'

Richard's mother answered the door and, once she recognised me, hugged me and asked me in. He'd be back soon. He'd be thrilled to see me; he was playing football at the recreation ground. 'Your old team. Claremont Station. Adam, Bobby, Patrick. And there are some new ones now.'

I sat in her kitchen, and she put the kettle on and brought out a tin of biscuits. She told me I looked bigger and more handsome and asked after my parents. I told her about them separating. She looked concerned; it wasn't for her to say, but she would imagine that my father would be a difficult man to live with. She ironed some shirts as we chatted.

'Look who's here.'

Richard looked startled, then took my hand and clapped me on the shoulder. He had grown more than I had; he was nearly six foot and looked broad and strong. His hair was the same, curly and sand-coloured, but there were dark patches on his upper lip and his jaw where he shaved. He hadn't much to say. He'd be leaving school next year. People in the town – Adam, Patrick and Dennis – were all OK. Claremont Station was second in the league.

'We could still use you.' He looked at me earnestly for a moment, and for a few seconds I had a strange feeling of elation.

It quickly disappeared. 'I can't. If I was lucky, I could play once every school holidays . . . No point, is there.'

He nodded and sipped his tea. 'Shame.'

'Do you know what happened to Deborah? Man in the sweetshop said they'd moved to Wiltshire.'

He smiled and raised his eyebrows knowingly. 'She didn't write and tell you? Her dad had a heart attack in the shop. Taken off in an ambulance . . . She told me she was writing to you all the time. Told me you hated that school . . . I told you not to go there.' He grinned and shook his head. 'I'm sorry I didn't write. I kept meaning to.'

'Was her dad OK? Where did they go?'

His mother answered. 'It wasn't too serious. He was in hospital in Wycombe for two weeks.' She put down her iron. 'But he was told to rest . . . retire if he could. They went to live near her family – Wiltshire, I believe.' She picked up a shirt and shook it.

'You don't know where in Wiltshire?'

I looked at them both, but neither of them knew. I couldn't think of much else to say to Richard. I left, telling them that I had to meet my father, but I had had another idea. It was possible that on a Saturday afternoon some of Deborah's girlfriends would be in the Sugar Bowl – and, anyway, now that I was sixteen, it would be fun to sit there for a while.

It was steamy and crowded and had hardly changed – the same chrome and red plastic, circular revolving stools, Formica tables and smell of sweet milk and tobacco smoke. I drank a chocolate milkshake and pretended to stare around aimlessly, while scrutinising the girls. I had only ever glimpsed the girls Deborah knew, in the street, as we passed and she waved or said 'Hi'. I tried to remember. Sometimes she had stopped and chatted, and I had loitered, paying no attention.

There was a girl at a table, with two other girls. I thought I had seen her before. Perhaps I had – by the river, in the street, at a bus stop. But I tended to forget faces I had only seen once, fleetingly. I finished my drink and stared into the mirror behind the bar, clenching my calves, fighting my nerves.

'Excuse me, but did you used to know Deborah Baylis?' She had short blonde hair, and looked surprised and suspicious at the same time. 'I was a good friend of hers until two years ago. I had to move away.'

She giggled then, and said she'd thought she'd seen me before. 'David, isn't it?' She had been Deborah's best friend at the grammar. Deborah had often talked about me. She had moved to Chippenham in Wiltshire.

'Do you know the address or phone—'

'No. She said she'd send it, but she didn't.'

I thanked her and started to leave.

'If you ever see her, tell her Teresa sends love.'

'I will. Thanks.'

'And tell her to send me a postcard.'

I called directory enquiries from my mother's telephone a few days later. My mother was in her bedroom.

'Name, please.'

'Geoffrey Baylis.'

'Address please.'

'He's in Chippenham . . . Wiltshire. I don't know the whole address.'

'I can't tell you the telephone number without the full address.' Her voice had the uninterested lilt of someone who says the same thing many times a day.

'There can't be many Geoffrey Baylises in Chippenham.'

'There might not be any, but I couldn't tell you without the address.'

'Do you mean there aren't any Geoffrey Baylises?'

'I'm sorry. I can't tell you if you don't know the address.'

'Please, it's very important.'

There was silence. 'I'm not supposed to tell you this.' She was speaking more quietly and in a normal voice. 'There's no one of that name listed.'

'No Geoffrey Baylises? What about G. Baylis?'

'None of them, either, dear. Sorry.'

'Thank you . . . Goodbye.'

I put the phone down and stared towards the window. 'Goodbye.' I repeated the word out loud and hurried across the hall and out of the front door, closing it quietly. I didn't want my mother to see me; I couldn't talk to her then. I had lost the person whom I now saw as my best friend.

That year, 1965, the shops in the King's Road changed rapidly. Sainsbury's closed and Lord John opened, a development deplored by my mother's elderly relatives, with the exception of Auntie Toto and Uncle Godfrey who liked 'the colourful young people' and anyway bought their food in Oakeshott's and Harrods. Pat and I followed the progress of the boutiques closely; Michael's Man Boutique on the corner of Tryon Street became my favourite and Pat's was Granny Takes A Trip which was about a mile down the road on the bend before the World's End. If either of us wanted to buy a shirt or a pair of trousers we would spend an afternoon walking from Sloane Square up to 'Granny's', examining the clothes in every shop before making a decision.

In the late summer we both wanted a pair of hipster trousers. Pat tried on a striped pair in Lord John and I tried a black pair, made of hairy, woolly material, in Michael's; they felt very strange, tight round the thighs and with the waist round the hips – I kept wanting to pull them up, but that made the legs too short and the crutch impossibly tight and ostentatious. We walked on, dropping in and trying on here and there.

After Chelsea Town Hall the boutiques stopped; Granny's was a lone outpost several blocks further on. My legs were aching by the time we got there and I sat on a chair while Pat tried on numerous pairs of hipsters and discussed them with me and the shop assistant, a girl in jeans with ironed blonde hair and false eyelashes. He eventually bought a pair with narrow green and brown stripes; I had decided to buy the black pair I had tried on in Michael's.

We took a bus back and sat upstairs on the right, smoking. The traffic moved slowly. Just after the bus passed Sydney Street we heard a man's voice say, 'Blimey! Look at that.' The people sitting on the left were all looking out of the windows. The bus was stationary. We stood up to see what was happening and everyone else on our side of the bus stood up as well. 'Chroist! Can you see that, Dave?' A tall girl with long blonde hair was walking past the Gaumont cinema wearing a white shirt and a light brown skirt. The skirt was at least a foot shorter than any skirt I – or, it seemed, anyone on the top of this bus – had ever seen.

On the pavement people were standing back and staring. On the bus people who didn't know each other were sharing their opinions.

'Beautiful! Look at her thighs!'

'Should be ashamed of herself.'

'Phwor! She can come back to my place any time.'

'You should be so lucky.'

'It's disgusting.'

'Mary Quant's miniskirt. Just launched.' A young woman with curly hair peered out of the window and spoke quietly to no one in particular.

The girl went on walking. The bus moved along slowly a few feet behind her. She crossed through the traffic and walked along the other side past the Chelsea Pet Stores. Pat and I sat down. People from the other side stood up and leaned over our heads. 'Did you see her thighs? Chroist!'

'Bloody amazing.' I was seeing in the street now something I had only expected to see somewhere very private sometime in the distant future.

The woman with curly hair turned round and put her hand beside her mouth. 'We'll all be wearing them next year.' She smiled.

'Chroist!'

~

Paul Snape dusted and polished La Frascetti regularly right up until we left school the next summer, 1966. Even when he and Pete became prefects, and a fag – to my embarrassment – cleaned our study, he insisted on looking after her himself. By then she had become a mascot to the whole house. To me she was still a symbol of freedom, but the artist had taken on as much significance as the subject, and the picture sometimes made me feel depressed; I would slouch in my worn-out chair and think about my 'lost friends' – I articulated the phrase often inside my head. I envisaged Deborah mainly, but also Richard, Adam, Patrick, Bobby the goalkeeper and Dennis. And, as the end of our schooldays came closer, I thought about my friendships with Pete, Dave, Pat, Paul and others. Would *they* last when we no longer had the grim institution to bind us together? Except for a couple of people whom Pat and I had met more than once in the Troubador – a coffee bar in Earl's Court where we listened to folk singers and had intense conversations with long-haired women and Australian men – I knew no one outside school and my old home town.

In the end Bird found me a disappointment. My 'A' levels wouldn't be good enough for the Oxford and Cambridge colleges he had entered me for, but, since I was not yet eighteen, I could stay at school another year and study for them again with more energy. The idea horrified me. I politely rejected it, and amid Bird's genuine show of sorrow sensed a measure of relief.

Without enthusiasm, I filled in a form applying to other universities. I had an idea of training to be a journalist, but my main aims were to be free, earn some money so that I wouldn't be dependent on my mother, wear jeans and open-necked shirts, and grow my hair.

17

Good Vibrations

PAT BEGAN WORKING for the agency first. We cleaned people's flats and houses for five shillings an hour. Pat seemed to get wealthy single men who wanted to sit and have a chat, whereas I got harassed mothers with large houses whose children's bedrooms had to be cleaned while they were at school. I found a copy of *Penthouse* under a teenage boy's bed, glanced at it and tucked it under his mattress. Later his mother rang the agency and said I was the best cleaner she'd ever had – could I come every week? It was dull work, but I couldn't see the point of doing it badly.

I was living at my mother's and spending some of my evenings with Pat. We often met at the Helvetia in Old Compton Street, a pub with free live music, and moved on to the Marquee to see groups like Manfred Mann or the Spencer Davis Group; if we wanted to stay up most of the night we'd squeeze ourselves into Les Cousins, a hot basement in Greek Street, and listen to folk and blues – Bert Jansch and Alexis Korner.

Dave Hunt rang unexpectedly. He was in London; he had got in to one of the medical schools and was living in a bedsit in Bayswater. Apart from me and Pat, the only person he knew in the city was his older brother who was a student. We went out drinking and were soon meeting up two or three times a week, usually in one of the pubs in the Fulham Road. We would move from Finch's to the Goat in Boots and back again, drinking Watney's Red Barrel very slowly. Dave was less wild than Pat, easier to be with, reliable and

almost always smiling, if not laughing. Sometimes the three of us would go to Soho and sometimes Pat would come to Finch's.

The Goat in Boots had bare floorboards, intricately engraved glass and worn panelling, the colour of chestnuts; it had been there nearly a hundred years and little seemed to have changed. There was a singsong around an upright piano most evenings – post-war hits and music-hall favourites. Dave and I loved that, but Pat wouldn't even drink in the place. Singing 'Daisy' while swinging a pint mug somehow connected me to the past, to the 1890s and the Norfolk Arms in Dalston, and to La Frascetti and my grandfather Tom Reynolds; this must be the kind of thing they had enjoyed.

I sometimes spent time standing alone with a pint at the bar in the Clifton, a small pub next door to the cinema. It was the name that attracted me initially, but its quiet ordinariness made me go back. It had no music, no decor, no pretensions and no crowds, just enough regulars to keep it going, and one person behind the bar – a blonde woman called Eileen – which was all it needed. Eileen was about thirty and had a certain elegance, with blonde hair swirled upwards and secured smoothly to the back of her head, black glasses with restrained wings, and a small gold cross which lay neatly on top of her red round-necked sweaters.

I went there after dinner, on evenings when I was at home with my mother. I would go out at ten, drink two pints and come back at eleven – when my mother would produce a pot of tea and a plate of bourbon biscuits and we would watch Joan Bakewell present *Late Night Line-up* or, on Saturdays, *The Late Show* with Eleanor Bron, John Bird, John Fortune and Barry Humphries.

I always stood in the same place at the bar, in front of a Rothmans ashtray with the beer pumps to my right. I would stare vacantly at the upside-down bottles and think – about girls and what to do with my life; letters had begun to arrive that suggested that the universities weren't impressed by me and my second-rate 'A' levels. Occasionally I talked to a civil but taciturn man called Cyril who regularly sat on a stool where the bar met the wall. He wore a jacket, shirt and tie and had scruffy shoes; he looked like the kind of man who would wear a brown coat over his shirt and tie at work – a warehouseman or a long-serving assistant in a hardware store.

Eileen told me that Cyril had flown in bombers during the war as a rear gunner. My slight knowledge of bomber crews came from the war comics I used to swap with Richard and Adam and from films, usually starring Richard Todd; the rear gunner lay flat on his stomach, isolated but for radio contact with his colleagues, and was in the most dangerous position of all. Eileen said that Cyril was a brave man; he had flown an almost record number of missions and had been shot down twice over the North Sea. But Cyril didn't want to talk about it; all he would say was, 'You 'ad to do it, didn' yer?' He was more interested in Fulham Football Club where he had a season ticket.

~

My mother didn't believe in God but she wanted to believe in something. She had a fondness for nature and beauty and believed, with a few reservations, that science could solve the world's problems, so she joined a group of like-minded people, the London branch of the British Humanist Association, and went to lectures and parties. Bits of their literature started to accumulate on the coffee table next to my bed, and she told me they were opposed to compulsory religion in schools – I agreed with them about that. As far as I could understand, the humanists were a descendant of the nineteenth-century rationalist societies and campaigned on behalf of agnostics and atheists and to limit the power of the church; some of the people I used to see on *The Brains Trust* –

Bertrand Russell and Julian Huxley – were involved, and I had the feeling that Sis and Old George and my grandfather Tom would have approved.

I was tiring of cleaning houses when my mother told me that the humanists were advertising for an assistant membership secretary, part-time. I applied and got the job, and worked there every weekday afternoon in an office near High Street Kensington, logging subscriptions and mailing the members. It was easy work, I was paid, and I liked my boss, Diane, who sat at a desk across the room from me and seemed very mature and sophisticated. I discovered that she was twenty-three, and was astonished when she told me that she lived with her boyfriend, John. It seemed very unusual and, when I told Pat and Dave, they were amazed; the idea of unmarried men and women living together was a novelty – and a rather appealing one.

Diane often chatted as she put on her lipstick at the end of our working day. She always had more than one lipstick and sometimes asked my opinion. 'John and I are going out for a few drinks. Then we're going to d'Aretusa's. What do you think?' She held two lipsticks in front of me: pink and purple.

'That one.' I had no idea what d'Aretusa's was, but pointed to the purple. I had seen it on her before and it went with her freckles and pale skin.

'Umm . . . maybe.' She went back to her desk and began putting it on to her lips as she stared into a tiny mirror. She looked over at me, grinning mischievously. 'You met any girls yet?' She had told me before that I ought to have a girlfriend.

'No . . . I'm trying though.' I smiled awkwardly.

'You ought to join the Young Humanists.' She giggled and blotted her mouth with a tissue. 'You'd meet some there.' She took out a tiny brush and started putting mascara on her eyelashes. 'Nice girls.' She smiled broadly, pushing her purple lips towards me. 'They have a party second Friday of every month. Wine and cheese. John and I go sometimes.'

I took her advice. The party was in a dull room used for lectures, on the floor below where I worked, and I wanted to leave as soon as I entered. At a glance I could see that Diane was the youngest of the young humanists, and her minidress – purple and yellow hoops – their only colourful feature. But I meekly accepted a glass of wine, and a pineapple chunk and a piece of cheese fixed together with a cocktail stick – and found that I couldn't get away from a short woman with enormous eyelids stuccoed with green eyeshadow. We discussed the virtues of humanism while an angular man with an intense expression looked on and said nothing. She talked a lot and had a standard reply to my small contributions to the conversation: 'Well. This is it.' She left the 't' off 'it' and drew out the vowel in an extended vibrato like an air-raid siren winding down. Except for Diane, the young humanists were too old for me.

~

I tried, and usually managed, to visit my father every third weekend – by then he had been retired for more than two years and would soon be seventy-five. I liked my room in Beaconsfield; it wasn't big and the wallpaper was brown and dowdy, but it was old with a sloping floor and a Georgian window, and it was the only room I had that was my own. I hung up Deborah's drawing of La Frascetti, and often gazed at her as I lay in bed.

It still amazed me to think that my father could remember her practising and performing so long ago, in the nineteenth century. Since his retirement, my father's shoulders had become rounder, his movements more ponderous and his hearing much worse – his game efforts to guess what people were saying when they spoke quietly sometimes provoked cruel merriment. When I stayed with him now, I often felt that *I* was looking after *him*; except for driving I could do all the dull, practical things – shopping, cooking, sweeping the carpet, turning on the television – more quickly than he could. And when he drove, I sometimes told him when to change gear because he couldn't hear the engine.

I began to wonder what the point of it all was, if in the end you just grew old and died. My father's answer was that we were all part of nature and that everyone had a duty to preserve and enhance the lives of their fellow men. That was the point. You could call nature God, if you liked, but it made no difference. This seemed to have given him a *raison d'être* and he felt that he had done his best for mankind with his involvement in politics and his efforts to make people think by writing books and talking to anyone who would listen. He also thought that one of his achievements was that he had made a lot of people laugh; he often said that he wanted to be remembered for that. It was true, I thought; when I was a child his sense of fun had seemed to balance his ability to be cruel.

And now he wasn't cruel; he seemed fairly content, more at ease than when he'd worked and lived with my mother. His temper had faded and he spent most of his time writing – essays, poems, observations and reworkings of bits of his life. We still drove to farms – betting on what we might see over the next hill – and I patted dogs while he discussed yields, leys and the Milk Marketing Board with old friends. We played games, discussed the big issues – current and eternal – and laughed at absurdities and our favourite comedies on television – *The Arthur Haynes Show*, Frankie Howerd and *Till Death Us Do Part*.

But now, when I left him after my short visits, he seemed small and vulnerable – and, though he never said it, lonely; he told me, without irony or self-pity, that the local chemist and the newsagent were his best friends. As I walked off to catch a bus or hitchhike back to London, I felt sadness – physically, in the bones of my arms and legs. It was a feeling close to pity, and I didn't want to feel that, but I couldn't help myself. I didn't expect him to die yet, but the physical effects of age had brought his death forward, from somewhere unimaginable beyond the horizon, to a blurred sort of focus in the middle distance.

In a sense his closest friend was a good-natured blue budgerigar called Joey, who had been given to him by Wing Commander Hayes. During daylight Joey had the freedom of my father's living-room and spent much time perched on his shoulder cheeping quietly into his ear. My father spoke to him frequently, not just to let him know what was happening but to inform him about important issues. I overheard Joey being made aware that 'Spinoza may have been a determinist, but he was a much nicer man than Leibniz' and that 'the Americans should never have been in Vietnam and they should get out *now*'. Joey usually replied 'Nice one, Cyril' – a reference to one of my father's and my great heroes, Cyril Knowles, the Tottenham Hotspur left back – but not always: 'Cogito ergo sum', 'God *strewth*!' and 'That's my son, David' were all repeated several times a day. When it got dark my father would get Joey to perch on his finger, return him to his cage and throw a thick cloth over it.

Even though he was less volatile than he used to be, I waited until he was in an obvious good mood before telling him that I probably wouldn't be going to university. I was certain that he would be angry; he valued education more than anything and would castigate me for wasting an opportunity. After a quiet afternoon reading, playing chess and talking, he put Joey to bed and began to poke the fire.

'Dad, you probably won't be very pleased about this but I don't think I'll be going to university. My "A" levels don't seem to be good enough, and I think—'

'You'd've got better "A" levels at a grammar school.' He

gestured despairingly with his hands. 'Wouldn't've been distracted by those idle toffs.' He shook his head and asked what I was going to do.

I told him about my job with the humanists for the first time and was going to mention journalism, but he interrupted.

'Well, I started as an office boy at sixteen. Can't do you any harm at eighteen.' He smiled, raised his eyebrows and leaned his elbow on the mantelpiece. 'Humanists are a good thing.' He didn't seem to mind about university; I was relieved, but at the same time almost disappointed. 'Self-help! That's the answer. I don't suppose you've read it yet?'

I shook my head. He had given me a copy of Samuel Smiles's Victorian classic, *Self-Help*, the previous Christmas. It was quarter-bound in leather and was inscribed: 'To Cliff from Mother, 10th December, 1910' – his nineteenth birthday. Underneath, my father had written: 'and to my son Bob on December 18th, 1930' and underneath that: 'and to my second son, David, at Xmas 1965'. I had wondered whether Bob had read it and how it had come back into my father's possession.

'Well, try to have a look at it.' He sat down in his armchair with a slight thump. 'It's very good advice. The bits about Arkwright, Stevenson . . . Peel, Disraeli . . . the *elder* Disraeli . . . are very good, very inspirational.'

'I've been thinking about being a journalist.'

'Ah!' He pushed himself more upright in his chair.

'But I'd like to be a fairly serious one . . . you know, a columnist or a leader writer.'

He looked at me and started rolling a cigarette. 'That's an excellent thing to aim at. If you could do that, you could write *and* influence things . . . a bit like I have . . . now and then. We ought to go and see Old Bowen.'

I had feared that he would say that. Old Bowen was very old indeed, deafer and less capable of walking than my father. The worst thing was that he dribbled and was always wiping his mouth with a handkerchief. He lived nearby with his wife and, as far I could understand, had once – a very long time ago – been 'almost the editor' of the *Daily Mail.* Although he was very deaf, he mumbled – unlike my father who shouted. My father and Old Bowen were unable to understand anything each other said; the last time we had been there Mrs Bowen and I had had to act as interpreters.

He tapped on the arm of his chair. 'Or Robbie Robertson?' This was a much better idea, except that Robbie Robertson lived on the east coast of Scotland, in Montrose where he was the editor of the local paper. I had only met him once; he was stocky and brusque and liked slapping people on the back.

Two years earlier it would have been easier to drive to Scotland than to spend an afternoon with Old Bowen; but now my father's driving had deteriorated to a point where I was in an almost permanent state of alarm. 'Rather long way to go, Dad . . . I mean, we don't *have* to gallivant all over the country *seeing* people just because I'm interested in journalism.'

'Well, there's no harm in it. Society should be a meritocracy, but it isn't, so you have to pull strings when you can. Anyway, I like gallivanting now and again.' He grinned like a naughty boy.

'I have to be at work on Monday. I work Monday to Friday. I can't go to Scotland.'

He looked disappointed. 'Well, perhaps I'll go.'

'Dad, you don't *have* to do anything.'

'I know. But I like to help you as much as I can . . .' He looked at me with watery eyes. 'I've no money to give you, and I'm sorry about that, but I've still got a good brain and a few of my friends still survive . . . some of them not without influence.'

'Well . . . "No person of quality esteems another merely because he is rich."' He laughed as I shrugged.

I managed to avoid a visit to Old Bowen, but the next day my father telephoned Robbie Robertson, talked for a while and then handed me the receiver.

'David. You've left school already – very grown up – and you want to be a journalist? Right: two things. Write to all the local newspapers in range of where you live – they're listed in the *UK Press Gazette* – and tell them you want to be a trainee reporter, tell them all you can about yourself and send any cuttings you have from anywhere including the school magazine. Second, try to go to a secretarial college and learn shorthand and typing. You'll need it, so you might as well learn it now. That's what you need to do. Got it? Good luck. Pass me back to your father, if you will.'

'Thanks, Mr Robertson. Goodbye.'

I arranged to do shorthand and typing at Pitman's secretarial college in Southampton Row, and wrote to the editors of newspapers and magazines. And I wrote, and rewrote, and eventually sent, a letter to a twenty-four-year-old Australian who had just come to London to start an English edition of a magazine called *Oz*, which he had founded in Sydney four years earlier. I had read an article about him in the *Evening Standard* where he was quoted saying, 'We aim at something between *Private Eye* and the *New Statesman*.' In the photograph alongside he had long, straight hair like Brian Jones and was with a slim girl in a minidress who was described in the caption as the magazine's secretary.

~

Dave and I bought a bottle of Spanish red in Praed Street. I was cold and nervous. 'Maybe I shouldn't come. I haven't been invited.'

'Don't be a berk! Might be fun . . . if it's not, we can go to the pub.'

'I won't know *anyone*.'

'You know Mart.'

'Slightly.' I'd met Dave's older brother Martin twice. He was twenty-one, enviably hip and had a dark-haired girlfriend who designed clothes. He and his flatmates, mostly students at the Architectural Association, were having a party in what Dave had told me was a huge flat on two floors. As we crossed Westbourne Terrace, the sound of a thousand people talking, mingled with the Kinks' 'Sunny Afternoon', came from open ground-floor windows; above, on a balcony, people were drinking, chatting and staring down at us. I tugged at the collar on my donkey jacket.

Inside, a long corridor was crowded with people moving in both directions. There was a wide staircase in front of us and an open door leading to the dimly lit room at the front where the music was playing. In another room a double bed and most of the floor were covered in coats.

I followed Dave as he pushed his way along the corridor to the kitchen. It was barn-like and painted brick-red, even on the ceiling and the window-frames. A man with shoulder-length hair was playing boogie-woogie on a bright blue upright piano, ringed by people jigging about, shouting and drumming on saucepan lids with knives and wooden spoons. A table was spread with food and another covered in bottles and cans.

Dave knew some of his brother's friends; there were quick greetings and I was briefly introduced.

I stood about tapping my foot, smoking and drinking red wine. After a while I refilled my glass and wandered off. The room at the front seemed dark and noisy. I climbed the stairs, picking my way through feet and knees. It was too soon to drag Dave away and go to the pub. I would explore the place and just maybe – though they all seemed remote and older than me – I would meet someone I could talk to. In a room with a polished parquet floor, six or seven people lolled on a bed, chatting and laughing. My heels clacked as I walked towards open french windows. A black girl smiled from the bed and waved with her fingers – goodbye, not hello. On the balcony, more people, talking and laughing. A girl leaned against the wall, her knee forward and her foot under her bottom, and a man loomed over her, his hand resting on the bricks beside her face. Through another window, another uncarpeted room, loud with people, and beyond, a high-ceilinged purple bathroom with an old-fashioned bath on claw-like feet. I stared into a long mirror and pulled a few faces.

Downstairs, in the kitchen, another man at the piano – playing slow blues. I helped myself to wine. In the room at the front, at least a hundred people – two hundred maybe – a perfumed, pungent smell, dim light from the floor in the corners and Van Morrison's voice behind the din of conversation – 'Here Comes the Night'. Faces half turned and then turned quickly away, as I squeezed close to them, glass by cheek, stopping and going, something splashing on my hand, carefully treading where the spaces allowed, inching aimlessly past scented hair and striped collars but in search of a destination, finding one, reaching it, a small table beside the wall with bottles and lighted candles.

I stretched for a bottle, filled my glass and turned back to face the room. Two girls were standing in front of me. Both had blonde hair falling around their shoulders and were dressed in black. The one closest to me was wearing something loose made of thin material that shimmered in the gloom. She smiled.

The other one spoke. 'Have you seen Johnny Holly?' She had an Australian accent and twisted her mouth hopefully.

'Don't know him. Sorry. I only know two people here.'

'Oh.' She looked disappointed. She had a wide face and a fringe. 'We don't know *anyone.* Johnny Holly invited us, but we can't find him.' She looked at the bottle I had just put down. Her friend was still smiling and staring at me. They held out empty glasses.

'I'm Dave.'

'I'm Kate. This is Bonnie.'

'Bonnie? Nice name.'

She explained that it wasn't her real name; her father had used it when she was a baby and it had lasted. She had a soft English voice. They were flatmates and worked together at Rediffusion Television. I said I was going to train to be a journalist, a writer. Kate was enthusiastic. She liked creative people. She wanted to be a painter, in a way was a painter; her father was a well-known artist in Australia. She asked how old I was. I had been eighteen two days before. 'Nineteen.'

They were both twenty, and I was glad I had lied.

Kate talked more, but Bonnie looked at me more directly and I had a sense that in some way I was gaining her approval. We chatted and smoked each other's cigarettes, ignoring the rest of the room, and they promised to wait while I fetched more wine from the kitchen. I uncorked a bottle and manoeuvred my way back to them, thinking of nothing but the fact that this was actually happening – a sophisticated party, with no one's parents lurking around, at which people could stay as long as they liked and, for the moment at least, I was with two beautiful girls whom I was still trying to tell apart. I looked at them closely and saw that Bonnie was slightly taller, her features more delicate and her hair a little more dishevelled; Kate's was carefully brushed and cut into a straight fringe.

As we talk, the lights blink – and go off. The walls are flooded with a rippling red glow. Two projectors, their beams crossing and illuminating the dust. Red, purple, blue, eerily undulating on walls, faces and clothes. And the Beach Boys' 'Good Vibrations' – so loud. Bonnie and Kate sway gracefully, their skin changing from blue to green. Bonnie drags her hands through the air in front of me. Men signal to Kate. She shakes her head; we form a tighter triangle. More music. More colours. Dancing, drinking and smoking hurriedly, more dancing, drinking . . . Light then dark. White light flashing on and off with the beat. Bonnie, Kate, everyone, gyrating in staccato jerks. Dave beside me, there and not there, there and not there, grinning and gone; first Kate's, then Bonnie's hair against my face as I shout introductions. A foursome, then a pair, Bonnie and me. Bonnie close to me, putting a hand on my shoulder, smiling. 'Good Vibrations' again.

We went to the kitchen where it was cool. Dave grinned and muttered, 'This is all right.' Bonnie put her hand on my forehead. I looked hot, she said. More wine, tap water and a slab of bread with Stilton.

We went out on the street at 4 a.m. It was cold and drizzling. Bonnie wore a red coat with fluffy white fur round the collar. I practised, 'Maybe we could meet again,' while she stood with Kate under the porch and Dave and I stopped a taxi.

'Maybe we could meet again.'

She smiled, tilting her head, 'That would be nice,' tore some paper, wrote and handed it to me. 'Ring in the evening.'

'I will.'

'Yes?'

'Yes.'

18

Dreaming in the Afternoon

THE AUSTRALIAN EDITOR rang. He was friendly and wanted to meet me and gave me an address, 'Clarendon Road near Notting Hill Gate'. It sounded familiar, but I couldn't think why; I had certainly never been there.

It was a street of old flat-fronted houses running north from Holland Park Avenue; some of the houses were posh and newly painted, others were grimy and peeling, with dark grey net curtains. As I got nearer, I thought how my knowledge of London would be useful to someone like this editor on his first trip to Europe. I imagined myself showing him – and the miniskirted secretary – the King's Road, Portobello Road, Soho, perhaps even Buckingham Palace and the Houses of Parliament. I was searching for something that I could offer this man who sounded so dynamic and self-confident, because I had little idea of what journalism really involved – Robbie Robertson hadn't helped at all with that.

The house was one of the smarter ones, there was a vase of yellow tulips in the window and I could see the gilded frame of a large dark painting. I walked past and back again, rehearsing what I would say when the editor opened the door. I rang twice, leaving a long interval so as not to seem rude or aggressive. No one came. I lifted the knocker and let it drop with a thud.

The door opened almost immediately. It was the secretary; she was wearing jeans and a loose sweater and had bare feet. She nodded when I said who I was, and led me into the living-room where Richard, the editor, was talking loudly on the telephone in Australian, and the Kinks were coming at low volume from two speakers. The furnishings were unexpectedly plush, thick carpet and antique chairs, and there was a smart-looking kitchen area at the further end of the room.

The secretary looked beautiful but tired. She told me to sit on a sofa and asked if I would like some lunch. She was going to cook some spaghetti; it would be no problem to do a little extra. It was 4 o'clock, an hour later than I had ever had lunch – even at Christmas. Her accent was softer than Richard's. I accepted enthusiastically; I wanted her to know that I was the kind of person who could eat lunch at any time.

Richard went on talking, smiling at me occasionally and mouthing 'sorry', and Ray Davies kept on repeating 'all day and all of the night'. A few feet away the secretary boiled water and chopped something up. I stared around, and picked up a copy of the *New Statesman*.

Richard put the phone down, leaped across the room and knelt on the floor in front of me. 'David Reynolds.' He said it very loudly, leant back on his hands and stared at me with a huge, teasing grin. 'Tell me about *David Reynolds*. Tell me *everything*.' He waved his arms in the air and laughed. 'I really want to know.' The photograph in the *Evening Standard* hadn't revealed the large mouth and the thick lower lip which formed a deep crescent when he smiled. He was wearing a thick cream-coloured woollen polo-neck, on to which his hair flopped enviably.

'Well . . . erm . . . I worked on my school magazine. I'm learning shorthand—'

'Yeah. You went to a public school.' He shook his head and smiled. 'We have those in Australia. You just left. I remember.' The secretary brought two mugs of black coffee. 'Thanks, Louise.' He took her hand and she leant her knees against his shoulder. 'So you like this idea of mine?'

'Yes. It sounds—'

'It's all happening, David. It's all happening already. Colin MacInnes is doing a piece about Malcolm X. Alex Cockburn's interviewing Paul Johnson. David Widgery, Peter Porter, Martin Seymour-Smith, er . . . Stan Gebler Davies. All over the UK, people are writing for us.'

'And Germaine.' Louise spoke softly.

'Yes, Germaine.' He hugged her knees and grinned as he drew out the second syllable.

I hadn't heard of any of these people and wondered whether Germaine had a surname. 'That sounds great.'

'Printers are falling over themselves to print it . . . So what could you do?' Louise wandered back to the kitchen.

'Er . . . well I could do lay-out, proofread . . . maybe—'

'Anything you want to write about?'

'Well . . . I do want to write about a man I know who was a rear gunner in bombers during the war.'

He grinned broadly and briefly and looked doubtful. A cloud of steam came from the kitchen. 'As long as it's relevant, David . . . Relevant to now . . . You know what I mean?'

I didn't. 'Yes. I think so.'

'And you could do proofreading, a bit of editing, all that stuff?'

'Yes. I've done that.'

'And there's no money . . . for now, anyway. Can you survive without money, David?'

'Well. I've got a job. Part-time. Clerking stuff at—'

'So you've got some spare time?'

'Yeah, except I'm learning shorthand typing in the mornings.'

'Shorthand typing!' He laughed. 'That's serious . . . Don't look so worried! Let's eat.' He touched me on the knee and stood up.

Richard ate with his head low over the plate and his hair brushing the table. I kept glancing at Louise. She hardly spoke and rarely smiled; she was slim and graceful, a deep-thinking Jean Shrimpton. I had never had food like it – spaghetti with tinned tomatoes, cheese, chunks of garlic, green peppers and cooked salami.

As we ate Richard passed me copies of American magazines I hadn't seen before – *The Village Voice*, *The East Village Other*, *The Berkeley Barb* – and asked me what I thought. They looked a bit like our unofficial school magazine, except for some thick wavy lettering that was hard to read.

'That's beaut.' Louise pointed to a group of pink letters shaped like a teardrop.

'Yeah.' I stared at the page as I twisted spaghetti round my fork. It seemed to be advertising a record by a group called the Grateful Dead.

A tall man came in and shuffled up to the table, smiling tightly as if he had a headache. He had long uncombed hair, a moustache like Marlon Brando's in *Viva Zapata*, small circular dark glasses and a shaggy white sheepskin waistcoat which he seemed to be wearing inside out. Apparently, he had been asleep upstairs. He looked at Louise. 'Any food?' He sat down, put his arms on the table and squinted around.

Richard smiled, showing lots of teeth. 'No. David ate yours. Martin, this is David.' Martin smiled – creases spread outwards from the corners of his eyes – and shook my hand. 'He's going to help us, aren't you, David . . . in your spare evenings and weekends?' He laughed. Martin started to roll a cigarette. 'I think we'll call you our trainee sub-editor. How's that sound?'

'Great. OK.' I smiled at the three of them, but somehow didn't want to show quite how thrilled I was. 'Thanks.' Martin put his cigarette in his mouth and shook my hand again. And Louise smiled for the first time.

'There'll be a probationary period, of course.' Richard laughed, and I must have looked worried; he leaned across the table and gently slapped my cheek. 'No, nothing too formal. We'll see how it goes.' He said that he'd phone me when I was needed, and that it would be soon.

~

Months earlier, a girl in Carnaby Street had handed me a printed card: 'Eat Delicious Food and Dance till 3 a.m. at Fanny's Bistro, London's First Bistrotheque'. There was a drawing of a man and woman dancing with their knees bent and their arms in the air. In smaller lettering it said that any customer presenting the card would get a free bottle of wine. I had kept it and had the impression that the trendiest places to eat were called bistros. I showed it to Dave and Pat and they agreed that Fanny's Bistro would be a good place to take Bonnie.

She sounded surprised when I said my name on the telephone, but her voice softened when I reminded her that we had met at the party in Westbourne Terrace. She wanted to have lunch rather than dinner, so I kept quiet about Fanny's Bistro and suggested an Italian restaurant in Notting Hill Gate. She didn't know it, but said she could get there in her lunch break from Rediffusion. I didn't know it, either – I had only mentioned it because I had passed it on my way to see Richard and could remember its name.

It was a stupid place to meet. She had to leave after half an hour to take the Central Line back to Holborn. We talked and ate fast – and, as I paid the bill and she waved perfunctorily through the plate glass, I wasn't sure that I still had her approval.

~

The next Saturday I was with my father. After lunch he fell asleep in his well-padded armchair, as he always did, with a book on his lap. Joey sat on his shoulder for a while, then on the back of my chair.

My father snored loudly with his mouth open and there was the usual clicking sound from his dry mouth as he woke up. I looked up from my book. He hadn't moved, but his eyes were open; he was staring at me and smiling. The shoulders of his jacket were up by his ears. He licked around the inside of his mouth, swallowed and pulled himself up in the chair. 'Dreamed about my father.' He yawned lengthily. 'We were on top of a bus in the Strand, but I was older than him – about the age I am now. I had my arm round him. I liked him.'

He yawned elaborately and looked towards the mantelpiece, at a black-and-white photograph of me, squinting into the sun with my hair hanging lankly over one eye. It was curling and brown with nicotine; he had taken it on the day we had climbed a hill and sat looking over the Bristol Channel.

He went off and came back after a few minutes with a pot of tea. As he rolled a cigarette, I went to my room and came back with my packet of Nelson. I waved it at him. 'Do you mind?'

'Of course not.' He clicked his Ronson and leaned forward to give me a light. 'You know, Uncle George wanted *me* to go to Swan River in Manitoba. He never gave any good reason why, and I am pretty sure nothing much happened there. But . . . I think he thought it would make me feel better . . . to see the place, to pay some kind of homage to where my father lived . . .' He sipped tea and stared at the unlit fire. 'I never much liked the idea. Cold and remote. We ought to light the fire. Are you cold?'

'No.' I was wearing two sweaters and two pairs of socks, as I normally did at my father's in winter. '*I'm* going to go . . . to Swan River.'

He looked at me and smiled. 'Maybe we should go together?'

'Maybe.' I smiled back, but I thought how travelling that

far with him – and his stiff limbs and his deafness – would make something that already, in my imaginings, seemed difficult almost impossibly arduous. But the negative thought passed quickly. It began to seem like an exciting idea. I could see us in a big American car with a bench seat in front, driving over compacted snow on a never-ending road.

I strolled around the room, smoking my cigarette and thinking about Swan River. I imagined it to be a cold, dark, spartan place, a valley in some wooded hills, hundreds of miles from anywhere. The nearest place on a map – Dauphin, to the south, in the direction of Winnipeg – was more than an inch away on an atlas page showing the whole of Canada. To make such a trip with my father seemed crazy – what if he became ill, or lost his temper with a mounted policeman or with a man in a bar with a gun? – but it was also appealing. We would be close and we always had good times in cars.

I pulled a book off a high shelf. My father had shown it to me once or twice, years before. It was small and very old and he called it 'the family Bible'. Inside the front cover was a line of beautiful copperplate writing in black ink: 'Thomas Reynolds, Clarendon Road, Notting Hill, 20th August, 1847'. Underneath was written – in the same writing, but in lighter-coloured ink – 'Married Eliza Phillips, 26th July, 1858, St John's Church, Westminster'. Below that was a list of twelve children, beginning with my grandfather: 'Thomas Clifton Reynolds, born 16th May, 1859'. The deaths of four of the children, who had died in infancy, were recorded, and against the name of another was the word 'stillborn'.

My father had sat down at his roll-top desk in the corner with his back to me; he was typing something. I carried the little Bible over to him. He looked up, took it from me and held it under his angle-poise light. 'Always meant to write in my parents' marriage, me and my sister and my children. I'll do that.'

I pointed to the top line. 'I went to that street, Clarendon

Road, last Monday to see that Australian editor. Nice houses. Quite posh.'

'Don't expect they were that posh then. Or maybe they were.' He pointed to the year 1847. 'This is back in the time of Dickens. The houses there now may not have been there then. My father's father was a portrait painter and engraver, you know.'

I did know. I had read about Tom Reynolds' father in Sis's diaries. 'Have you ever thought that if your mother's mother and your father's father hadn't died in the same year, you and me might not be here?'

He looked puzzled and tapped his fingers on the sides of his typewriter. As I explained – that the close deaths of *their* parents had made a bond between *his* parents – he began to smile. 'I never thought of that.'

I looked at the deep lines on his face in the sharp light of the angle-poise. He was so old. I wanted to do something to make him happy and thought of asking my mother to give him a little more money – so he didn't have to eat fish heads and could buy himself a car with automatic gears. But why should she? She was working and hadn't much herself, and he would just spend it quickly on some spree or other. If I could earn more, I could save up and take him to Swan River.

That night, after we had gone upstairs and said goodnight, I took Sis's diary for 1897 from its shelf in my room. The last entry I had read – almost two years earlier – had been for 13 February, the day my father's sister was born. Sis wrote a lot that year. She adored her new baby, and her new baby smiled a lot. In the middle of April my eyes began to close.

19

Sleepless in Highgate

BONNIE'S VOICE WAS breathy and warm. 'Fanny's Bistro? I've read about it somewhere. Sounds great.'

'It's a bistrotheque. Dancing as well as eating. Is that OK?'

'I *love* dancing . . .' She giggled. '*You* know that.'

When I put down the telephone, I found that my palm was sweating. The last thing she had said was 'Look after yourself', slowly as though she meant it and it mattered. I wiped my hand and the receiver on one of my mother's cushions.

Richard rang. 'David. We're doing a photo shoot. Kind of a story about a dull kind of man, a sort of Norman Normal, you know, who decides to give up his job and become a groover, go off on the hippie trail, get stoned, the whole hippie thing, you know?'

'Yup. Right.' He had used several words that I had not heard before; what was a 'groover' and what did 'hippie' and 'get stoned' mean?

'Anyway. We need someone to hold lights and be an extra and generally help out – this is next Saturday, starting very early, about six o'clock, or whenever it gets light. Should be finished about lunch-time. Can you join us? It'll be fun, I promise.'

'Sure.'

He told me where to go, a photographer's studio near the King's Road, although most of the photography would be out of doors.

I met Pat at the Chelsea Drug Store. The building had been coated in scaffolding and its opening trumpeted for months; the press had told us that it would follow the American tradition of combining a bar with a chemist's shop. But it wasn't like the drug stores in James Stewart movies; it was brass, chrome, mirrors and loud music, with the paracetamol downstairs and the beer upstairs. The drugs were on sale all night, but the drinking had to stop at eleven.

Pat had enrolled at a drama school, and always seemed to wear the same shirt – black with little pink roses. He was the first man I saw wearing anything floral and for a while, with his long hair, I thought it made him look like a girl, but in time I liked it enough to borrow it. With the shirt and his Jackie Kennedy dark glasses, Pat got stared at a lot, especially in the Chelsea Drug Store where everyone seemed to stare anyway. I eclipsed him in only one respect; my sideburns were long and thick while his pale face seemed to grow almost no hair.

He explained some of what Richard had said and, a little patronisingly, told me to read the American magazines that Richard had shown me and to listen to Jimi Hendrix and Jefferson Airplane instead of the Stones and the Animals. But I liked what he said about the hippies; peace and love, especially free love, were obvious ideals that had somehow escaped the politicians, and to campaign for them by growing one's hair, wearing beads and strange clothes and attending rock concerts sounded like a lot more fun than the Labour Party or the Young Humanists.

I wasn't sure that I wanted to get stoned, though Pat had tried it with some of his drama-school friends and was going to do it again. There was nothing to be frightened of, he said; he had felt peaceful and dreamy, although at the same time what he called his 'awareness' had been heightened. He told me about Aldous Huxley's *The Doors of Perception*. I was surprised; if Aldous Huxley, whose books I had had to read at school and whose brother used to be on *The Brains Trust*, got stoned, there must be something worthwhile about it – and maybe whatever that was had caused Dylan to sing 'Everybody must get stoned'.

~

At 6 a.m. on Saturday I walked quickly through empty side streets towards the King's Road. There was frost on the grass in the squares and plants killed by the cold stood out limp and blackened. A damp mist blew around in the trees and the sky was light grey. There was no sign of dawn or of the day warming up.

Richard, Louise, Martin and a man in a short leather jacket were standing in the street outside a tall house drinking coffee. Martin smiled and offered me his coffee mug; he was wearing gloves and clapped his hands together. The coffee steamed; I gulped at it and handed it back.

Louise was visibly shivering inside a long coat; she went into the house as a man wearing dark glasses and a long and very obvious wig came out. He spread his arms wide and said, 'Hey! What do you think?'

'Fantastic.'

'Groovy.' Everyone laughed.

Richard turned to me. 'Now this is Bob.' He pointed to the man in the leather jacket. 'Bob, David. David, Bob's in charge . . . well, except for me, that is.' He tittered softly. 'Do what he asks, hold lights, light-meters, whatever. OK?'

'OK.'

Bob had long hair and waxy skin. He led me into an alleyway beside the house where a mound of empty cans, eggshells, tea leaves, cigarette butts, bottles and old newspapers lay beside some overturned dustbins which seemed to have been attacked by a starving animal in the night; two dish-like lights, set on spindly stands, towered above this detritus. Bob flicked a switch and the drab tableau was suddenly sharp and colourful and filled with shadows. He studied the scene approvingly, with his hand on his chin. 'Been up since four arranging that.'

'Incredible.'

He glanced at me curiously for a second. Then he flicked off the lights, climbed a ladder and showed me how to adjust their direction by swivelling them around. 'There's only one ladder. You'll have to keep coming down, moving it and going up again.' He shrugged apologetically, and shouted to the others. 'If we've got Louise, we're ready.'

The lights came back on. Louise walked in front of them and squinted towards us. 'Now?'

'Yes.' Bob picked up a camera and looked through the viewfinder. 'Just for a minute at first. Lie against that dustbin.'

'Coat off?'

'Please.'

Richard stepped forward to take Louise's coat. Underneath she was naked except for a pair of black knickers. I stared for a second before looking away. When I looked again she was lying among the rubbish with her back against a dustbin, smiling tiredly. 'OK. You don't all have to stare.' Someone laughed. I turned away again. If I didn't count a visit to a strip club with Pete Connolly, this was the first time I had seen a woman nearly naked.

'Right light, David. Move it slightly left.' I started to climb the ladder. 'No, the whole thing. Move the stand.' Martin helped me. 'OK. Up the ladder. Down an inch.'

To keep her warm Louise was covered with her coat while I moved the lights around, but soon she was exposed again and Bob told me to hold a sheet of silvered cardboard low down about three feet from her right side. The light reflected from it and her left side was thrown into shadow. He told me to alter the angle several times, moving the line where light turned to shade across her torso.

With a thick felt-tip, Martin drew a gap-toothed pair of

lips on Louise's stomach and arrows on her breasts pointing to her nipples. The man with the wig, whose name was Chester, lay on his back with his head between her knees pointing a home-movie camera at her over his shoulder.

My arms ached. Bob moved around, crouching, clicking the shutter and changing cameras. No one was paying any attention to me. Almost idly, I studied Louise's breasts. They seemed cold and unthreatening – rounded, practical pouches with nothing frivolous or entertaining about them. I looked at her slender arms, her neck and her torso, and noticed a small roll of flesh above her navel where her body was bent against the dustbin. With her clothes on, she was striking and beautiful. Naked in the cold morning air, artificially lit and surrounded by rubbish and people telling her where to put her limbs, she seemed ordinary – even her solemn, pretty face was unremarkable.

Without Louise – her day's work was over – we moved around London in two cars, setting up and taking other bizarre photographs – outside the pet shop in the King's Road, in the Brompton cemetery, by a traffic island on a dual carriageway in Chiswick.

We went to a bookshop called Indica in Southampton Row; it stocked the American magazines that Richard had shown me and Pat had told me to read, and upstairs were the offices of the new underground newspaper, *International Times*. Richard said it was London's most radical bookshop; I had been passing it every day, unaware, on my way to my shorthand-and-typing classes.

Chester was photographed without his wig, wearing a dark suit, white shirt and plain tie. I saw that the real Chester had short hair and black-rimmed glasses and looked like a conventional office worker – the kind of man whom Richard called Norman Normal – and I discovered, belatedly, that the story we were telling was a satire on the hippie lifestyle, about someone from 'straight society' who got 'turned on' after a chance visit to a radical bookshop. It was the last shot of the day. I had to be an extra and smoke a large roll-up prepared by Martin. Bob told me to point it towards the ceiling, suck hard and inhale very deeply; it was supposed to be a 'joint'.

Afterwards, I travelled home alone on the tube. It was three o'clock and I was tired and hungry. I felt satisfied but unsure of myself – I had played my small part in something new and revolutionary and I seemed to get on with Richard and Martin, but I wondered whether I would ever catch up with them; they were already satirising a lifestyle that I had first heard about – from Pat – the previous evening.

At five to eight I was at Oxford Circus, leaning against the wall watching the crowds coming off the Central Line escalator – mostly hopeful, excited people, on their way to a night out. At eight o'clock Bonnie's head rose above the moving banister; she had a black ribbon in her hair. I glimpsed her knees through the gap in her long coat as she came towards me smiling. She pressed her cheek against mine.

We walked down Regent Street and she took my arm and pointed at things in shop windows. She wore a white fluffy scarf which brushed against my face. We turned into Maddox Street and up the steps to Fanny's Bistro; I had booked a table and had walked past one lunch-time so that I would know where it was.

The walls seemed to be black, the lighting was dim and every table had a small light with a red shade; ours was on the edge of the dance floor. Bonnie gave her coat to a waitress and I saw that she was wearing a loose and very short pink dress; it was shiny with a subtle pattern and the sleeves fell back to her elbows when she rested them on the table.

We ordered wine, and slow music played quietly as we

smoked and talked. She told me about her father. He was quite old – though years younger than mine – and she was an only child; he worried about her and she had had to fight to leave home and live with Kate in London.

'He disapproves of me.' A small wrinkle appeared between her eyebrows. 'He thinks all these terrible things – that I stay up too late, drink too much . . .' – she waved a hand in the air – '. . . smoke too much, go to all-night parties, have thousands of boyfriends.' She lit a cigarette, looked at the floor and shook her head. 'Some of it's true, of course . . .' – she looked up and touched my wrist – '. . . but not the boyfriends.' She put her hand over mine where it lay on the table and looked down at the menu.

I stared at her – examining her face, searching for an expression – and turned my hand over under hers so that I could feel her fingers. The black ribbon was pulling long blonde tresses away from her face to somewhere behind her ears, and hair was falling forward on to her collar bones. She looked up at me blankly – perhaps curiously. I wanted to lean across and kiss her, but instead I picked up a fork, tried to grin casually and looked down. She let go of my hand and half turned in her seat. The ribbon was velvet; its ends were cut at an angle and trailed over the hair that fell down her back.

The place became busier and noisier; every table was occupied and waitresses dressed in black were taking orders. I copied Bonnie and ordered avocado; I had heard of them but I had never seen one. We talked about *Blow Up* and *Doctor Zhivago* and Bonnie said that I must see *Un Homme et Une Femme* because it was 'beautiful and romantic'. She tasted her avocado and said it was perfect; mine tasted like mushy peas mixed with oil and vinegar, but I did what she did and scraped every scrap from the skin.

We danced while we waited for the main course to arrive. The floor was small and there were two or three other couples moving stiffly in an inhibited, early-evening way. The DJ, a man in a Donovan cap under a light at the back of the room, put on 'Good Vibrations'. Bonnie put her mouth to my ear. 'Our song.' She laughed, and jerked and swayed; her tights were transparent and her legs were slim and pale. As we went back to our table, heads and eyes followed her – and one or two men glanced at me.

We finished the wine with the main course, ordered another glass each and danced again. The music grew louder and shafts of coloured light roved the room like wartime searchlights. We danced on and when we weren't dancing we consumed chocolate mousse, more wine, cigarettes, coffee, and Cointreau – something else I had only heard of – and talked excitedly about how to change the world by spreading peace and love, and by working towards an environment where people could find their uninhibited, creative selves. We were interrupted by a woman selling red roses – I bought one for Bonnie – and again by an itinerant photographer whom I paid to take our picture, with artificial grins and hands clasped across the table.

Later, the lights and the music were slower – the Walker Brothers and Dusty Springfield. We drank water with our Cointreau and danced cheek to cheek. I could feel Bonnie's thighs shifting gently against mine; I wondered whether to kiss her, but her head was resting on my shoulder and she seemed dreamy and content.

We left at three o'clock. It was raining and we stood under the awning outside. Bonnie waved at a taxi which didn't stop and I thought hazily about where I could get a night bus back to Chelsea. A taxi pulled over and Bonnie leaned in and spoke to the driver. I badly wanted to kiss her goodbye. She turned with her hand on the door. 'Do you want to come back?' She smiled and climbed in. I followed.

The windows were opaque with condensation. She put her arm through mine and gripped my hand. I sat back, wondering and apprehensive. What was in her mind? She lived in Highgate, a part of London I had never been to and knew nothing about except that it was miles north. She knew I lived in Chelsea. How would I get back from Highgate later? This was our first date, so she couldn't be inviting me to stay; if she was, she must like me and have an idea that it would be fun to have breakfast together and maybe go for a walk in the morning.

I had never been in a taxi with anyone other than my mother and grandmother. As it swung round a corner, Bonnie fell against me and somehow we started kissing. Her tongue was smooth and sugary and the kissing went on and on until eventually I looked up. The taxi was moving fast through traffic lights, windscreen wipers slapping from side to side. I could see the driver's eyes in the mirror and felt embarrassed; what would he think – these people who weren't able to stop kissing each other? I turned back to Bonnie.

Minutes later, she sat up and called directions to the driver. I wiped the window and glimpsed a privet hedge and a red door. The taxi stopped. We were on a hill.

The driver gave me a big smile as he drove off. Bonnie put a finger to her lips, unlocked the red door and led me across a hall. There were rugs and pictures; it seemed like a normal house but she opened another door with a key. She put her finger to her lips again and signalled that I should follow her; we tiptoed across a dark room and through another door; she closed it behind her and clicked the light on. We were in a small kitchen.

'Kate's asleep in there.' She whispered and pointed to the room we had just crossed. 'There's only one room and this, and a loo outside. Kate and I share a bed.' I must have looked startled. She took hold of my chin and shook it. 'We sleep head to toe – I'll make you a bed on the floor. Kate's going out early. Then you can come in with me and get comfortable.' She shook my chin again, but more gently. 'Don't look so worried.'

With my eyes closed, I lay on a thin piece of foam listening to the steady breathing of two women. The floor was hard, and I was cold even though Bonnie had tucked blankets around me and spread an eiderdown over them. I had been awake for twenty-four hours but couldn't sleep. My brain shifted randomly, out of my control, from memory to memory, image to image: Bonnie's beautiful hair, the Indica bookshop, Louise's hand on an eggshell, Bonnie's serious face as she talked about her father, Bonnie smiling as she danced. I opened my eyes and, in time, found I could see the dim shapes of a table, an armchair and, on the other side of the room, a bed; it was large with the long side against the wall.

I was wearing my shirt and pants. My other clothes were on the armchair. I got up quietly, put my socks back on and spread my donkey jacket over the eiderdown. I lay down and still felt cold. I wondered how long it would be before Kate went out. I could get warm then and sleep for a bit, perhaps cuddled up to Bonnie, before we got up and had breakfast – or lunch, depending what time it was.

I was lying on my side facing the wall; someone was moving about. I opened my eyes; I must have been asleep. It would be Kate. I shut my eyes again to avoid the embarrassment of having to say hello to her. She went into the kitchen and I could hear her washing and brushing her teeth, a kettle boiling and a door opening and closing. She came quietly in and out of the room two or three times, dressing and drinking coffee. There was a long silence when I thought perhaps she had gone without my hearing the door, but there were more sounds – a zip and hair being brushed very thoroughly. Finally, the door to the hall opened and closed.

I waited a minute or two before opening my eyes and turning over. I heard Bonnie moving. 'Come in and get warm . . . Get Kate's pillow . . . and tuck in the blankets.' She sounded sleepy. I took my socks off and walked towards the bed. She was lying on her side looking at me with only her face above the sheets. I thought momentarily about my pants; I still had my y-fronts from school. My shirt was hanging over them, but I wished I had bought some of the striped briefs I had seen in shops in the King's Road. The sheets and pillowcases were sky blue and there was a printed Indian bedspread. I moved the pillow and tucked the blankets firmly in around the corner where Kate had slept. Bonnie pulled back the sheet and I got in.

The bed was warm and she put her arm around me and kissed me. I felt pleasantly overwhelmed as I had in the back of the taxi, but now there was heat and sleepiness, and I could feel the smoothness of her back and that all she was wearing was a T-shirt. She stroked me lazily, and we dozed in each other's arms.

Still lazily, she undid the few buttons on my shirt and suggested I take it off; I'd be more comfortable. I dropped it on the floor. We stroked and felt most of each other's bodies, until, lifting up my head, I saw my watch on my wrist beside her hair on the pillow.

It was a quarter to eleven and I remembered my mother. I hadn't told her I would be out all night. She would be worried, panicking and would have rung the police. I kissed Bonnie quickly and sat up. 'I ought to phone my mother.'

She brushed her hair aside and gazed at me curiously. 'Your mother?'

'Yes. It's just that I didn't tell—'

'All right.'

I got out of bed, suddenly feeling foolish, and walked towards the telephone. 'I'm sorry.'

'You have to go across the road to the phone box.' She

was sitting up, staring at me and frowning. 'That phone only takes incoming calls.' She lay down again and said tiredly, perhaps irritably, 'And you'll need a sixpence . . . There are some on the kitchen table.' I quickly pulled on trousers, shirt, shoes and donkey jacket and picked up a sixpence. 'I'll have to let you in. Ring the top bell.'

'I could take the key.'

'No.' She sighed. 'You might meet the old bag.' She turned her back to me.

A cold wind blew through the broken panes of the telephone box and the phone itself took the warmth from my hand. It rang for a long time before my mother picked it up.

'Hi, Mum. Just ringing to say that I stayed at a friend's—'

'I thought you must have, dear. How nice of you to call. Are you having a good time?'

'Yes. Thanks. I'll see you later.'

'All right, dear. Bye now.'

I put the phone down and stamped my feet, stalling my longing to rush down the hill, get back into bed and get warm. I thought about what had just been happening and about Bonnie. She was two years older than me. I stopped stamping, and stared at the glass without focusing. My ideas about first dates might be wrong; and my impression that women never made the first move – the first move with any serious implications anyway.

I pulled my jacket around me, ran down the road and rang the bell. Bonnie opened the door and sprinted back across the hall to her flat; her T-shirt just covered her bottom. Another door opened. An old lady was standing inside it, looking at me.

'Who are you?'

Bonnie had disappeared. 'I'm a friend of Bonnie's.'

'Did you stay the night?' She frowned. 'I don't allow that.' She had straggly hair and thick damp lips.

'No. I just arrived.'

There was a pause while she seemed to examine my clothes. 'All right.' She shut the door with an emphatic click.

Bonnie was sitting on the side of the bed giggling.

I shut the door. 'Who's that old woman?'

'Landlady. Bloody old cow.' She giggled more loudly and made a snorting noise. 'Shall we go back to bed?' She smiled.

'Er, sure . . . If that's OK?'

She came towards me and spoke slowly, emphasising each syllable. 'It is O . . . K.' She kissed me and pressed herself against me. Again, she spoke slowly. 'You are *so* stupid.' She stepped backwards, crossed her arms and pulled her T-shirt over her head. She turned away quickly and got into bed. I glimpsed her small breasts and saw that her pubic hair was golden.

~

That evening my mother wrote Christmas cards while I watched *Perry Mason*. She had to finish the cards that night because Christmas was in eight days' time. She had numerous cousins whom I knew vaguely and she kept passing cards to me and asking me to write my name; I complied perfunctorily, thinking that each one would be the last.

Della Street was stalking an ugly man in a pork-pie hat, but I was finding it hard to think about anything but Bonnie. We had parted saying that we would meet again before Christmas and I had said that I would telephone. On the tube back from Highgate I had decided I was in love with her. We now had an important bond between us and I wanted to be with her all the time. Several times that evening I had almost telephoned, but had held back; she would probably think me silly. I was intensely aware now of the age gap between us – though she thought it was only one year, a lie I would have to own up to.

'What would you say if I was to say I wanted to get married?'

My mother stopped writing and looked up at me. Her mouth was a little open, but she looked thoughtful rather than surprised. She looked down at her Christmas card and finished signing it. In one part of my mind I knew it was a daft question, but in another I knew I would never love any woman other than Bonnie; she was perfect.

'I'd say that it might be better to wait a little. You are just eighteen and there—'

'Lots of people get married when they're eighteen . . . or younger.'

'I know, but I think on the whole it's better, if possible, to wait. Marriage ties you to one person . . . for ever . . . for the rest of your life is the—'

'I know that.'

'Well, you asked me what I thought, darling.'

'Sure.'

She started to write another Christmas card. Della Street had been locked in a room with bars across the windows.

'Of course, I'd give you my blessing whatever you—'

'I don't need your blessing. I'm eighteen.'

She went back to her cards. I knew I was being obnoxious, but I didn't know why; somehow, she made me feel irritable. I went to the kitchen to make a cup of coffee and came back and asked her if she wanted one.

'No thanks, dear.' She smiled. She was licking envelopes. It suddenly annoyed me that she called me 'dear' and 'darling'.

I sipped coffee and thought about Bonnie: how beautiful she was; how free; how uninhibited; how willing, it seemed to me, to do anything.

'Did you have anyone in mind? To get married to?'

I didn't answer. She was sitting back in her chair with a pile of envelopes on her lap, licking stamps.

'Well. You don't have to tell me.'

'No, I don't.' I was shocked by the harshness of my voice. I knew she didn't deserve it. I lit a cigarette. I was happier than I had ever been, but I was being rude to my mother, the kindest and most equable person I knew. *Perry Mason* ended and the news came on; Harold Wilson had done something dull and children were being napalmed in Vietnam. 'God! I'd like to make the world a better place.' I stretched, and stubbed my cigarette.

'You can.'

'Yeah?' I shrugged.

'Probably in small ways . . . at first.'

'Yeah, maybe.' I smiled tiredly.

She started to write yet more cards. 'You know, if you got married, you would have a responsibility to your wife and that might prevent you doing other things . . . like travelling or . . . you still might go to university.'

I grunted. I knew she was right.

'Can you sign this? It's to Auntie Evelyn.'

I wrote 'David' in the space after 'Mary and', and imagined piles of cards that said 'Bonnie and'.

20

Half a Turkey

DIANE CAME OVER to my desk. She was grinning and showing her tiny upper teeth, and was shaking her hands down by her sides; she had been applying puce nail varnish. 'So what's she like?'

'Who?'

'Your girlfriend.' She laughed and shook her head as well as her hands. 'It's so obvious.'

'Is it? . . . How come?'

'Everything about you. You keep smiling to yourself. You're walking differently. You keep patting your hair.' She strutted across the room with her chest thrust out, tapping the back of her head. 'Come on! Tell!'

I was amazed that she knew. She said she had just been guessing, but she had been working in offices for a few years and always watched the other people, wondering whether they were happy or not. I told her about Bonnie and laughingly confessed that I was in love.

She sat down on the corner of my desk and looked serious. 'Have you told her you love her?'

I shook my head. 'No.'

'Well, don't . . . yet. Honestly, it's not a good idea. Even if she thinks she loves you, she'll be put off by you talking about love. It puts pressure on her, makes the whole thing kind of heavy. She probably just likes you, you know? And wants to have fun.' She looked very concerned and I felt grateful. 'Don't say you love her for at least three months.' She leaned forward and stared into my face. 'I'm so happy for you . . . but I'm right, honest. Forget about being in love – for now anyway, and enjoy yourself.'

I thought about this as I walked down to Finch's to meet Pat and Dave. It was hard. Bonnie mattered more than anything. That had to be what people meant by love, people like Shelley and Keats and Graham Greene, and John Lennon and Paul McCartney.

Pat was dismissive of the whole idea and told me not to be silly and romantic. Dave was more interested and sympathetic, and I was pleased when Pat left the pub early after fixing an evening when we would go to *Un Homme et Une Femme*.

Dave hadn't felt like I felt, but he said he could imagine it. We crossed the road to the Goat in Boots where we had a few friends, principally Peter the Pianist and Peter the Painter. Peter the Pianist was plinking the piano; he looked up and waved. Peter the Painter was a graduate art student who funded himself by selling meticulous paintings of pretty landscapes on the railings at Green Park. He had a big nose and long wavy hair and looked like Charles I. He joined us at a small circular table and Dave told him that I was in love.

'Oh, no. Stop it.' He smacked my hand. 'It's just misery, mate, I promise you. How long's this been going on?'

'Since Saturday.'

He laughed affectedly and looked at me with a sagging grin, as though I was something amusing but slightly offensive. 'I suppose you can't think about anything else, and you don't know what to do next.' He slapped my thigh. 'I know. I know, Dave. It's happened to me.' He took several gulps from his pint. 'More than once.' He started to shake his head. 'Calm down. Treat her like a friend . . . well . . . bit more than a friend . . . *if you can*.' He chuckled. 'Honestly mate, I feel for you. Fucking agony.' He put his hands on his hips, sat up straight and stared around the pub, as if that was all he had to say.

It was, for the moment, and he soon went to talk to

someone else. Dave fetched fresh pints and we drank in silence for a while before the routine began.

'Dave?'

'Yes Dave.'

'I was thinking, Dave.'

'What Dave?'

'I was thinking, Dave, that I'm fed up with living in that dark little bed-sit, and that I should look for a flat, Dave. What do you think, Dave?'

'Sounds good, Dave.'

'Would you be interested in sharing, Dave?' The routine had begun at school – probably because we were both amused by our friends calling us Dave – and had become a habit; it was supposed to be mildly satirical, but now he was frowning at me and stroking his chin.

I had liked Dave since my first day at school when he had shown me where to go and had cycled to the river and back with me – and I liked him even more now; he was a romantic without being a drip. I quickly got excited about the idea of a flat; I had been worrying about having no room of my own where Bonnie and I could be together, and I would soon finish the shorthand-and-typing course and would be able to work full-time, so I thought I would be able to afford it. As Dave and I discussed the merits of different parts of London, I wondered how my mother would feel. We agreed on the edge of Chelsea where it merged into the World's End and Fulham, an area with the Goat in Boots, Finch's and the Fulham Forum cinema at its centre – and my mother's flat not too distant.

Two nights later Dave, Bonnie and I went to the Architectural Association's Christmas Ball in their building in Bedford Square – Dave's brother Martin had given us tickets. The attraction was a group called the Pink Floyd whom Pat and I had seen a few weeks earlier at a strange all-night event at the Chalk Farm Round House; they had made no records, but Bonnie knew who they were and wanted to see them. She was wearing blue jeans and a check shirt, and no ribbon – her hair fell freely around her face.

Dave left us and we strolled around the elegant old building arm in arm for hours waiting for the Pink Floyd to appear in the open space in the basement. We ate, drank, chatted to people we didn't know and spent time kissing at the bottom of a flight of stairs.

Very late, with about fifty others, we stood watching shapes and colours moving and merging on the walls, and a frenetic, wiry man with a guitar making strange noises that echoed for long seconds – while the rest of the group played as if they were the Animals or Manfred Mann. I looked at Bonnie and wanted to tell her she was perfect, but I had thought about what Diane had said – that I mustn't be 'heavy'; I would tell her that I loved her on 18 March, three months from last Sunday.

~

On Friday evening, the day before Christmas Eve, I went to her flat carrying a bottle of Nuits-Saint-Georges, a wine that my mother had told me was always good, and a pair of silver earrings in a box wrapped in red paper. I had thought of buying a ring of some kind but Diane had advised earrings – a ring was too 'heavy' – and had suggested Kensington Market as a good place to get them.

I arrived at eight, as Bonnie had asked; the food was almost ready to serve and Kate would be out until late. The room was lit by two candles – one on the table where we ate and one on a shelf above the bed. Dave Brubeck's 'Take Five' was playing. She had cooked fish pie and bought cheesecake from somewhere in Soho.

After supper we opened our presents. She liked the

earrings and put them on. She had bought me a Penguin paperback of *Tender Is the Night* by F. Scott Fitzgerald.

We were lying on the bed listening to a slow, breathy saxophone – a sensuous, thought-stopping sound, unlike anything I had heard before – when the phone rang. The candles had burned down and there was a whiff of burning wax; Bonnie was resting her head on my chest and pulling gently at the hairs behind my ear. She raised her head and listened; the phone went silent after the third pair of rings. She smiled and looked down at me, pushing my hair back from my forehead. 'Kate'll be here in fifteen minutes . . . Have to get up . . . soon.'

We drank coffee with Kate, who came in cold, red-faced and chattering. Before I left I looked at the LP cover – *West Coast Jazz with Stan Getz*.

The humanists were shutting their office until the new year; Bonnie and my other friends were spending time with their families. I decided to go to my father's after Christmas and stay there until I had to go back to work. Rather than shout on the telephone, I had written to him telling him my plans and he had replied on a postcard: 'Delighted. Come for ever, if you want.' I looked forward to spending time with him – and perhaps some time alone, walking, or sitting in a pub.

I wasn't expecting him to do anything special, but there was a Christmas tree with a gold star at the top and some red baubles hanging off it. It was on the table next to the television where Joey's cage usually was – Joey was on the floor – and there were presents in Christmas paper underneath. With a lot of grunting, my father bent down behind the television and found a switch. Coloured lights flashed all over the tree – some of them carefully buried among the needles. He put his hand on my shoulder. 'Nice, don't you think? Got it cheap on Christmas Eve. Lights came from Woolworth's, three and six . . . They don't have to flash though.' He unscrewed one of the bulbs and the lights went out while he put in another one that made them shine without flashing.

He held up the bulb he had removed. 'There's a resistor in there. Metal strips expand and contract – very clever . . . Now, I've bought half a turkey, and we're going to have a party on New Year's Eve.'

'*Half* a turkey?'

'We can't eat a whole turkey, just you and me.' He pointed over his shoulder with his thumb. 'I got it from the pub. They've got thousands there. I stood the chap a lager and he split it down the middle with an axe. Paid him eight shillings. He said not to tell anyone or everyone would want half a turkey.' He grinned and led me into the kitchen. The half-turkey was in the fridge – lying on its flat side in a rectangular metal tray. It looked plump and fresh and a little purple. 'I'm not sure whether to roast it like that, or somehow prop it the right way up. I've got stuffing and sausage meat.'

'How're you going to stuff it?'

He raised his arms in the air and made a kissing noise with his lips. 'There'll be a way.'

'Is this for the party?'

'No. This is just for you and me. I thought we'd have Christmas lunch tomorrow . . . Then we can eat it cold for the rest of the week. And I can casserole the leftovers, make soup from the bones – all that, like your mother used to do. I've got potatoes and parsnips – for roasting – and peas and carrots. But no sprouts. I hate sprouts.'

'No. I don't like them either.'

'Horrible – taste like farts.' He grinned and looked away.

'Right.' I tried not to laugh but, for no good reason, our giggles soon reached the soundless level where neither of us could speak. I went into the living-room and held on to the back of a chair. It took me a minute or two to recover.

Back in the kitchen, he was smiling at the glass in the back door. He turned. 'You mustn't make me laugh like that.'

'You started it.' There was a box on the floor with some bottles in it. I peered in. 'Is this for the party?'

'That's the drink for it . . . except this.' He pulled out a bottle of cherry brandy. 'This *isn't* for the party. It's for us. I've got an Arctic Roll.' He grinned and put his hand on my shoulder.

'Great!' We hadn't had Arctic Roll for two years.

I examined the contents of the box; there were three bottles of sherry, four half-pint bottles of Carlsberg and a bottle of Quosh. 'Who's coming then?'

He told me while he put the kettle on and warmed the teapot. The chemist and the newsagent were both coming with their wives, and Wing Commander Hayes would be driving over from Marlow. He had invited Old Bowen, but Mrs Bowen had said it would be too much for him; however, she might come herself if the old man was in the mood to be left on his own.

'And Mrs Harris.' He smiled, as if there were something naughty about Mrs Harris.

'Who's she?'

'Runs the florist down the road.' He waved his hand vaguely towards the east. 'Edwina, to me. Very nice—'

'I didn't know you knew her.'

He was still smiling cheekily. 'Oh, I've got lots of friends.'

'Ooh. You and Edwina, eh?' I nudged him.

'She's got a daughter actually – Arabella – very pretty. She's coming too. Almost exactly your age.'

'Oh God! Da-ad!'

'She's a peach – an absolute peach. You'll like her.'

'Dad! It'll be incredibly embarrassing.'

'No, it won't. She's a nice girl. Intelligent, makes jokes . . . Just left convent school, Our Lady of . . . Misery and

Dolours . . . or whatever it's called . . . You know? Up towards Amersham.' He looked as if he might giggle again; we both knew that it was called Our Lady of the Assumption.

'Dolours . . .? What are they?'

'Sorrow . . . lamentation, tears . . . suffering, privation, pain, agony and absolute bloody misery . . . all that sort of—' He was silent for a moment, then made a spluttering noise, followed by a series of full-throated guffaws, during which he held on to the kitchen cabinet and bobbed his head up and down.

I was catching his hysteria again, but managed to say, 'So you thought coming to our party might cheer her up?'

'She doesn't—' His laugh became a cough. He gulped and the coughing got worse, deep and bronchial. His face turned red and he hurried to the lavatory, hoicked and spat, and came back wiping his mouth with his handkerchief. 'Oh dear. That's terrible. Mustn't laugh so much . . . I was going to say that Arabella is very cheerful. Takes the Pope with a pinch of salt. I asked her.'

I could imagine her; I knew the kind of girl he liked – she was not far from the kind of girl I liked. Despite his coughing fit, I wanted him to laugh again. I looked at him with raised eyebrows.

He was smiling and shaking his head and filling a glass from the tap. He drank it quickly. 'Don't get me going again, Sunny Jim.'

He filled another glass with water and I gave up trying to be funny. 'So we have to stay up most of the night with these people?'

'No. No. They're coming at six. Otherwise we'd have to do proper food. They'll go at about eight . . . I hope.' He'd bought some crisps and planned to spread Gentleman's Relish on triangular pieces of toast – Old Bowen had given him a large jar of it for Christmas.

We drank tea and opened presents, and he seemed very

lively and energetic. I had bought him a scarf and a paperback by Bertrand Russell called *Roads to Freedom* – about anarchism, syndicalism and socialism – which I was keen to read myself. He had got me a *Concise Oxford Dictionary*, some socks from Woolworth's, a record token, and a book called *Purity and Danger* by someone called Mary Douglas. It was a hardback, recently published, which he had bought because he had read about it in *New Society*. He took it back from me and told me in detail what it was about, thumbing through it and reading bits out; it was obvious that he had read it before wrapping it for me.

It seemed to be a study of social groupings and of how taboos and rituals reflect power structures. My father kept talking about people who lived in the margins – sometimes he used the word interstices – of formally ordered groups and who through no fault of their own were blamed for things that went wrong. Apparently Mary Douglas mentioned Joan of Arc and the Jews, but also the fathers of families in the Trobriand Islands, where inheritance passed through women; she called these people outcasts and likened them to beetles and spiders living innocently in the cracks of walls. Primitive – and some supposedly civilised – groups cast such people as witches and oppressed them unfairly.

He talked about this for almost an hour before handing me the book back and telling me I *must* read it, and, if I couldn't read it all right away, I must read chapter six, at least. I wanted to read it, but I had another book to read first, *Tender Is the Night*, and I had thought that I might get round to the rest of my grandmother's diaries.

There were five quiet days before New Year's Eve and his party. On one of them the morning was bright and clear; we drove across the Thames at Cookham and on to Winter Hill, where there was a view back across the river to the Chilterns. As I knew he would, he pointed to a patch of terracotta, buried in trees, on a hill five miles away – the farm where he had lived with my mother during the war and about which he had written the books that had earned him his Rolls-Royce and his yacht. We walked a hundred yards or so along the ridge and went back to the car; he had decided that he didn't want to climb hills any more – he *could* climb them, but he didn't want to.

On the other days we stayed at home, throwing logs on the fire, watching television, playing cards and chess, reading and eating turkey. During his afternoon naps I sat across from him, deep in *Tender Is the Night*. He snored with his mouth open and a book or a journal on his lap; I looked at him from time to time, pondering his age, the achievements – and the follies and the petty cruelties.

Some nights I sat up late reading Sis's diaries, and opened the green folder to leaf through the hundred or so pages of my father's recollections to find his accounts of the same events. I began where I had left off, soon after Gladys's birth in 1897.

The new baby was loved by all the inhabitants of 59 Norfolk Road, and their affection for her grew as she did. At first her presence had small, practical repercussions. Cliffie's narrow bed was moved from its place beside his mother and put under the window, and Gladys slept next to Sis in Cliffie's old cot. Cliffie didn't mind about this – he was five years old and liked to kneel on his bed and stare down at the people and the horses in the street – and he soon became attached to his little sister: he was not so much older than her as to make him indifferent or disdainful, but he was old enough to feel responsible and loving.

The room that for so long had been Sis's own was now shared by four people. Sis, who had often said that there was plenty of space in the house, found it cramped, but she didn't think of moving elsewhere: she was as devoted to her father as ever and the memory of Tom's drunken behaviour was very recent; she wanted her father's and brothers' protection.

And, anyway, soon after Gladys's birth Tom told her how happy he was, with their situation as well as their children. While Gladys was a small baby, he kept up the habit he had resumed while Sis was pregnant of buying flowers in the evenings as he passed through Liverpool Street Station – and he got out his camera again and took photographs of his newly expanded family. For several months his drinking seemed to be controlled, and the number of whiskies tossed down on his Sunday morning walks with Cliffie stayed at the two that he had set himself before Gladys was born.

Sometimes he took Cliffie on longer outings, while Sis stayed at home with the baby. In April they went on the top of an open horse-drawn bus from Liverpool Street to Charing Cross to see the decorations for Queen Victoria's diamond jubilee. It was the first time Cliffie had seen the grander and busier parts of London. There were horses everywhere and the air was filled with their smell; he was intrigued by the small boys with dustpans and brushes who ran about in the street collecting dung and flinging it into iron bins on the kerb. He asked his father if they ever got run over and couldn't wait to tell Toppy about them. St Paul's Cathedral overwhelmed him and he nearly cried when Tom asked him what he thought of it, and his amazement grew as they walked around Trafalgar Square and down Whitehall to the Houses of Parliament and Westminster Abbey.

Everywhere Cliffie saw flags and coloured glass globes, lit with nightlights and etched with the legend 'V Crown R', but the decoration that caused him to point with wonder was a sequence of letters which lit up one at a time before revealing the whole word, after which the sequence was repeated in a different colour. It was opposite Broad Street Station and the word was 'Bovril'. He asked his father if this was part of the jubilee decorations and was disappointed to hear about beef-tea, the marvels of electricity and the resistors that made the lights flash. The Queen's glass globes seemed dreary by comparison. In the late afternoon they went to Hyde Park and saw the Queen herself being driven in a carriage. Again Cliffie was disappointed. The famous and important Queen Victoria had no crown; she looked like Aunt Suey, just a little old lady in black wearing a bonnet.

Later in the year Tom took him to see his office. Cliffie was fascinated, both by the grandeur of the district – the Welsbach Incandescent Gas Light Company had offices off Victoria Street near St James's Park underground station – and by the gadgets that his father used. Cliffie saw a telephone and a typewriter for the first time, and was allowed to listen to someone's voice coming from miles away and to take away a piece of paper on which he had typed his name.

Tom introduced him to a dignified man with white hair and gold-rimmed spectacles, and the man felt in his pocket and handed him a shilling. Cliffie was awestruck; he wasn't sure what it was for and whispered was it for him to spend? The man smiled and said, 'Yes, but don't get tight on it.' Cliffie asked what 'tight' was. The man went on smiling and said, 'Ask your father. He should know.'

The next year, at the beginning of May, Cliffie became a pupil at the Birkbeck School. It was a short walk from Norfolk Road and Tom went with him on the first morning. Cliffie was six and a little anxious because the Birkbeck, a vast red-brick building with several playgrounds, was very different from the dame's schools he had been to; it had five hundred pupils, half of whom were girls. His father kept squeezing his hand and saying, 'Don't you worry, old chap.' And he reminded him that his uncles, George and Ernest, had gone to the school when they were six and stayed until they were fifteen; they had both liked it and had told Cliffie that he would be all right. For the first two terms he was able to go home for lunch. Little Alice collected him and, on that first day, unexpectedly and to Cliffie's delight, Toppy, who had not yet been to any school, came with her.

In the summer of that year, 1898, Gladys outgrew the cot and Young George gave up his room across the landing from Sis's so that it could be shared by the children; until his wedding to Marie Potts in 1900 – they had become engaged in 1894 – he slept on a narrow bed in a corner of the living-room.

From then on Cliffie and Gladys, like many siblings, shared a bed – and Gladys would only sleep wrapped in her brother's arms. She called Cliffie 'Boy', and they played together on the stairs and landings and on the large, rectangular lid of the WC which served them as a table. There Cliffie taught her to play chess, and by the time she was three – and he was eight – she could beat him, sometimes. If someone wanted to use the WC, they would move the chessboard and play on the floor in the hall outside.

Looking back, Cliffie saw that he had lived for five years as an only child among many grown-ups; Gladys was both a welcome companion, who adored and looked up to him, and a source of some freedom because she drew the attention of the adults. The house continued to be a focus for Old George's many brothers, sisters and sisters-in-law, and also for two of Tom's brothers – Bill, who had been at the dinner where Tom and Sis first met, and Bertie, who came to play chess. All of these visitors – even the most dour, the deaf retired policeman, Uncle Johnson – were charmed by Gladys. They would sit her on their knees, cuddle her, play with her and bring her presents. And she always responded sweetly and politely.

Drunken Aunt Suey called every Saturday – to receive five shillings, a weekly contribution to her maintenance from Old George – and made a point of seeking out Cliffie and Gladys. She would fumble in her voluminous, dingy skirt and present each of them with a paper bag full of bull's-eyes; they were then required to kiss her. Cliffie could manage this only by holding his breath – Aunt Suey gave off a sickly stench that Sis said was caused by gin – but Gladys happily complied and sometimes even hugged the smelly woman.

Apart from her parents, Gladys's favourite adult was Rose; unlike Cliffie, she seemed to realise when she was a small baby that there was something unusual about a woman who walked about on her hands and somersaulted backwards through doorways, and she soon tried to imitate her – something Cliffie had never done. Rose taught her to dance and cartwheel and do headstands and handstands, but it was a private matter; Gladys didn't like to have an audience. She danced with Rose in the drawing-room with the door shut, to tunes produced by a device like a musical box, and, though Sis was admitted to play Gladys's favourite tune, 'Daisy', on the piano, no one else could join in or watch. She would turn cartwheels for her own pleasure in the garden, and sometimes Cliffie found her standing on her head beside their bed – and then she would say, 'You do it, Boy,' but, though he would do most things she asked, he wouldn't, because he didn't like being upside down.

On Mondays Cliffie and Gladys would stand at the breakfast-room window waiting for bubbles to rise from the drain in the corner of the basement area at the front of the house; bubbles appeared on Mondays because it was washing day and the drain was clogged with leaves. While the Alices boiled water in the copper in the scullery, and washed and rinsed clothes and linen in galvanised baths with scrubbing boards and Rickett's Blue, Gladys and Cliffie watched and waited, without telling anyone, as the bubbles came, closely followed by soapy water which slowly flooded the basement area and slithered towards the door. Only when it came under the door and crept along the passage would they sound the alarm – and watch with delight as one of the Alices waded across the area and unblocked the drain with a stick.

When Old George was away, he would send his washing home in a parcel and always put in small presents for Cliffie and Gladys. The postman always knocked twice when he had a parcel to deliver and the children would rush to the door yelling, 'The dirty!' Cliffie would get there first and begin tearing off the paper and string on the breakfast-room floor while Gladys danced around, excited and trying to help. On one occasion Sis appeared and told Cliffie that they must take turns and that Gladys should be allowed to open this one.

Sixty years later, Cliffie remembered what Gladys said then, and gave it as an example of his sister's sweet and gentle nature: 'No. Let Boy open it. He likes doing it, don't you, Boy?'

Cliffie recalled that his attachment to Gladys persisted and grew stronger. Writing in 1960 – with the benefit, of course, of sixty years in which to coalesce his memories – he described their young life together as an idyll in which 'she loved me as I loved her'. She was 'adorable, pretty and somehow possessed an unearthly quality of grace'.

21
Gladys

THE SUMMER OF 1898 should have been a good time for Tom. The Welsbach company promoted him to the prestigious and highly paid position of Chief Accountant and, for the first time for six years, he and his wife were able to sleep in a bedroom free of children. However, the new job brought new time-consuming pressures, and Sis seemed to find being alone with him at night more of a nuisance than a blessing.

Old George told Sis of a conversation he had with Tom, in which Tom said repeatedly that he was 'exasperated' by Sis's attitude towards him. Old George had been unsure of what he meant, but told Sis that an exasperated man who drank was a potentially dangerous man. He assumed that, with his yet higher income, Tom was again wanting to find a home; surely Sis *must* now look for one with him. But Sis seized on her father's use of the word 'dangerous'. In her opinion Tom *was* dangerous; did her father know that that summer he had tried to slap her face, raised his fist to her and, more than once, come home with blood on him after brawling who knew where? Her first responsibility was to her children; it would be wrong for her to take them from a home where they were happy, and where there were adults who cared for them, to live alone with her and a drunk.

By the autumn of 1898 Tom was again drinking heavily and regularly.

On 5 November, Cliffie, who would be seven the next month, was very excited; his family always had a party on

Guy Fawkes night, with a large bonfire and a guy. He had bought his own fireworks with pocket money saved over many weeks and had been gloating over them for days; he would be allowed to let them off before the main display provided by the grown-ups. It was a Saturday, and when his father came home from work he helped him make the guy out of old sacks, straw and string; it was a proper one with legs, arms, a body and a head, and he was struck by the care his father took to get the proportions right by adding and taking away handfuls of straw, and by how skilful he was with the string. Cliffie dressed it in an old shirt, jacket, trousers and peaked cap that his father had saved specially.

Later, his father went to the Norfolk Arms and he helped his grandfather and Uncle George build the bonfire while Gladys, who was not yet two, struggled to carry pieces of kindling chopped by Uncle Ernest. That evening would be Gladys's first sight of fireworks – she had been asleep in her cot the previous year – and she was excited but apprehensive; she didn't like loud bangs.

As it grew dark, the garden filled with relations, friends and neighbours. The children from next door hung over the wall, and Toppy lurked in the shadows under the trees at the end.

Gladys watched with Sis from the kitchen window and flinched when Cliffie ran up with a golden rain and waved the sparks at her from beyond the glass, but she was soon laughing and clapping as he set off starlights and Prince of Wales feathers. Afflicted by some demon, Cliffie lit a squib on the kitchen window sill; Gladys pointed with delight at the brief shower of silver sparks but the sudden bang as they went out made her scream and cry and bury her head in Sis's shoulder. Furious, Sis ran out of the house and chased Cliffie up the garden until she was diverted by Ernest tossing a firecracker at her feet.

While Young George minded the bonfire, Tom took

charge of the fireworks and soon began to have a row with the father of the children next door; the man was annoying him by telling his children to watch their eyes whenever Tom let off a rocket. Cliffie recalled his father saying, 'I'll soon show you' – and briefly wondering what he would show him.

The man had the same thought. 'What will you show me?'

'This.' Tom held up his fist in the firelight – to Cliffie's eyes it was much larger than usual – and started to climb over the wall. Young George and Ernest rushed up and, after a struggle, managed to hold him back.

When the fireworks were over, Sis rebuked Tom and accused him of being drunk. There were moments of angry shouting before Tom strode out of the house slamming the front gate so hard that it fell off its hinges.

For weeks the gate lay on the ground in the basement area. It embarrassed Cliffie; he knew now that being drunk was something to be ashamed of and the broken gate was a public declaration of his father's weakness.

Cliffie often witnessed, or overheard, his mother accusing his father of being drunk. His father would protest, either angrily or in a hurt way, and reply with one of two favourite expressions: 'Unmitigated rot' or 'I'm right as ninepence.' In time, Cliffie came to regard both these ripostes as confirmation that he was, indeed, drunk.

On 6 January, Twelfth Night, 1899, Little Alice took down the many holly branches that had festooned the house over Christmas and left them, bundled with string, at the bottom of the stairs to the basement. Late that night, after everyone was asleep, Tom came in, cursing noisily and knocking over the furniture. When Young George asked him to be quiet, he swung a punch at him, and was subdued only when Old George pushed him down the stairs – where he stayed until morning asleep on the holly.

The event stayed in Cliffie's memory – he found it hard

to understand how his father could sleep on a pile of holly. But he was more dismayed when his father wet the breakfast-room sofa. He found him in the scullery shamefacedly washing the loose covers and learned the truth by eavesdropping. After that, he knew what had happened when his father's trousers and long johns were hanging on the line beside the sofa covers.

In Sis's diary, references to Tom were brief. His degradation was recorded in short, clipped notes buried among descriptions of Sis's own activities and those of Gladys and Cliffie: 'Tom fell on basement steps. Father and George had to go down and carry him'; 'Tom drunk. Punched Ernest and swore at Rose, 1 a.m. Apologised after lunch'; 'Vile night. Tom threw up in his sleep. Alice helped me wash. Father away so slept, tried to, in his bed.'

Tom was always penitent, and said that he would reform and that whatever had happened wouldn't happen again, but Sis didn't believe him. Even when she was aware that he was trying hard to conquer his craving, and for a few days or weeks he drank less or stopped drinking altogether, she had very little faith. She was tired of broken promises; the only thing that he could say that touched her – and he said it often – was that he loved her and Cliffie and Gladys; she believed that he did, but now such declarations – as she confided to Kate and to her diary – only made her sad.

For a while Tom claimed to have turned to God, to have signed the pledge and to be praying for release from what he described as an affliction. Sis scoffed privately, but took Cliffie to St Mark's Church where he joined the Band of Hope, signed the same pledge and attended gatherings where he and a large group of children recited: 'I have promised, with God's help, to abstain from all intoxicating drinks and beverages.' At Sis's insistence, Tom had to explain to Cliffie what 'abstain', 'intoxicating' and 'beverages' meant.

In March 1899 the Welsbach company demoted Tom

from chief accountant to assistant accountant, with a reduced salary, on the grounds that he was no longer competent to fulfil his former role and that he had lost the respect of his subordinates. Sis recorded that he seemed almost grateful and that he stopped drinking – although she viewed even this latest effort cynically.

In June the board in Germany told their manager in London – the white-haired man who had given Cliffie a shilling – to sack Tom. Tom wrote to him, stating that he had 'taken himself in hand' with the help of a priest, who himself wrote a letter promising to hold Tom to his undertaking. Sis saw the manager's reply and described its contents as shameful, despite its main import: that the manager had reversed the board's decision and given Tom a last chance. To his employer, Tom had resolved to renounce his 'miserable and unworthy past by rigid sobriety and honesty in the future'; the implication that his drinking had led him to be dishonest at work disturbed her, but she had a small hope that this close confrontation with the prospect of unemployment – something men feared more than anything – might be Tom's salvation.

Cliffie was seven then. He was aware of the crisis and of the importance of his father's job and had prayed earnestly on his knees for its preservation, but this didn't stop him having fun with his sister and his friends. In February 1899 Sis was concerned that he was spending too much time with Toppy and, in particular, that he had gone with him to a football match in Tottenham without asking her permission.

I reread my father's account of his escapades with Toppy and felt envious of his friendship with someone so loyal and daring. My explorations of the little town I had grown up in by the Thames seemed tame compared with the adventures he and Toppy had had all over London and the risks they had

taken. And I realised that it was Toppy, rather than my grandfather Tom or great-uncle George, who had triggered my father's enthusiasm for the Spurs.

To get to the Tottenham Hotspur football ground at Northumberland Park would have cost Toppy and Cliffie a penny ha'penny each return by horse-drawn tram, but they could rarely afford that; instead, they travelled free by hanging on to the ladders at the backs of brewers' drays or by jumping on to the axles of the four-wheeled cabs known as growlers. They had to be quick and alert; there was an ever-present danger of being seen by the driver and lashed by his whip, and there were malicious urchins in the street who would yell, 'Whip behind, guvnor.'

Toppy earned regular money by lighting fires in the homes of orthodox Jews on Saturdays and paid the sixpence it cost to get him and Cliffie into the Spurs ground, and a penny for five Woodbines or Ogden's Tabs to be shared during the game – my father's penny-a-week pocket money would have already gone on sweets. And Toppy funded much longer excursions; he knew that, as long as you didn't leave a station, you could travel every branch of the North London Railway and come home again on a child's half-price ticket bought for a penny at Dalston Junction. In this way Toppy and my father saw large swathes of London from the windows of railway carriages, from the ships in the docks at Poplar to the pagoda at Kew and the Thames at Richmond.

Cliffie and Toppy had an enemy, the local bully, Bert Rapley – and that summer of 1899 Rapley had something to taunt Cliffie about, a fact that Cliffie could not dispute: that his family was pro-Boer. Since the death of Gladstone the previous year, Old George and the rest of them, including Tom, had given credence to the views of Keir Hardie, Robert Burns and Robert Blatchford, the editor of the radical *Clarion*. By listening to discussions around Old George's bed, Cliffie learned that his family's long-standing bugbear, Joe

Chamberlain, had conspired by means of a secret telegram with someone called Cecil Rhodes to deprive the Boers of gold that they had found on their own land in a place called the Transvaal; the Boers had invaded some British territory called Natal only because Chamberlain and Rhodes had sent soldiers into their country.

When he expressed this view at school, Cliffie encountered bewilderment and even jeering, so he decided to keep quiet about it. However, Rapley remembered what Cliffie had said. On a Thursday band night on Hackney Downs in August, after an argument about a cricket bat, he chased Cliffie into the crowd around the bandstand. There, just as Rapley caught up with him, Cliffie found his father – with his mother, his uncle Ernest and his sister in her pram. Deprived of his prey, Rapley danced about a few feet away, jeering and pointing at the whole family. 'Pro-Boers! Pro-Boers! Bloody pro-Boers! That's what they are!' It was a serious stigma and the crowd stared, some of them angrily. Uncle Ernest wanted to give Rapley a thick ear, but Tom told him to calm down and said that *he* would deal with him. But first he ushered Sis, Gladys, Cliffie and Ernest into the penny seats – which were green deckchairs, close to the bandstand and separated from the crowd by a rope.

Rapley stood by the rope shouting, 'See them! Bloody pro-Boers, they are.' Tom went up to him and spoke in a friendly voice: 'If you keep shouting like that, I'll call a policeman. You're a naughty boy. I know where you live and I know your father and I'll call round and tell him. Do you like jumbles?' Jumbles were cakes, three for a penny at a shed nearby. Tom put a penny in Rapley's hand. The bully, who was only nine years old, looked at him, dazed, then turned and walked away.

Tom had not had a drink for two months, and Sis dared to hope that, with the constant threat of the sack, his resolution might last. She didn't speak to him on the subject because he had asked her not to mention it. He stayed sober for another month and then something happened – Sis never knew what, but presumed it was something at work. On an evening in October she smelled whisky on his breath. He wasn't drunk then, but he was ten days later, and the following week the pattern of staggering down the basement steps late at night and sleeping on the breakfast-room sofa began once again.

This time Sis decided to say nothing, to go away to another room when he was drunk, to ignore him as her father always had.

In January 1900 the Welsbach company sacked Tom and allowed no discussion.

Cliffie found out on the day it happened. He was playing cricket with Toppy against a lamppost in a side street and saw his father walk past the end of the road; it was a Saturday morning and normally he returned from work much later. There was a strained atmosphere at lunch and Cliffie knew something was wrong. His father had promised to buy him some white mice that afternoon – and had already made a cage for them out of a soapbox. When they went to buy the mice, his father told him. Cliffie started to cry; he knew that this was the worst thing that could possibly happen. But his father seemed all right; he told him not to worry, and called him 'old chap' as he always did when Cliffie was bothered about something or sad.

Everyone except Sis was sympathetic and tried to help Tom. He curtailed his drinking and sat every day at the kitchen table writing letters to companies who were advertising jobs. Over the next few months he was interviewed several times and his references were taken up, but he didn't receive a single offer. The problem was his reference from the Welsbach company; it praised his work over the fifteen years he had been there, testified to his skills as an accountant and a manager of others and even listed his professional qualifications – exams that Tom had passed years earlier – and his ability to speak and read German. The man with the white hair had done his best, but, probably because he was a good man with a conscience, he had written a final sentence: 'I cannot testify to his sobriety.' A man of forty could not get a job without a reference from his previous employer.

In April 1900 Uncle George at last married his fiancée, Marie, and they moved into their own house, a mile away in Upper Clapton; he had saved for it for seven years. Sis was bereft; for a large part of his life she had played the part of his mother, and more recently – through what she now saw as her unfortunate marriage – he, unlike her father or Ernest, had always been there. And he had contributed to the family's expenses.

In the summer, after months of effort, Tom gave up answering advertisements and earned a little money mending watches and writing letters applying for jobs for other people – he had fine handwriting and a reputation for being able to write a good letter – but the money was not enough.

At the end of the summer term Cliffie was taken away from the Birkbeck School, which he had grown to like and where he was in his third year, and was registered at Sigdon Road Board School, for which there were no fees. Although Toppy was there, Cliffie had a sense of dread every time he walked up the three flights of stairs, 'tiled in white like a public lavatory', to the boys' classrooms on the top floor. Many of the children came from the nearby slums and were dirty, scruffily dressed and unruly, and Cliffie didn't like their constant swearing and their thick Cockney accents. Most of the teachers' time was taken up with trying to keep order, and the cane was their ever-ready weapon.

Lack of money soon forced those who remained at Norfolk Road to do without servants. Little Alice left to marry her long-time sweetheart – Little Bennett who worked in the ticket office at Hackney Downs station – and was not replaced; and Big Alice, who had been living in since Gladys was born, was asked to leave. This seemed to hurt Sis even more than the departure of her brother. Although the bright and popular Cousin Minnie, who always looked after the small children at family gatherings, joined the household in the role of mother's help, this was not the same as having servants.

~

That summer, 1900, Gladys was three and allowed to play with friends in the street. Cliffie was told to look after her and make sure she didn't get her clothes dirty, a responsibility he undertook willingly and with pride, even though he had to watch and stay alert while she and her friends played with hoops and a skipping rope. He would stand in the road, just beyond the gutter, ready to catch Gladys in his arms when she slipped off the pavement, as she often did, towards the mud and dung on the street. Sometimes he pulled her around in a cart, which Tom had made out of a wooden soapbox and some old pram wheels, but this led to trouble with his mother; traces of dirt were found on Gladys's skirt after he and Toppy had filled the cart with buckets of horse dung, scraped from the street, for sale to keen gardeners at a penny a bucketful.

Tom's drinking took hold again that summer and Sis's diary filled with cryptic reports of violence and verbal abuse. This time she was unable to ignore him, because the rows were about money as well as drunkenness. He would plead, sometimes in tears, for her to give him twopence, the price of a drink at the Norfolk Arms, and sometimes she would throw it at him. The money had been earned by her father, and not by him, but she would give it to him to get him out of the house, although she knew that, if he could buy himself one drink, he could win the price of others at billiards – he was an excellent player, drunk or sober – or sponge off friends and acquaintances. If Sis wouldn't give him money, he would approach others including Little Alice and some of the other neighbours – but never Old George.

A row broke out when Sis saw him leaving the house with a toy steam engine that he had given Cliffie for his birthday the previous December. He confessed that he was intending to raise a few shillings by pawning it. In Cliffie's presence, Sis demanded to know what he had paid for it. The answer was twenty-five shillings. Cliffie blubbered that it was all right, Daddy could have it, but Sis took the money from her purse and threw it at Tom, screaming at him to go away and get drunk.

A day or two later Cliffie was alone with his father in the breakfast-room. 'Daddy, why do you get drunk?' he asked. Tom looked at him for a long time before his face collapsed and he muttered, 'Shame on me. I don't know. I can't help myself.'

On a Saturday in October, Tom came into the kitchen after drinking in the middle of the day. He was hungry and Sis passed him an open tin of salmon. He tasted it and asked how long the tin had been open.

'Long enough to go bad and poison you, I hope.'

Tom swung his fist at her. She jumped out of the way and his hand smashed into the glass of a large framed map of the British Isles. His hand was cut severely and he was led to the nearby hospital by Cousin Minnie. When he had gone, Sis wept and Cliffie knelt down by the wall and prayed.

Sis had written before that she wished Tom would go away and never come back. That night, she wrote, 'I cannot bear it any longer. We must get rid of him.' In the morning she and her father discussed how they might get Tom to leave what was still legally – and, in Sis's view at least, morally – their home.

The next year, 1901, on 22 January, a Tuesday, Tom came into the kitchen and announced, 'Daisy is dead.' Cliffie didn't find out till later that Daisy was Queen Victoria. His mother was more concerned about a persistent cough that Gladys had developed, and Tom was sent to fetch Dr White.

Cliffie watched the white-haired doctor look into Gladys's throat while holding her tongue down with a teaspoon. He looked grave and, after what seemed a long time, turned to Sis and said, 'Diphtheria, I'm afraid. She must be taken away.' He asked Cliffie to run downstairs and fetch another teaspoon, which he used to look into Cliffie's throat. He pronounced him free of infection, but said he must not go near his sister while they waited for her to be taken to hospital. The bedroom he shared with her must be sealed up until it could be sterilised; he would have to sleep somewhere else.

Cliffie watched from his parents' bedroom window as Gladys, wrapped in a cream blanket, was carried to an ambulance. After she had gone, he sat with his parents and Minnie in the kitchen. No one else was at home and there wasn't much talk. Everyone, including Cliffie, knew that diphtheria was a disease that killed small children. His father told him that Gladys had been taken to the fever hospital in Homerton, beyond Mare Street. No one – not even her parents or her brother – was allowed to visit her.

The next day Cliffie walked with his father across Mare Street and through the gloomy graveyard of Hackney parish church to the hospital. He waited outside while his father enquired about Gladys; she was neither better nor worse.

Wednesday, January 23rd. No news. I want to be with her but they have guards at that place.

Tom and Cliffie went the next day and the day after and received the same message.

Thursday, January 24th. No news. I am in purgatory. Cliffie lies on the sofa staring at the floor. Tom fiddled all day with the Herfords' clock, drank small glass of port when I had one. That was all. Minnie does everything.

Friday, January 25th. No news. Father home now. Sat with him. He is philosophical, says it is not my fault. I will make it up to Cliffie if my darling lives. And to Tom – poor man.

On the fourth day, Saturday, Tom came out of the hospital smiling. He hugged Cliffie. 'The crisis is passed. She's out of danger.' When they told his mother and his grandfather – who had returned from some distant place after receiving a telegram – Cliffie saw his mother break down in tears and smile for the first time since Gladys had been taken away.

Saturday, January 26th. They say my darling is out of danger. Can this be really true? I must *believe it. Cliffie with George. Father and Tom play chess. No drink.*

The good news quickly spread around the family, and Auntie Marie asked Cliffie to come and stay with her and Uncle George in their new house until Gladys was completely better and home again. Cliffie was glad to go there. As well as a servant called Clara whom he liked, they had the new electric light; he marvelled at the dim glow of the carbon lamps and was allowed to play with the switches as much as he liked.

On Sunday evening Uncle George was even kinder to Cliffie than he usually was. Since his marriage he had visited his old home every Saturday and had always taken Cliffie a packet of chocolate cigarettes; Cliffie was pleased, but a little puzzled, when he gave him this same gift on a Sunday and he wondered why his aunt's eyes were watering.

Uncle George didn't go to his office the next morning. He told Cliffie that his mother was coming to see him. She arrived with his father, and hugged him and called him her darling boy and said that she would never be unkind to him again. His father stood looking on, and Cliffie saw the familiar lines on his temples as he tried to smile. He sensed that something was wrong. He enquired eagerly about his sister.

Gladys had died the day before.

Monday, January 28th. My darling is dead.

~

On 2 February Sis noted mechanically that there had been a funeral service that afternoon at a cemetery in Friern Barnet called the Great Northern, and that Gladys was buried afterwards. She wrote a list of the seventy-three people who attended the funeral. She wrote nothing about how she felt.

Then she gave up diary-writing for ever.

22

The Vanishing Lady

I READ SIS'S LAST diary entries on the day before New Year's Eve, 1966, in my room, at my father's home. He was downstairs, cleaning and hoovering in preparation for his party the next day. I looked out of the window at the bare apple trees, and then back at my room, at Deborah's drawing of La Frascetti; she had been at Gladys's funeral. I had only my father's account of what happened next and I hadn't read it since soon after he wrote it, when I was thirteen. I picked it up and read it again.

He was nine when his sister died and he wrote that he remembered little of the grief that followed because he was taken away from home and spent much of the next year travelling with his grandfather, and sometimes with his mother as well, in Britain and Ireland, and he stayed for a long period with Aunt Kate and Uncle Gibson and his cousin Kathleen in Braintree. He was taken away because the drinking and the rows started again soon after his sister's funeral, and grew so bad that, at times, Old George and Sis abandoned their own home to escape from Tom.

Cliffie barely went to school that year, but he can't have been away all the time, because he remembered things that happened in London – and time spent with his father. They went together to the Oval to watch Surrey play Middlesex and saw a famous batsman called Bobby Abel take a diving catch right in front of them. On the way Cliffie had his first ride on the tube, travelling under the Thames from Old Street to Elephant and Castle; when he asked what would happen if the tunnel burst and the river came flooding in, his father took his hand and said, 'Don't you worry, old chap.'

He helped his father with his watch-mending, and saw him spend days emptying and cleaning the outdoor water tank, which was thought to have been the source of his sister's infection. At the same time a plumber installed a pipe that brought mains water directly into the house for the first time. Above the new tap, his father fixed an enamel label that said 'Drinking water'.

Uncle Ernest and Aunt Rose moved away, not far, to their own flat in Islington, and it felt as if another cornerstone of his life had been removed. But they still paid him a lot of attention, bringing him presents from their travels and, most excitingly, taking him to the music hall. He remembered riding on a tram with Uncle Ernest from Dalston, along Essex Road, to Collins's Music Hall on Islington Green; his uncle told him that, as well as playing the xylophone during Aunt Rose's act, he now did conjuring tricks – and his best trick, which Cliffie would see later, was called the vanishing lady: 'Auntie Rose is the vanishing lady, but she don't always vanish when she should.' Cliffie liked his uncle's funny way of speaking; he knew he had caught it from Aunt Rose and that his mother disapproved.

That evening, Cliffie stood in the wings and was surprised and proud to see hundreds of people shouting and clapping while his aunt did what she did at home as his uncle played cheeky little flourishes and dramatic rolls on his xylophone. He was even more astonished when the audience stood up and sang and swayed from side to side as, followed by a spotlight, his aunt walked on her hands down a flight of stairs playing 'Daisy' on her violin; he had seen her do that lots of times, but nobody in his family sang when she did it.

Uncle Ernest reappeared wearing a top hat and tails and

showed the audience a box which seemed to have no holes or hidden compartments. The audience clapped as Aunt Rose squeezed herself into it with her knees beside her ears; Uncle Ernest closed it, strapped down the lid and played a tune on the xylophone which ended with a long roll; then, holding his hat high in the air, he revealed that the box was empty. From his viewpoint in the wings, Cliffie was thrilled – and was startled a second time a few seconds later, when his aunt tapped him on the shoulder.

Ernest and Rose's room was taken by Cousin Bertie, a vacant youth, whose father, rich Uncle Charlie, paid Old George for the inconvenience of putting up with his son. Bertie was nineteen, had been thrown out of the army and was now, at his father's insistence, training to be a stockbroker. He was much disapproved of by Sis because he went out drinking with Tom, whom he called 'squire', and she was certain that Bertie paid for the drinks. When Old George heard of this, Bertie was summoned to his bedside. Cliffie was tucked into bed beside his grandfather, and watched Bertie stare awkwardly at his feet as Old George told him in his deepest rumble never to go drinking with Tom again. 'Do you not understand that his only hope is to give up the drink? Cliffie here understands that.'

After Bertie had gone, Old George told Cliffie that it was his brother Charlie's fault that Bertie was a wastrel; Charlie had brought him up to believe that money was more important than anything else. Cliffie remembered what he said next because he had heard it before, and was to hear it again: 'No person of quality esteems another merely because he is rich.'

On a Sunday afternoon in the spring of 1902 there was a big row in the kitchen. Cliffie listened from the top of the stairs. It wasn't just his mother and father who were shouting; he could hear deep bass bellowing from his grandfather – a frightening sound that he had never heard before. The kitchen door was shut, so he couldn't make out what they were saying. Cousin Minnie came and stood behind him with her hands on his shoulders. She led him into the drawing-room and stayed with him after shutting the door; she said that he shouldn't worry. Soon he heard the slamming of doors and rapid footsteps on the basement steps. He looked out of the window and saw his father hurrying away.

In the evening his father returned, spoke to his grandfather and packed two suitcases. Cliffie stayed in the kitchen with his mother, who seemed pale and nervous, but hugged him and told him that his father was going to live somewhere else for a while, not far away.

His grandfather called him to the basement door, where his father kissed him and said, 'Goodbye, old chap. Don't worry. I'll see you before long.' Turning away, his grandfather took Cliffie by the arm – but Cliffie resisted, lingered and watched his father walk up the basement steps and along the pavement with a suitcase in each hand.

He didn't see him again.

~

The next afternoon, as my father napped in his armchair, I found it hard to concentrate on *Tender Is the Night*. I stared out of the window at the unmelted frost, poked the fire from time to time and walked about the room, picking things up and putting them down. I had never had a sister and no one close to me had died, and I had always been in touch with both my parents, so I couldn't imagine how my father had felt. I wondered when he had realised that he would never see his father again.

I was standing by the cabinet that held the *Encyclopaedia Britannica* when my father opened his eyes and smiled. 'What are . . .' He croaked and swallowed and started again. 'What are you doing over there?'

'Nothing. Just thinking.' He went on looking at me. 'I finished reading your mother's diaries yesterday . . . It's a pity she stopped writing after Gladys died.'

He pulled himself up in his chair and reached for his tobacco tin. 'She'd had enough. She was distraught for . . .' He opened the tin and teased out some tobacco. 'For ever really . . . She lived till 1942, you know.'

'I know.' I hadn't meant to talk to him about his mother or Gladys's death – but it didn't seem to upset him, though there was a silence, during which he lit up, inhaled and stared into the fire. I sat down in my usual chair opposite him. He yawned loudly and leaned forward with his hands on his knees. He would soon remember that people would be arriving in an hour to drink sherry and eat Gentleman's Relish. I wanted to say something, about his sister – or his father – to keep the conversation alive. 'It's a shame your father didn't write anything.'

He yawned and grunted, stood up and stretched his arms elaborately. 'Actually, he did. Not much . . . about five letters. I'll try and find them for you if you like.'

I was surprised and said I'd like to read them – and was about to ask why he hadn't mentioned them before, when he looked at his watch.

'God *strewth*! Those blasted people will be here soon. You should have woken me up.'

He put on a new tie that my half-sister Ann had given him for Christmas, and we borrowed chairs and sherry glasses from the woman who lived at the front of the house. He toasted bread and I cut it into triangles and spread them with Gentleman's Relish. The party went well, in the senses that my father considered it a success, Old Bowen's wife didn't come, and Arabella and I got on and talked quietly in a corner.

Later we had turkey sandwiches and Arctic Roll with cherry brandy, and watched Scottish dancing on television.

My father promised to look for his father's letters, but said he wasn't sure where they were; he hadn't read them since soon after his mother had died.

We toasted the New Year with cherry brandy and went upstairs at about half past twelve. I felt a little drunk, and lay in bed thinking once again about Gladys's death and Tom's departure and how, at the age of ten, my father had been left with only his mother and his grandfather, after a short lifetime filled with love, people and fun – as well as drunkenness and squabbling.

~

The next day I returned to London and met Pat outside the Academy Cinema in Oxford Street. He was leaning against the wall near the end of a long queue with his hands in his pockets. A cold wind blew along the street from the east and paper bags and newspapers swirled around our feet. The shops were shut, their windows filled with banners announcing sales, but the Christmas illuminations – a smiling Father Christmas, slung high above the road and flanked by gaudy, geometric snowflakes – lit up the dampness in the evening air.

Pat told me about his Christmas and New Year in Dorset; he and his parents had drunk a lot, and his serious-minded sister had disapproved. I didn't bother to tell him about Christmas lunch with my mother and just four old ladies; Uncle Godfrey and the 105-year-old Auntie Georgie had died and been cremated during 1966. Christmas seemed a long time ago.

The queue didn't move and I thought about Bonnie – still at home with her parents. I imagined her on a sofa facing a flaming fire with her parents either side of her in chintz-covered armchairs; they were drinking sherry and her father was raising a toast to the new year.

'Chroist! I'm so bloody cold.' Pat put his hands in his

armpits underneath his jacket and stamped his feet. A minute later he held something in front of me. It was a roll-up.

'I've got some fags, thanks.'

He leaned against me. 'Go on. It's a joint.'

I saw that it was lit. 'Here? Now?' I looked casually around. It was a drab setting for my initiation; I associated this sort of thing with white rooms, Aldous Huxley, joss sticks and music. Behind us a man with wavy grey hair was holding the arm of a woman in a leopard-skin coat; she was carrying a patent-leather handbag and wearing a small black hat. In front was a group of about six people in jeans and scruffy coats.

'Just take a drag and hold it in deep. No one'll know.'

I took it, inhaled, handed it back and exhaled slowly without moving my shoulder away from his. 'Why not do this somewhere more private?'

'Where? Can't smoke this at home. The old man might smell it.'

The queue started to move. He passed it back to me twice before we came to the ticket office, where he licked his thumb and forefinger and pinched it out.

I felt a little strange as we walked down the stairs, and leaned against Pat until we were sitting down. Straight away I was absorbed in the trailers and advertisements. There were narrow strips of white light at the edge of the screen; perfect droplets of water hung in the air as beautiful people sat on rocks smoking beside a waterfall.

Later, after a *delicious* ice cream, I seemed almost to become Jean-Louis Trintignant standing on the beach wondering at Anouk Aimée who was Bonnie's darker-haired elder sister and the most beautiful woman I had ever seen. Drops of rain made shapes on the windscreen and I was eventually lulled to sleep by the rhythm of the windscreen wipers and the sound of a thousand beautiful voices.

'Chroist! That was beautiful, man. Great music.'

'Dubba dubba dub, dubba dubba dub, da da da, dubba dubba dub . . .'

We laughed a lot as we wandered slowly to the Golden Egg and ordered mixed grills with chips. I ate fast and asked Pat whether he had heard of Stan Getz. He had, but knew only what I had already assumed – that he played the saxophone.

Bonnie and I started to see each other two or three times a week, going out – like a proper couple – for drinks, meals, films and pop concerts, and staying in with Stan Getz when Kate was out. We were warm and physical and paid each other compliments – but I managed not to say the word 'love'.

The Woodman, a busy low-ceilinged pub with floral upholstery, near Bonnie's flat and Highgate tube station, became our regular meeting place.

On a Wednesday towards the end of February I arrived there five minutes early, bought a pint and waited at our favourite table – by the window overlooking the traffic lights on Archway Road. I kept glancing at the door. Half an hour later, Bonnie still hadn't arrived and I was wondering which to do first, phone her or buy another pint, when Kate sat down in front of me. She was pale and out of breath.

'David, Bonnie's not coming.' She was biting her lip. 'She's not well. Can I get you a drink?' She stood up.

'What's wrong with her?'

She looked embarrassed. 'Oh . . . some flu thing. I'll get you a drink.' She picked up my glass, walked away and turned back. 'Red Barrel?'

'Sure.' I lit a cigarette. Bonnie had put off a night out we had planned the previous Friday because she had to work late typing a script; she was going home to her parents' for the weekend, so we had rearranged to Monday; then she had postponed Monday – the script still wasn't finished. Tonight would have been the first time I had seen her for a week.

Kate came back carrying my pint and a Bloody Mary.

'Thanks. Nice of you to come.' We sipped our drinks.

She was frowning. She sat back and crossed her legs, then uncrossed them and leaned forward with her elbows on the table. She looked into my eyes and then away and back again. She put her palms either side of the ashtray and moved it slightly. 'David, this is really unfair . . . and hard to say. Bonnie isn't ill.' She looked down at her hands and up again. 'She's got a new boyfriend . . . I'm really sorry.'

A shiver surged through my body; I could feel it on my face, in my arms, everywhere. I sat up, tried to swallow and reached for my beer. 'Just like that. You mean . . . she doesn't want to see me again? . . . *Just like that.*'

'She's behaving really badly. She should be here to tell you. She rang me from somewhere and asked me to come and tell you she was ill. I said I wouldn't. I would only tell the truth—'

'She doesn't want to see me again? What? *Ever?* You *know* that?'

'Yes.' She reached across the table and put her hand over mine.

'How do you *know*, if she just asked you to say she was ill?'

'She's been talking about nothing else for about two weeks: how to let you down lightly . . . her new bloke . . . on and on.'

I drank some beer. Two weeks: that meant we had seen each other twice – and slept together – since she had met this other man. 'Who is he?'

'Oh, just someone she met at work.' She swallowed a mouthful of Bloody Mary. 'An American, a producer who just started working at Rediffusion.'

'Producer. How old is he?'

'About thirty. Bit of a creep, *I* think.'

I drank some more beer. I found what she was saying hard to believe. Bonnie was twenty, and she thought I was nineteen; why would she want to be with someone who was thirty?

'I'm sorry, David.' Her eyes were slanting downwards; she looked miserable. 'You're such a beaut bloke. It's unfair.' She looked away, out of the window.

I stood up. 'I'll be back in a minute.' I picked up my cigarettes and left the pub. I walked down the hill towards Archway, stopped and stared at my reflection, murky but complete, in an unlit shop window. I went a little further, leaned one arm against a bus stop and stared down into the gutter. She couldn't just end our relationship like that; we were such good friends – I had even met her parents over a stiff Sunday lunch. I dropped a cigarette butt at the foot of the bus stop, trod on it, and walked slowly back up the hill.

Kate was still sitting by the window. She was smoking. She didn't see me. I stood outside the door for a few moments, then went back in.

'Are you sure?'

She pulled my hands towards her across the table. 'Look. She would have told you herself . . . some time. I just wasn't going to come here and lie about her being ill, so it's ended up being me who's told you . . . Perhaps I was wrong. Perhaps I—' Her expression changed; she was looking at something behind me.

Bonnie was standing there in the red coat with the white furry collar that she had worn on the night we first met. There were tears on her cheeks. I stood up and hugged her. She sobbed into my shoulder, and kept saying, 'I'm sorry.'

While Kate bought her a drink, she told me through tears that it was true: she loved this other man; she loved me too in a way, but not the same way; she had to choose; she couldn't have two boyfriends; she hated to hurt me.

'Why choose him?'

She had been holding my lapels. She let go, her face puckered and there were more tears. My question had been angry and futile. I regretted it.

When Kate came back, I whispered to Bonnie, 'I love you too,' kissed her and left.

I sat on the tube facing my own image distorted in the blackness of the window opposite, and paying attention to nothing except my own angry thoughts. I wanted to tell Bonnie to go to hell and I wanted to punch the smooth jaw of the American producer whose image was firmly in my mind – he had short dark hair with a sheen to it, like something I had seen in a hairdresser's window, and a perfectly pressed pink shirt with a button-down collar; at the same time I was going through the possible ways of rescuing my love for Bonnie and what I thought was hers for me – she had said she loved me.

Dave and I had found a flat around the corner from my mother and the Goat in Boots. It had two rooms: one with armchairs in the middle and a bed at each end; the other a kitchen with an old dining table on which Dave laid out his medical books and I put my new second-hand typewriter. We shared a bathroom with a pair of male Canadian accountants from the floor below and became adept at cooking eggs and bacon while shaving at the kitchen sink.

I had got a full-time job as an editorial assistant on *Humanist* magazine, which was published monthly by the Rationalist Press Association, an organisation with its roots in the nineteenth century – loosely allied to the British Humanist Association. It had ten or so employees and a narrow Georgian building in Islington. On the magazine, apart from me, there was just the editor, a genial man of about sixty, respected among humanists for his books and lectures and known to everyone as HH. I was taught how to put the magazine together using articles he gave me. As long as the magazine came out on time and looked as it usually did, he and the rest of the staff were happy. This was fortunate because, under the pretext of having to check proofs at the printer in Tufnell Park, I was soon spending time at the flat of a woman who came in to the office twice a day to make tea and coffee. She was twenty-eight and hid provocative messages under my teacup. For a few days I was surprised at myself; she was so old.

Sometimes at weekends and in the evenings I did the same sort of work for nothing for Richard, the Australian, but there was a big difference. The design of *Humanist* followed a pre-ordained style, and much subbing work was needed to make the text and pictures fit the page precisely; *Oz* was created by a long-haired designer called Jon, to whom every page was a work of art and the idea of a column of text aligning with the one next to it was anathema.

For both magazines I worked away quietly with a scalpel, Cow gum and a plastic spatula, but I had to go out in search of pictures – to picture agencies for *Humanist* and to Martin's flat above the Pheasantry in the King's Road for Richard and Jon. The picture agencies were little bureaucracies where I had a coffee and a cigarette with people who became friends while I searched their files and they filled in forms. Martin would be either alone, hatching and cross-hatching and showering the bare floor with ink, or surrounded by rock stars and models who were friendly in a restrained, you-look-a-bit-young-and-I'm-not-quite-sure-who-you-are way. Whether he was alone or not, there would be music and marijuana and sometimes charades, as I waited – often for hours – for the completion of a drawing or collage which would blow the minds of incipient hippies. Over several months I read a battered copy of Herman Hesse's *Steppenwolf* in Martin's flat, in between making coffee, rolling joints and looking for pictures he couldn't find.

Soon after my idyll with Bonnie ended, I had a drink with Peter the Painter. He listened to me bemoaning her treachery, nodded sympathetically and said that a similar thing had happened to him. 'You didn't *really* know her, Dave. If you had, you'd have known she was the sort of girl who would come across all lovey-dovey – and, fair enough, let you fuck her, but I bet she enjoyed that too – while all the time she was on the look-out for something better, or maybe not better, just something that would build her career.'

'No, Bonnie wasn't like that. She just—'

'You'd be surprised, mate.'

'All right, maybe I didn't know her well enough, therefore I shouldn't have fallen in love – but how could I have helped myself?'

He shook his head and his long curls flapped around his chin. 'It wasn't love Dave. It was lust.' He swallowed a third of a pint, put the glass down and wiped his mouth with the back of his hand. 'There's a difference.'

'What about love at first sight?'

'It's bollocks. It's what sensitive souls, like your good self, call lust. It's better just to accept that you and all of us men and quite a lot of women' – he laughed roguishly – 'are lustful, and just act on it – not try to dress the whole thing up as something fancy and poetic and spiritual and all that bollocks.'

23

Lost in Earls Court

Peter the Painter played rhythm guitar in a rock group called Ocean Daydream. He had talked about it a lot – it sounded like an English Jefferson Airplane – and had shown me a sketchbook, in which he wrote lyrics in large, clear handwriting in black ink, but, despite invitations to remote venues on the edge of London, I had never seen them perform.

On a cold evening in the spring of 1967, he took me to meet the other members of Ocean Daydream – friends of his from art school who lived together in Earls Court. They had got a recording contract; the record would be coming out quickly and Peter and the others were placing an advertisement in Richard's magazine, at their own expense. Being artists, they had designed the advertisement themselves and wanted to hand it over to me personally.

The flat was in the basement of a Victorian mansion block in a side street. We walked down a wide stone staircase littered with chewing-gum wrappers and cigarette packets. The door was ajar, lights were on and somewhere, someone was playing an electric guitar. Inside, we crossed the hall to a large room which looked as if it had been painted white a long time ago; there was a sofa, some upright chairs and a table covered in small bottles of paint, but no people. I followed Peter back into the hall where he pushed lightly on a door that wasn't quite shut. He put his head in and quickly pulled it out again. A man's voice said, 'Come in Pete, it's OK.'

A man with long wavy hair was lying in bed under some

blankets; his face was open and friendly. There was a woman lying on top of him; I could see bare shoulders and straight reddish hair. 'Hi, come on in.' The woman moved sideways and pushed her nose into his neck.

'This is Dave . . . about the ad. That's Eric. And that's Julia.'

Julia had turned her face away. She waved the back of her hand towards us. Eric laughed. 'Go make some coffee, or get a beer. I'll see you in a minute.' He laughed again.

There was a large fridge in a large dirty kitchen, but no beer. As Peter filled a kettle, a man with straggly thin hair and tight trousers came in. A red electric guitar hung on a strap from his shoulder and glittered in the light; he was fiddling with the tuning. 'Hello, mate.' He looked up at Peter and back at the guitar. 'Who's this, then?' He glanced at me.

'This is Dave.'

'Hello, Dave. How are you, mate?' His face was pale and flat; he had brown eyes and it looked as if his nose had been broken.

'Fine, thanks.'

'He's come to talk about the art for the ad . . . remember? This is Chas, by the way.'

I nodded.

'Yeah, I'll get the stuff.' He finished tuning the guitar and went away.

Peter told me that Chas was the one who cared most about the look of the ad. 'He's got a visual concept. It'll be on the LP, posters, everything.'

Chas came back with a sheet of white cardboard and Eric appeared – dressed, with bare feet – and moved mugs and plates off the kitchen table into the sink. Chas brushed crumbs on to the floor with the back of his hand and put the cardboard down. A grainy black and white photograph of a calm sea, with a sandy beach in the foreground, was pasted on to it; in the sky, in square capital letters, were the words

'Ocean Daydream' and underneath in smaller letters 'is coming'. 'What do you think?'

'Great. Is it going to be in colour?'

'Oh yeah. As colourful as possible.' He smiled laconically. 'The transparency and camera-ready art for the type, with the colours specified, are in here.' He turned the cardboard over; there was an envelope taped to the back. 'I'd like to see a proof . . . if that's OK.'

Two girls came into the room. One was Julia who had been in bed with Eric – I recognised her hair.

The other was Deborah.

'Is that OK? To see a proof?' Chas had picked up his piece of cardboard and was holding it in front of me.

'Er . . . yes. Fine . . .' I mumbled at him and walked towards her. 'Deborah?' She was a lot taller than when I had last seen her – and, when I got closer, I saw that she was a lot thinner.

She looked at me and put her hands up to her ears. 'David? What are *you* doing here?' She shook her head and laughed. 'God! That's amazing.' She held my arms and kissed me quickly on the lips.

I saw that I was holding Chas's artwork. 'Picking this up. What are *you* doing here?'

'I sort of live here, most of the time. It's incredible to see you.' She was gaping with wide eyes, and looked around at the others. 'Everyone, this is my old friend – from when I was little. My oldest friend . . . We sort of lost each other.' The others smiled and looked at me with new curiosity.

I smiled back and shrugged. 'Long time.'

Deborah touched my arm and frowned teasingly. 'Where've you *been*?'

We left the others and went into the room with the sofa. I found it hard to stop staring at her, marvelling both that it was *her* and at how she was now, definitely, an adult. Her face had angles that hadn't been there before – a hardening of her nose and cheekbones – and her brown hair was longer and fell thickly to her shoulders. And she was so tall. She seemed taller than me – I looked, we were the same height, but she was so slim she seemed taller.

She chuckled, showing her gums and wrinkling her nose; that hadn't changed, but her gestures, and the way she moved her eyes, were more mature – graceful and feminine. She shook her head. 'You look just the same . . . It's incredible . . . I didn't think I'd see you again – ever.'

'Nor did I . . . Think I'd see *you*, I mean. You look great . . . You're so . . . tall.'

We were standing a foot or two apart. She came closer and hugged me, her arms around my neck and her cheek against mine. I held her waist lightly, our bodies not touching. I felt oddly elated, a little as though I had suddenly found a favourite object, a book or a picture – something that had intrigued me long ago – that I had mislaid and forgotten about. But I was wary; naturally, she had changed. Would I like the new Deborah? I had been so fond of the old Deborah. Was this sufficiently the same person?

We sat down on the sofa and talked. Her father had died a year after they left Marlow, and she had lived with her mother and grandmother in Chippenham. She had gone to school, made some friends, but it had never felt like home – and still didn't. Then she had won a scholarship to Chelsea Art School; she loved London, the galleries, the people, the streets and shops. Chas was her boyfriend – he did some teaching at Chelsea – and, though she had a room in a hall of residence, she spent most of her time here, in his flat. I told her what had happened to me and my parents, and we spent some time working out how long it was since we had last seen each other.

Chas came in. 'I've known this man since I was a little girl, but haven't seen him for more than four years.'

'Incredible.' He smiled as though he meant it, and sat

down on the arm of the sofa. 'Maybe tonight was preordained by the great Yahweh.' He looked upwards and pointed towards the ceiling. He wasn't good-looking, but there was humour and kindness in his mouth and in the way he moved his eyes. I guessed he was about Peter's age, twenty-five. He put his arm round Deborah and looked at me. 'We're going out to get something to eat. Come along, if you want . . . Pete's coming. Probably go to Dino's.'

Before we left the flat, Chas wrapped his artwork carefully in brown paper and handed it to me formally. 'Don't leave it in the caff. That transparency is unique. *I* took it.' He laughed. 'In California.'

Crammed together in a booth, six of us ate spaghetti and drank Valpolicella. I sat at the end by the aisle, opposite Peter and next to Deborah. I kept glancing at her profile; there was a gently curving ridge in her nose that hadn't been there when she was a child. I caught her looking at me and we both smiled. I felt more confident. This *was* my old friend, wasn't it? She had just grown up a little; that was all. I apologised for not answering her letter all that time ago, and told her about the day I had gone to look for her and found a strange man behind the sweetshop counter.

We listened to the others talking about their LP. All the songs had been recorded on to a master tape, and Chas and Peter were arguing about the ordering of the tracks. Eric didn't seem to care; Deborah whispered that he played the bass and was very easy-going. Chas and Peter wrote all the songs; some of them were joint compositions, but some, it was obvious, weren't. Deborah told me quietly that it didn't matter what order the songs came in; they were all good, Chas was a brilliant guitarist and she was certain the record would be a hit.

She ate very slowly, apparently avoiding the spaghetti, picking out just the cheese and tomatoes and olives, and told me about Chris, the group's drummer, who modelled himself on someone called Joe Morello who drummed with Dave Brubeck. Chris lived in the flat too. I wondered whether Peter, who lived alone in a big, chaotic room in the Fulham Road, was in some ways an outsider.

A sharp wind blew in our faces as we wandered back down Earls Court Road. Deborah and I arranged to meet at Finch's the next Saturday at eight – Chas and the others would be playing a concert in St Albans that night. As we said goodbye, she touched my shoulders and, for a moment, rested her cheek against mine; she was cold and shivering.

Peter and I walked down Redcliffe Gardens. 'Can't tell you how great it is to have found Deborah again. Fantastic luck that you play with Chas and the others.' I had the brown paper parcel in one hand and slapped Peter's back with the other.

'She's a sweetie, Deborah. But she's got a problem. You ought to know.' He swept his hair behind his shoulder. 'She's too keen on the old smack.'

'Smack!'

'Heroin.'

'Jesus.' I knew what smack was. 'What do you mean? She's an addict?'

He nodded. 'Looks that way. Chas thinks so. He's worried about it, very . . . and feels guilty.'

'Shit. Shit, shit, shit.' I hated the idea of Deborah being taken over by a drug. I started walking more slowly. 'Why's he feel guilty?'

'Well, he gave her her first hit, didn't he? He just didn't think she'd get so keen . . . We all do it now and again. Well, I don't any more, actually.'

'So . . . can he do anything about it? Chas.'

'They don't keep any there any more. She cleaned them out anyway. But she gets it. She stole some money the other week.'

'Jesus.'

'From another kid in college. Chas took her to a doctor. So she gets prescriptions for methadone, but they say it's not working . . . It's a bloody shame, mate. She's such a sweet kid – and can she draw! She'd be a star if she could get hold of herself.'

We turned into the Fulham Road and walked on for a minute in silence. 'Well, what can *I* do? I must be her oldest friend. We were almost brother and sister.'

'Dunno . . . Talk to her. Be her friend . . . We all do that. We're like a bunch of uncles and aunts. She's so young.'

'She's eighteen.'

'I know.'

'She's only been in London about six months.'

'It doesn't take long, if you really like it . . . And don't ever give her money – however much she whines and wheedles.'

We reached his flat and he asked me in. It was late and I had work the next morning. We stood on the doorstep for a while talking about Deborah and heroin, but I learned nothing more – except that Chas had repaid the money she had stolen and persuaded the college to take no action; and that if it happened again, the police could be involved.

~

I waited for Deborah for more than an hour at Finch's that Saturday. Then I walked over to the flat. As before, the front door was open, but the only light came from the end of a corridor off the hall. I peered round a door into a room dimly lit by a standard lamp. It had a bare wood floor. An easel with a pencil drawing of a still life stood in one corner, three or four guitars were leaning against the wall and several speakers and amplifiers were piled on top of each other.

Someone was lying under some blankets on a low double

bed. I knocked on the door and the person moved a little, but didn't look up or speak. I tiptoed to the bed.

'Deborah.' I said her name quietly in the silence.

She sat up, stared at me and put her hand on her forehead. 'My God. My God. David. What time is it?'

'Just after half-past nine.'

'What are you doing here?'

'We were going to meet. It's Saturday. Remember?'

Her eyes were open very wide and she was staring at me, as though my presence was alarming or even frightening. She was wearing a black T-shirt. 'I'm sorry. Yes. I must have fallen asleep.' She lay back down.

'Do you want to go out? Or do you just want to go back to sleep?'

She frowned. 'I can't go out. I can't.' She put her hand over her eyes. 'I'm not very well.'

'What's wrong?' I thought of sitting down beside her, but decided to stay standing up.

'Don't know. Don't feel good at all . . . Some kind of bug.' She sat up again and stared around the room. She seemed a little panicky.

'Can I get you anything?'

She leant over the side of the bed and rapidly pulled things out of a small leather bag, dropping them on the floor. It was as though she was angry about something and was taking it out on her keys, address book, make-up, comb. She found a brown envelope, pulled a piece of paper from it, and held it towards me. 'Please, get this for me.' I took it and she lay down. It was a prescription from a doctor in Lillie Road.

I looked at my watch. 'It's quarter to ten.'

She turned on her side and hugged her knees under the blankets. 'There'll be somewhere open.' I looked at her and down at the prescription. The doctor's writing was the usual scrawl, but there was a word that looked like methadone. 'I'm sorry . . . David. I'm really ill. If there is nowhere else, could you get to Boots, Piccadilly Circus? It never shuts.'

'The Chelsea Drug Store is open.'

'Yeah? Never been there.' She stared at me. 'Anywhere. Please.' She turned away again. 'I think I'm going to die otherwise.'

I wondered what would have happened if I hadn't come round. Would she have gone on sleeping and not wanted the drug? Would Chas have come back and gone to Piccadilly Circus at one o'clock in the morning? 'All right.' I put the blanket over her. She had shut her eyes. On a whim, I kissed her forehead; it was cold and I could feel her sweat on my lips. I went down to the Chelsea Drug Store to get her prescription filled.

I got back just before midnight. I had stood for an hour in a slow-moving queue with other methadone users – or perhaps their friends – and a couple of men whose children needed cough medicine; the pharmacist had had to hand-write a label with detailed dosage instructions for every opaque brown bottle.

Deborah didn't seem to have moved but she was awake, blinking rapidly and clenching and unclenching her fingers on the sheet. She raised her head, said 'thanks' very loudly and reached for the bottle. It was in a white paper bag.

'I'll pour it for you in the kitchen.' I walked towards the door.

'I can swig it. I know the dose.' She sat up.

'No. I might as well make sure it's right.' I walked to the kitchen and rinsed a glass and a spoon. She came and stood beside me. She tapped on the draining board and I could see her shivering. I measured the liquid into the glass and put the cap back on the bottle.

'That's not enough, David.' She frowned at me and stamped her feet. She was wearing just the black T-shirt and a pair of knickers; her legs were long and too thin.

'It's what it says on the label, which is what your doctor wrote on the prescription.' I tried to sound unconcerned and held out the glass.

She took it, drank the methadone straight down and stood with her eyes raised to the ceiling and the glass in her hand. I put the bottle in my pocket. 'OK. Thanks.' She swilled out the glass in the sink and walked quickly from the room. 'I'll be back in a minute.' I put the bottle in a cupboard beside a jar of Marmite and filled the kettle.

As I sipped scalding instant coffee, I could hear her running a bath. I sat down and looked idly at a three-day-old copy of the *Evening Standard*. Minutes later, I heard her walking about the flat and then the sound of *Sergeant Pepper*.

She came into the kitchen. She still seemed tense, but she looked better; she had combed her wet hair and was wearing blue jeans, a thick grey sweater over a white T-shirt, socks – or tights – and scuffed brown shoes. She looked at me with a taut, apologetic smile. 'Would you like some more coffee?' She picked up my mug.

'Sure.'

I stood beside her as the kettle boiled. 'I'm sorry.' She spoke without looking at me.

'It's all right.' I didn't know what else to say. I had been shocked when Peter had told me of her addiction, but that hadn't prepared me for what I had felt earlier – when I found her and as I tramped the streets and returned with the bottle – fear, anger, and a little pity. Now I felt some relief as well.

She carried the coffee to the living-room and sat down on a rug beside the stereo, and turned the sound down a little. I sat on the sofa, facing her. 'I know what you're doing. Peter told me.'

'He wouldn't know.'

'He does. They all know – the whole group, they're very worried about you . . . You must know that.' She drank her coffee and looked at the floor without speaking. '*I'm* worried about you too.'

'Well, it's all right. I've stopped.' She shook her head angrily. 'It's over. I'm doing the methadone . . . thing. Have you got any cigarettes?' I handed her one and lit it. 'There's nothing else to say . . . It's under control.' She pulled nervously on the cigarette.

'Three hours ago you said you were going to die.' She turned *Sergeant Pepper* up, and picked at a strand of her hair and stared at it. 'Look, I'm your oldest friend. Maybe I can help.'

She went on playing with her hair.

I remembered something. 'By the way, Teresa sends her love and said to send her a postcard.'

'Teresa?' She looked up at me, frowning.

'From Marlow. She said she was your best friend.'

'When—?' She was looking at her hair again, holding it in front of her face. I saw that she was crying, though she made no sound. The record ended and the pick-up clicked back into place. She stood up with her fists clenched by her sides. 'Oh God!' It was a high-pitched whine.

I stood up. 'Deborah?' She ran from the room. I followed more slowly. 'You all right?' A door slammed. I could hear a tap running.

I went back into the room with the sofa and thought about turning *Sergeant Pepper* over – and decided not to. After a few minutes she returned and smiled properly for the first time that evening. 'I'm sorry.'

I said it was OK and we sat down at either end of the sofa.

'I'm a fool, but I'm trying not to be any more.' She got up and turned the record over.

'Sure.' I didn't know her as I once had. I wondered whether we would ever get back to the easy friendship where she said things I wasn't expecting and held my hand as if she hardly noticed it. It didn't seem likely. I had been going to ask whether she remembered our plan to go to Swan River, Manitoba – but that had been when I had thought we would meet for a drink and a chat. A part of me wanted to take her away somewhere and look after her, feed her methadone until she was better, and let her out into the wild again like a beautiful bird with a mended wing – she was beautiful now, even though she was so thin. But I knew it was a stupid dream; I knew nothing about addiction or heroin, had nowhere for her to live – and didn't even know her very well any more. And she had Chas. He seemed nice. He could look after her – as long as he kept caring. I wondered when he would come back.

'What's the matter? You look sad.'

'Oh, I'm all right. I was just . . .' – I wondered if I should say it – '. . . thinking . . . I don't know you so well any more.'

'Oh! . . . Well, you will. We can see each other a lot.' She reached over and took my hand, squeezed it and put it down gently. 'I'm so glad you're around again . . . You've been great tonight. I'm sorry I was such a mess . . . but I'm still me . . . and you're you.' Perhaps I didn't look convinced. 'You are. You're just older . . . that's all . . . and so am I, but I'm no different, whatever you might think.'

Maybe she was right; people didn't change that much. I forced a smile, leaned forward and slapped my knees. 'You're right.'

'Why don't we meet one evening next week? I promise I'll be there.'

'OK, but . . .' I smiled more genuinely. 'I'll take the phone number, just in case.'

She went into the kitchen and came back with two glasses and the remains of a bottle of red wine.

'Is it OK for you to drink with the . . . you know?'

'Yeah. There's not much here anyway.'

We drank and talked – about drawing, Chas, our parents, our old town. She said she'd love to see my mother again, and my father, and maybe go back to Marlow sometime. She seemed lively then, more like my old friend. When the wine was finished, she said there was no need for me to stay; Chas and the others would be back soon and she would be all right. I said that I'd stay until they arrived.

She smiled. 'Don't you trust me? I don't even know where you put my methadone.'

'Of course I do.' I wasn't sure whether I did or not. 'It's next to the Marmite.'

I asked whether she remembered our plan to go to Swan River, Manitoba.

She did and she mentioned my grandfather and La Frascetti, though she had forgotten her name.

I told her that her drawing was now hanging in my room at my father's, how I had had it all through school, how Snape had polished the glass and that boys used to touch La Frascetti's chest for good luck.

She laughed and suggested we go to Swan River when I had my holiday from work in the summer.

I was wondering how serious she was – and whether I, or she, could afford the trip – when we heard footsteps and voices in the hall. The rock group had returned, tired and grumbling about their audience. Peter was taking the van home and offered me a lift. Deborah wrote down the phone number and kissed my cheek.

In the van I told Peter what had happened and how Deborah had said that she would follow the methadone treatment.

'Well . . . let's hope she sticks to it.' He didn't sound hopeful.

April was cool that year, but from the beginning of May the London air warmed slowly to a long climax of hot days and nights which lasted from the end of June until well into September. The King's Road boutiques were filled with beads, kaftans, bells and colourful cotton scarves – for men to wear knotted around their necks. Pat wore all of the gear most of the time; Peter the Painter had a bell around his neck that made him sound like a cow on a Swiss mountainside, and happily endured the barracking of the older regulars in the Goat in Boots; I hid a tiny bell on a strip of leather under my shirt and a red cotton scarf, and pretended to be surprised when people heard its subtle tinkle. The scent of joss sticks and marijuana and the sounds of 'A Whiter Shade Of Pale' and 'San Francisco – Be Sure To Wear Some Flowers In Your Hair' pervaded Chelsea, Kensington and Notting Hill, and people were buying the magazine that I helped to stick together with Cow gum.

Though I didn't dress like an archetypal hippie, I embraced what they believed in and had the exhilarating feeling that the world was changing for the better, that I was part of something significant and was, myself, helping a little to bring it about.

Drugs were a part of it. But to me, they weren't important. I consumed other people's from time to time, but the overreaction of the establishment – made known to all by the sentencing of Mick Jagger to prison for possessing four tablets of speed, bought legally in a chemist's shop in Italy – reinforced the view that the authorities were oppressive and too cynical to believe in the possibility of peace, let alone universal love.

It all seemed very straightforward to me, as it did to many of my peers: those who wanted to imprison Jagger were the allies of those who were so keen to destroy communism that they would kill and maim children in Vietnam and send their own sons to do it. As Martin put it in one of the cartoon strips I sat waiting for him to complete, they were imprisoned by their own tiny minds. Those people, we thought, couldn't imagine a world where everyone loved everyone and there was no need for nationalism or wars. We could see that – and bring it about: by example, by having fun, and by defining everyone as our neighbour.

Personally, I thought the new world should be organised on the principles of anarchism as described by Bertrand Russell in *Roads to Freedom*. That no one agreed with me on that detail didn't reduce the excitement and energy that came from believing – for a short time, but for longer than just that summer – that somehow people would understand the bigger message and that the world would change.

~

Deborah and I met often for a while, and gradually I came to see her objectively for the first time. When I was younger, she had just been there, my supportive friend, who was funny and had a vivid imagination. Now I saw that she was exceptional – talented and clever – and had an unusual desire to explore and understand things, many of which I knew nothing about. She was interested in R. D. Laing and Marshall McLuhan, and lent me a book that I struggled to make sense of: *Memories, Dreams, Reflections* by Carl Jung. And she came closer than anyone to agreeing with me about anarchism – and was the only person who, on my recommendation, actually read *Roads to Freedom*.

When I told my mother that I had found Deborah she immediately asked us both to dinner at her flat. She provided wine and the two of them talked animatedly about art. Later, when we were alone, my mother said she thought Deborah and I would make 'a good pair' – even though she was concerned about her thinness and the way she picked at her food. We were certainly good friends again but, even if Chas had not been around, I couldn't imagine any other form of relationship.

I took to dropping in at the flat in Earls Court and became friendly with Chas, and realised that, to a degree, he was her mentor as well as her lover. He looked at me with sad eyes and said how much he regretted making her aware of smack. He admired her talent and her intelligence and said he thought she was on some kind of quest, which he hoped she would resolve. Meanwhile she was vulnerable; he wanted to make her happy, but wasn't sure how.

I had seen no more signs of smack; when we arranged to meet, she always turned up, pale and smiling, in an afghan coat, with a red and black knitted bag on her shoulder. But then one night her head kept drooping and she fell asleep while I was talking to her in Finch's; it was only half past eight. She seemed groggy when I woke her, and I walked her home. On another occasion, late at my flat, she asked me to lend her a pound for a taxi, and became angry, almost panic-stricken, when I didn't respond instantly. Ruefully, Chas told me that she was back on smack. There seemed nothing I could do, except talk to her.

Late one evening, she told me that she expected to kill herself within a year; she saw no point in life. She was frighteningly lucid and, though I argued for most of the night, I couldn't convince her – or indeed myself – that there was a point. It seemed to be a matter of belief, rather than reason.

She didn't mention suicide again, and there were times when she was wholly the person I knew and used to rely on, but other times when it seemed that part of her was obliterated, replaced by panic or by the drug which made her seem as if she were sleepwalking. Unintentionally, imperceptibly, I began to see her less often.

~

On a warm night, late that summer, I went to a party in Battersea and stood holding a wine glass in a garden as darkness came on. A woman came towards me, peering into the gloom; she was holding a lighted cigarette. 'That you, David?' She had an Australian accent. It was Kate, Bonnie's flatmate. We moved towards a light. Her skin was brown and her blonde hair had got blonder. As we talked, she said how sorry she was about what had happened with Bonnie.

I raised my shoulders. 'It's in the past.'

She told me that Bonnie had moved in with Bob, the American producer, and that, though they still worked in the same office, she had grown tired of Bonnie; she was too openly ambitious, and too frivolous at the same time. Kate raised her eyebrows and pulled down her mouth, and apologised for being bitchy.

We got bored with the party and went for dinner at an Indian restaurant, where she talked about her boyfriend who only came to London once a month from Warwick where he was a graduate student. His name was Johnny Holly.

After that evening, we went out together often for many months. She loved music and dancing and our favourite places were the new psychedelic ones, UFO and Middle Earth, and sometimes, after midnight, we went to hear jazz at Ronnie Scott's. I discovered that Bonnie's Stan Getz and Dave Brubeck records were in fact Kate's. 'Bonnie had never heard of Stan Getz until she met me.' With Kate, I felt free to confess that, until I met Bonnie, I hadn't heard of him either.

She was faithful to Johnny Holly and I tried to convince myself that I was content with that. But during the winter, when we had been close for some time, I found that I was in love with her. It was an obsession that had accrued gradually; I loved her company and her view of life – and I wanted more of her. I knew that I was in love because I just couldn't stop myself taking the bold steps of saying so and writing letters telling her why and how wonderful she was. I dismissed what I had felt for Bonnie just a year earlier as a delusion. This was real love, not a sudden passion.

But Kate couldn't reciprocate; she loved Johnny Holly. She couldn't give me back what I wanted to give her, and I couldn't stop demanding it. A few weeks after I declared my love, I ended our friendship because it made me miserable. She told me I was mad.

As they had done about a year before, Dave fed me pints of beer and Peter the Painter gave me advice. 'What you felt for Kate really *was* love – not lust. I can see that, because you went out with her for months without thinking about lust, didn't you?'

I nodded feebly, wondering whether that was really true.

24

Treading Softly

DURING THOSE HOT months of 1967 I visited my father from time to time, but always felt that I didn't go often enough. He was grateful for my sporadic appearances and made a show of not putting pressure on me to see him more often which, of course, added to my feelings of guilt.

On a Saturday afternoon in August, I suggested we drive to Marlow and perhaps walk by the river. I felt like being outside; the temperature was in the eighties and the sky was clear. By then, driving somewhere and taking a short, slow stroll was the best way to be outdoors with him; he had taken to walking with a stick – though he stressed that his stick didn't have a rubber knob on the end, unlike those of real geriatrics.

He liked the idea. 'We could go to the lock and buy ice creams, like we did when you were little.'

Before we started I wound down all the Cresta's windows, and my father handed me his tobacco tin and took his jacket off; he was wearing his hat, a white shirt and royal blue braces. We drove slowly along the A40 towards High Wycombe among the caravans and loaded roof racks of an endless stream of holidaymakers. As the fan blew the warm air from outside into our faces, my father cursed the caravan in front of us and all the other traffic and threw his hat over his shoulder on to the back seat.

Rolling him a cigarette, I asked what he thought about anarchism, thinking he would broadly approve.

'Anarchism! More right-wing than the bloody Tories.' He

pulled out in the hope of overtaking the caravan. 'Traffic both ways. Curse it.' He lifted his hands momentarily from the steering wheel.

'I thought it was more left-wing than communism.'

He pulled back in line with the caravan. 'Well, it's total *laissez faire*, isn't it? And isn't that a recipe for rich people doing what they like – devil take the hindmost?'

'But, if everyone behaved decently—'

'The trouble is they won't.' He tapped his ash out of the window and glanced at me quickly; I must have looked disappointed. He smiled. 'That's the problem, Sunny Jim. The only thing that will interfere with the greed of the rich is giving power to the poor.' He flicked the indicator; we were taking the side road from Holtspur to Bourne End. 'Anarchism is all very well as a model, but it could only ever be achieved by changing human nature – completely and utterly.'

He turned off the A40 and suddenly we could see for three or four miles, across the Thames to Winter Hill and the woods around Cookham. The sun was high above the trees across the river and my father flipped down the sun visor.

We were soon sitting in stationary traffic in Bourne End, and I persisted in arguing that anarchism could work and that human nature – whatever that was – could change. My father was gently dismissive; possibly it could change a little, but only very slowly indeed, imperceptibly, as people became better educated. He had read *Roads to Freedom* soon after I gave it to him at Christmas, and pointed out that Bertrand Russell had written the book long ago, in 1918, and, even then, had thought that anarchism was an impractical dream.

The traffic still didn't move, and he cursed and wiped sweat from his forehead as a police car edged past, its siren wailing. He talked about Bakunin, whom he called the father of anarchism, and Rousseau who had advocated that everyone should live in the woods, like primitive tribesmen; eventually Rousseau had gone mad. He smiled. 'You won't go mad old chap, will you? You can't save the world by yourself, you know.'

I didn't answer. I watched some children queuing to buy ice creams and felt hot and irritated.

He turned the engine off and pulled on the hand-brake. 'I like that new magazine you're working on, but – and I know I've said it before – I wish they'd stop telling people to take drugs. You aren't taking any of those drugs are you? Pot, lysergic acid?'

I lied to reassure him, as another police car squeezed past.

He pointed at it and said he hoped they would hurry up and get the traffic moving. He nudged me in the ribs. 'In an anarchic state, we would sit here for ever.'

'No, everyone would get out of the way without needing the police to tell them.'

He laughed. 'And there'd be no traffic lights, and everyone would wave each other on out of sheer good nature, I suppose.'

I couldn't help smiling, but I was still worrying away at anarchism and the hippies and universal love. As the traffic started to move, I asked him *why* he didn't have more faith in human nature. The answer seemed to involve original sin.

We passed a motorbike lying on its side amid an array of flashing blue lights. Two men in white coats squatted beside a man on a stretcher at the side of the road. As we drove on, along the flat road to Marlow, a warm breeze came through the windows. A group of Friesians moved lazily in the shade of some trees towards the river, and the Marlow Donkey, the two-carriage train that shuttled between Marlow and Bourne End, chuffed by going the other way. I trailed my hand outside the window, cooling it in the wind. His mention of original sin was somehow demoralising; it made me wonder whether it was possible ever to have a new idea – whether it hadn't all been thought already, hacked over interminably since Aristotle and Plato.

As we came into Marlow, my father turned off the main road and deftly found his way through the familiar little streets. He stopped the car beside an old brick wall, a few yards from the gravel path that led to the lock. I wound the windows up while he stretched, picked up his stick and put his hat on. He gazed down the road at the cedar tree, the smooth lawn and the big, old house that had been Uncle George's home. He waved his stick towards it, saluted with his left hand and muttered, 'God bless you.'

We bought ice creams from the van at the end of the path. It had its bonnet open and its engine running. My father told the man inside how, when he had been an ice-cream man, he had been able to turn the engine off at every stop because the fridges were cooled by huge blocks of ice. The man nodded politely and turned away to serve some children.

We licked at our 99s as we climbed to the crest of the curved wooden footbridge. There my father stopped to survey the river, the weir, the bridge and the church. He waved his stick. 'One of my favourite views in all the world.' It was a scene that he had painted and photographed several times. It also appeared on postcards and tea towels. He took a deep breath through his nose and let it out through his mouth. 'Beautiful day for it, Sunny Jim.' He hooked his stick over the balustrade and put his arm on my shoulder. A line of pleasure boats was waiting to use the lock, and four or five swans were paddling by the bank near the yew tree in the graveyard. I put my arm lightly round his waist – and realised that I was taller than him, just a little; my eyes were level with the brim of his hat.

We walked on and sat on a bench beside the lock. The ice cream was dripping on to our fingers. Eight small boats filled the lock and we watched them rise gradually towards us, as water poured in through the sluices. A fat man in a peaked cap sat on a stool behind the wheel of a boat called *Lorelei*, and shouted self-importantly to a tired-looking girl with a rope in her hand. The lock-keeper smiled and looked on with his hands on his hips.

I became aware that my father was looking in my direction, and saw that he was frowning – not at me, but at the ground by my feet, or at something he was thinking. He looked up at me with a curious smile. 'Tread softly because you tread on my dreams.'

'What?'

'That's what you're thinking, isn't it? Yeats. I've been treading on your dreams. I'm sorry.' He put his hand on my shoulder. 'You are a clever boy. You must dream your dreams – and put them into practice if you can. Take no notice of what an old man thinks.'

He must have seen something in my face. I felt sad, but tried not to show it. He was seventy-five and I was nearing nineteen. I gripped his arm near his shoulder; I could feel hard muscle – formed by the daily typing of his thoughts.

Later, after he had chatted to the lock-keeper and I had helped to push the heavy grey beams that opened the lock gates, we sat on the other side and he told me that he had, at last, found his father's letters. He had gone through all his desk drawers, his two four-drawer filing cabinets and numerous cardboard boxes. They had been in the bottom drawer of the chest where he kept his clothes, in his bedroom. He thought they had probably been there since 1942, though the chest had been moved many times; he would have put them there after reading them, soon after his mother died.

'I've read through them. There are only five from Swan River, but they give a little idea of what his life was like, if you're still interested. Rough and hard, I would say.'

'I *am* still interested. What about our idea of going there?'

He looked at the ground and didn't answer.

'Remember?'

He shook his head slightly and looked at me sideways. 'I'm too old. I really am. I'd slow you down . . . but you go, if you want to. Take photographs and tell me about it.'

'I'll go some time. I'm not sure when, but I'll go. But you come with me – you'd be all right – if you want to.'

He shook his head again. 'No. I'm not up to it. It's too far.'

I looked past him; a group of children were pushing on a beam, slowly opening one of the giant gates. He had never before declared himself incapable of doing anything.

Beyond the footbridge, on the lawn outside the big room where I had first heard the words 'Swan River, Manitoba', old people were sitting at tables having tea; a man in a white jacket stood in the doorway holding a jug of orange squash.

Back at home, my father handed me a brown envelope. 'Have a look. They don't tell you much, but you might be interested.' He went off to the kitchen to make tea. The envelope was addressed to him at an office in High Wycombe; it had been posted in London in 1942. There seemed to be about ten letters, old and folded, written on flimsy paper of different sizes. I unfolded one carefully. There were several cream-coloured sheets, about the size of a page in a paperback book and faintly lined in green. The first page was headed 'Durban, Manitoba, Canada' and dated 14 October 1906, the year my mother was born – she would have been four months old then, and my father would have been two months from his fifteenth birthday.

My grandfather had small, sloping handwriting, and used black ink and a nib that produced fat strokes in one direction and thin ones in the other. The letter began 'Dear George' – presumably Uncle George – 'After leaving Winnipeg I got to Swan River, 319 miles at 11 p.m.' It went on to say that the next day he had walked twelve miles to Durban, where he had started work on the Thunder Hill branch of the Canadian Northern Railway. I looked at the last page. The writing was larger. There was a bold number 6 at the top, in the middle. At the bottom, with some flourishes on the capitals, was written 'Yours sincerely T. Clifton Reynolds'.

My father came in with tea and a packet of fruit shortcake biscuits, and I asked him why the letter came from Durban and not Swan River. He said that Tom had actually lived in Durban; that had been his address: just Durban, Manitoba, Canada. Durban was a small village and Swan River was the local town. I would see, if I read the letters.

I knew my father had last seen Tom in 1902, on the night he left with two suitcases and said, 'I'll see you before long.' The date of the letter revealed that four years had passed before Tom went to Swan River. I asked my father what had happened in those four years.

He sat back with Joey on his shoulder and told me that Sis and Old George hadn't allowed Tom to see him, and that Tom hadn't known where he lived. They had moved from Norfolk Road after Tom left – not far, to some rooms, upstairs in a house in Rectory Road, Stoke Newington. This had been a come-down for Sis, but was also a relief, quiet and peaceful with no rows or drunkenness – just her and Cliffie much of the time, and Old George when he was at home. Sis did all the housework; there were no servants and no mother's help. They had no gas, just candles and oil lamps which blew black smuts on to the walls and ceilings. Cliffie was ten years old and responsible for lighting the fires and the range, and he often fetched food.

My father laughed and talked about 'sheep's jimmies', which were half a boiled sheep's head and cost threepence ha'penny. They looked awful – he said I'd've hated them – but tasted delicious. He also remembered buying hot boiled pork with a pennyworth of pease pudding from a shop called Robinson's in Stoke Newington High Street. For that, he had often stood in a long queue with a bowl he brought from home.

He smiled as he bit into a fruit shortcake and recalled how on Saturdays Stoke Newington High Street had been full of hawkers. 'My grandfather would take us and say, "Come on, Sis. Let's you and me and Jim spend a golden sovereign." He was a spendthrift . . . like me, though not so bad.' He shook his head and went on smiling as he told me about 'the sixpenny ha'penny shop' where everything – chamber pots, kettles, rugs, huge boxes of candles – cost that curious sum. The shop was lit by paraffin flares, and customers had a clipper card which was clipped every time they bought something. For ten clips Sis used to get a free hardback book; she usually chose Dickens.

My father went to his bookshelves, pulled down a book and handed it to me – a small, fat copy of *Martin Chuzzlewit* with a dark blue binding. It had come from the sixpenny ha'penny shop. The type was tiny and black, and I tried to imagine Sis reading it in the light of an oil lamp. My father said they'd had lots of them when he was a boy; Tom had collected them too.

I asked about Tom – where had he been in those years before he went to Canada? Most of the time, my father told me, he had been homeless, a vagrant living on the streets of London. Sometimes he slept outdoors – on the embankment, my father guessed – and sometimes in a hostel for the poor, of which there were many, but even the poor had to pay something. He ate in soup kitchens where a meal cost a penny. He tried to get work of any kind, but there was a surfeit, even of labourers. His mother had died, and it seemed that only three people kept in touch with him: Uncle George, La Frascetti and his brother Bertie, the chess-player – his other brothers and sisters wouldn't see him because he was a drunk and an embarrassment. Old George had him sent away when he came to beg at his office in Shoreditch. But Uncle George gave him money from time to time, and La Frascetti took him out for meals and bought him clothes.

I was amazed that my grandfather had had to live like that, and the shock no doubt showed on my face.

My father stopped talking and stared at me for a few moments. 'You have to understand that there were lots of men in his situation then – and women and children. Thousands of them with nowhere to live, and many of them actually starving. I saw them when I went wandering in the real East End with Toppy, in East and West Ham, Canning Town, the docks, Plaistow; it was like Calcutta . . . There was a famous case where a starving man was arrested for stealing a few oats from a horse's nosebag.' He shook his head. 'It's not surprising the Labour movement got going around then.' He sat back and smiled a little. 'And my father was a well-qualified, reasonably educated man. He went to Canada to fill his belly. You read those letters . . . You'll see. Just about the only good thing he has to say about it is that he got good food and plenty of it.'

'I thought he went because he wanted to start a whole new life, or something. He just went for food?'

He raised his hands and shrugged, and explained that the Canadian government had been offering subsidised passages to Europeans who wanted to go there to work – especially on the railways which were rapidly expanding west. A ticket for Tom by boat and train from Liverpool to Winnipeg – which was where they had wanted people – had cost four pounds, a lot of money, despite the subsidy. Uncle George and a wealthy friend of Tom's brother Bertie had paid two pounds each.

I was surprised that I hadn't heard about this before.

My father held out his forefinger and Joey hopped on to it. He stroked the top of the bird's head for a few seconds, with his nose on his beak, then moved him away and looked back at me. 'You see, I didn't know any of this till years later.

They just told me he was all right and living in London, but that it was better if I didn't see him, and then that he had decided to go to Canada because he might be able to get a job there.' He waved his free arm towards the table. 'I didn't know those letters existed until years after he died. Two of them are to me. They just put them away and didn't tell me.' He was animated, but he didn't seem to mind that his father's letters had been kept from him. 'I don't blame them. He was just trying to make trouble; you'll see if you read them.'

I felt annoyed with Old George and Sis – on my father's behalf. 'Why didn't you tell me all this before?'

He seemed surprised. 'Well, I wrote all that stuff.'

'I know . . . That's great . . . Sorry, I'm not complaining.'

'Well . . . I suppose I didn't write about my father after he left, because there wasn't much to say – and it didn't involve me.' He stroked Joey again, and looked at the clock. 'Let's watch the six o'clock news. Keep those letters. Read them in London when you've got time.'

We didn't often watch the six o'clock news. He seemed tired. He hadn't had his usual nap and had been talking all afternoon.

~

On a Saturday early in the next year, 1968, my father called at our new London flat with a middle-aged woman and her eight-year-old son. The visit had been arranged several days before, and they arrived on time at noon. He had met the woman and the boy for the first time less than half an hour earlier on the steps of the Royal Court Theatre, and had driven them round to meet me – and, coincidentally, Dave. The idea was that he would marry this woman.

He had told me he wanted to get married because he wanted companionship and someone to cook for him – and, I gathered from his letters, he hoped for sex as well. He didn't know any women who would be likely to marry him, so he filled in a form and sent it to a marriage bureau with a cheque and his photograph, the studio portrait taken in 1947 for the cover of his *Autobiography* – the one that had sat, facing a photograph of my mother, close to my bed at boarding school.

I was required to make a good impression on my potential stepmother, and supply coffee and biscuits. I felt extremely uncomfortable. I would have been pleased if, in a more natural way, he had come across a nice woman – one who thoroughly understood what she was letting herself in for – and married her. But this approach to marriage seemed crazy and very unlikely to succeed. As well as supplying a deceptive photograph, he had lied about his age on the form; the woman would be expecting a fit man in his early sixties, instead of a very deaf one, aged seventy-six, who walked with a stick. I felt sorry for the woman, even before I met her.

Dave – who could easily have stayed in his room, or gone out, for an hour – was supportive and amused; we dusted and hoovered the flat and went shopping for biscuits. When the bell rang, Dave lit the gas under the kettle and I opened the door. My father was wearing a white shirt and the tie he had worn on the New Year's Eve before last, his old suit and a tight, beige overcoat with brown leather buttons that was someone else's cast-off – and he wasn't carrying his stick. The woman had a hat and looked cross, and my sense that she disapproved of me, as well as of my father, was intensified by the black-rimmed glasses that rose at a steep angle from the bridge of her nose. The boy was small with an intelligent face and looked awkward in a grey flannel suit with short trousers.

There was no sitting-room, so I led them into my bedroom and invited the woman to sit down in my rickety armchair. My father sat on my desk chair and the boy and I sat next to each other on a low sofa. We managed to talk for a minute or two about the GPO sorting office next to our building and how the vans made a lot of noise during the night. Then I found out that the woman lived in Chiswick and my father talked about one of his cousins who had once lived there. The little boy turned his head sideways and stared at my 'Legalise Cannabis – The Putting Together of the Heads – Hyde Park Stone Free Concert' poster, from the previous summer; Dave and I had discussed taking it down, but had decided that the lettering was so psychedelic that none of our guests would be able to read it.

It was a lugubrious gathering until Dave came in carrying a tray. 'Don't often have coffee parties.' He beamed at everyone with raised eyebrows. 'Thought perhaps I should wear an apron. Now, what would sir like? Custard cream or chocolate digestive?' He bent over the little boy who smiled for the first time and took a biscuit. 'And would sir like coffee, or I have a very good orange squash?' Even the woman smiled a little, while retaining her pained expression.

Somehow, we got through half an hour and then, at last, they left to have lunch at a restaurant in Battersea Park. I shut the door on them and went back to Dave. He looked at me, and started to make a hooting noise and wave his arms about.

I didn't think it was funny. 'What does he think he's doing? That poor woman and that sweet little boy.'

'That woman's face. Oh dear, I think I'm going to die.' He held his stomach. 'I've never seen anything . . .' – his face was screwed up and the hooting continued – 'like it . . . Did you see her when . . . when . . . your dad . . . said how he admired . . . Lenin?'

'What's going to happen now? She won't want to marry him.'

He shook his head and went on laughing. 'And he won't want to marry her. Oh dear . . . I don't think I'll ever recover.'

We went to the pub and recalled every agonising moment. I relaxed and began to laugh along with Dave; I could see that we had been involved in an exquisite farce, as well as a pathetic tragedy.

When we came back to the flat, my father was sitting alone in the Cresta outside. There had been no plan for him to return. He climbed out of the car, frowning. 'I've been sitting there for an hour. Was about to give up. Can I come in for a minute?'

I touched his shoulder. 'What happened?'

'I couldn't see behind properly in the car park at Battersea. Backed into another car. There was a bit of a bang, and she just got out and walked off with her boy. Didn't say a word.'

'Oh dear . . . I'm sorry about that.' I looked at the back of the car. There was a new dent in the bumper.

He glanced at it and shrugged. 'It's nothing serious. I'm dying for a pee.' Dave and I followed him slowly up the stairs. 'Ghastly woman, didn't you think? Unsmiling harridan. Wouldn't have married her for all the tea in Joe Lyons.'

'No, she wasn't my type – or yours, I wouldn't have thought.'

He went into the bathroom and left the door open. Dave disappeared and I hovered outside. He shouted over his shoulder. 'Nice little boy. Shame about his mother.'

He followed me into the kitchen and sat down. I made some tea and Dave came in and leaned against the wall. My father rolled a cigarette, drank the tea quickly and asked for another cup. He looked at Dave. 'Well, Dave. A narrow escape, I think, but thank you for doing the coffee and all that . . . Just sorry I wasted your time.'

Dave smiled. 'That's all right. It's nice to see you.'

My father looked round at me. 'I'm meeting another one next week.' He smiled.

25

Awareness Ends

I THOUGHT ABOUT GOING to Swan River that summer – I had two weeks' holiday before starting a new job. I decided, with some sadness, that I didn't want to go with Deborah; I didn't want to be alone with her for that long – at the moment, anyway. In the end I couldn't afford to go at all, and went to the Channel Islands with Dave and Pat instead.

When I returned, I found a letter from my half-sister Ann asking me to telephone her; my father had had a stroke and was in a hospital in Aylesbury. I sat on my bed with the letter in my hand. I felt weak and nauseous. I imagined he would soon die, if he hadn't already; the letter was a few days old.

I had contemplated his death often; for most of my life I had thought of it as something that would happen one day but not in any foreseeable future, and had wondered vaguely how I would feel. Since he retired, four years before, my sense of his death as a real possibility had grown gradually until, a year or two ago, I had begun to feel glad that he was alive every time I saw him or heard from him. When I parted from him, usually on his front doorstep, I felt sadness in a tingling wave through my arms and legs, not just because he seemed lonely, but because I was thinking, without willing to, that I might not see him again.

Ann said that he wasn't about to die, but that it was serious – he seemed to have lost some movement in his arms and legs and, though she couldn't define it, his brain appeared to have been affected a little; he didn't seem quite the same, though he could talk and even joke. He had been found lying on the floor in front of the fire by the woman who lived in the front part of the house; she had noticed the light on all night and hadn't heard him walking about as usual. He had been conscious, but hadn't been able to speak, and had been taken to Aylesbury in an ambulance. He had been there a week and had recovered to the point where he thought he should go home, but, Ann said, he certainly couldn't look after himself – not yet, and perhaps not ever.

I told her that I would go to see him the next day, Sunday, and she warned me that the hospital was grim and depressing; it catered for the elderly and incapable, and the mentally ill. She had been trying to get him moved to somewhere nicer and nearer to her.

~

It was a gabled, late-Victorian building on the edge of the town. A few shrubs flanked a tarmac entrance that led to a grimy swing door. I was taken to the threshold of a badly lit, high-ceilinged room with bare floorboards, in which there was nothing except a row of wooden chairs against each of the longer walls. I saw him immediately. He was sitting very upright on the nearest chair, some feet away, with his hand on his stick and his mouth open. His hair, which for years had been a steely grey, had turned almost white. I looked across the room to see what he was staring at; a young man in a grubby double-breasted jacket was rhythmically flicking his tie, up and down.

He smiled sweetly as soon as he saw me, and made an effort to stand up. I saw that someone had fitted a rubber knob on the end of his stick. 'So glad to see you.' His voice was hoarse. 'Thought you'd never come.' He grasped my hands.

'I'm sorry. I was on holiday. Ann didn't know where I was.' I sat down beside him and pulled the chair round so I could see him properly.

'I've got to get out of here. It's full of lunatics. Look at him.' He gestured towards the young man playing with his tie. 'He does that all day long – and I watch him.'

'Isn't there a television?'

'No. There's a dormitory, this place . . . and we eat in there.' He waved his stick towards a pair of swing doors. 'Horrible food. I've got to get out. It's killing me.'

'I know Ann's trying to arrange something. I'll talk to her. We'll get you somewhere better as soon as possible.'

'I want to go home.' He cleared his throat, but his voice remained a loud whisper. 'I'm all right. I shouldn't be here. Look at these people.' He glanced down the row beyond me. 'The old ones are senile and the young ones are mad.' He gestured at the other side of the room. I noticed for the first time that on my father's side of the room there were about eight old men staring into space and on the other side a similar number of younger men, many of whom I could see were handicapped.

He put his hand in his jacket pocket and took a long time to pull out his tobacco tin. 'Could you roll as many as you can with that?' I took it from him. 'Good chap. I find it difficult at the moment.' The tin was almost full of tobacco. I started rolling and asked him if he had any books. 'Ann brought some. They're in my cupboard. Find it hard to concentrate if I read for very long. She brought a Simenon. I like that.'

I handed him a cigarette and, with some difficulty and a little swearing, he managed to light it with his Ronson. I told him about my holiday and he seemed interested and told me he had dreamed that he was driving his car in Scotland; he thought he had been on his way to see his friend Robbie Robertson in Montrose. 'I'd like to be out driving my car . . . You could call a taxi and we could go home now.'

'Better not. You need looking after for a bit longer. You don't want all the trouble of cooking and washing up . . . and all that.' He shrugged with one hand; the other remained on his stick. I tried hard to think of something to talk about and made a comment about Czechoslovakia – the Russians had driven tanks into Prague two days before – though I didn't expect him to know about it.

'Disgraceful. I'm quite a fan of Dubçek. I'm losing faith in Russia – again. They're not proper communists; they're nearly as bad as Joe Stalin.'

'How did you know about that?'

'The *Guardian*. I get it every day. Read all of it before lunch . . . even the horse racing.' He smiled. 'Nothing else to do. I read that that awful man Nixon is likely to be the next President of the United States. God help us! . . . No *Guardian* today, though.' He raised his hand from his knee again. 'Look at that poor devil.' Across the room a man was screwing up his face and making grunting noises. 'I'll show you where I sleep.'

I helped him to stand up, and he took my arm as we walked slowly out the way I had come in and along a cream-painted corridor. He slept on an iron bedstead, the second in a row of six with six others facing. An old man was lying in the bed opposite looking at us. My father smiled, let go of my arm and raised his hand in a salute. The man's lips moved; he seemed to be trying to speak but there was no sound. My father turned away and said, 'Completely senile. Pop off soon, I expect.' He raised his eyebrows without smiling and pointed at the bed at the end of the row, next to his. It had no bedclothes – just a striped cotton sheet which fell to the floor on both sides. 'Chap in that bed died last night. Woke me up when they came and took him away . . . Though they tried to be quiet.'

I looked at the bed and back at the old man on the other side of the room.

My father sat down on his bed. 'Got my children here . . . some of them anyway.' He laughed. There was a frame on the cupboard beside his bed, with photographs of Ann, Madeline, my elder half-sister, and me on top of the hill in Somerset. 'Madeline's been to see me. She's marvellous; she knows how to talk to these people.' Madeline and her brother Bob, whose photograph wasn't in the frame, were his children from his first marriage. 'She'll get me out of here, if Ann doesn't.'

I hadn't seen Madeline for a few years; she was a physiotherapist who worked in a hospital for children with cerebral palsy – my father often described her as a saint.

'It all has to be kept tidy. The nurses are very bossy.' He opened the cupboard. The previous day's *Guardian* was underneath his washbag and a small pile of books. On a higher shelf were three one-ounce packets of A1 tobacco, some green Rizla papers, two bananas and a packet of fruit shortcake biscuits.

We wandered back to what was called the day room and soon afterwards I was politely asked to leave; visiting time was over and the patients had to have their tea. My father grasped both my hands. 'Come back quickly. There's a good chap.'

'I will.' I kissed his cheek.

'Ann's got Joey, you know.'

'Yes, I know.'

'Bye, old chap.'

I waved as I left the room. He lifted his arm and smiled.

I walked around the ground floor of the building, looking for a doctor, and found myself in a kitchen where a man directed me to the sisters' office. My father's ward sister was a small, energetic woman who readily agreed that he shouldn't be on her ward or in her hospital – which was for the mentally disturbed; they were trying to find him a room in an old people's home, but they were scarce and it could take time. When I asked if she thought he would get back to normal, she said that he had made progress but she wasn't qualified to say more.

I walked slowly towards the station with my eyes on the ground and my hands in my pockets. My eyelids felt heavy and I looked forward to closing them on the train – perhaps I would even sleep, though it was only six o'clock. I wanted him to get back his speed and his energy and his sense of fun – the humour he had shown today had been cynical and at times macabre. But then, a week ago he couldn't speak, and there was nothing funny about that place that wasn't related to madness or death – so perhaps it would all come back.

I phoned Ann when I got home. She had no more idea than I did whether he would get better, but didn't sound very confident. She said that she would keep badgering the county authorities to get him into a normal old people's home. I asked if she and her husband, Adrian, had any money to pay for him to go to a private one. She laughed drily. 'We've got two sons, David. The only person who might do that is your mother. Anyway, he wouldn't approve; he's a socialist.' She laughed again. I thought of reminding her of something he often used to say – 'I am not going to suffer from a system I despise' – but decided not to.

I didn't think my mother had any spare money – she was over sixty now and had stopped working – but I phoned to tell her what had happened to my father. She sounded concerned – a little for him, but mostly for me. I told her that I didn't feel like starting my new job – as editor of a small weekly paper called the *Freethinker* – the next day. I had been flattered that the managers of the National Secular Society who published it had placed their faith in me, and had been looking forward to it. But now it seemed like a nuisance; it was just something I had to do. She said that she was sure my father was proud of me and my new job – which I knew to be true – and would hate the idea of his illness sapping my energy.

A few days later my father was moved to an old people's home on the edge of Slough, and I went there the next weekend. He had his own room with white walls, a white bedspread and a window overlooking a large garden. He smiled more readily and was actually pleased with some aspects of the place. He liked some of the nurses and beamed with pride as he told me he had become friendly with a fellow patient, a woman who had read some of the books he had written – men and women were allowed to mix. Later, as we walked slowly along a path outside, he pointed to an old lady knitting on a bench; he put his hand beside his mouth and whispered loudly, 'My fan.' He nudged me and grinned.

We were told that, as well as the effects of his stroke, which made him clumsy and forgetful, he was suffering from hardening of the arteries which slowed all his movements. For a time I kept faith in the possibility of his getting better – back to normal, back to his home and his car, back to me. But soon, even I couldn't ignore the truth: drugs might keep his arteries open, but the part of his brain that had been destroyed would never grow back.

He became an amiable old man who took a long time – and often needed help – to do simple things such as eat or undo the zip on his trousers; but, as he always had, he continued to think, albeit very slowly, about the things that he thought mattered and to send me his ideas in letters and on postcards. And he took trouble to read the *Freethinker*, particularly my editorials, and send comments and messages of praise. He couldn't work his typewriter and his handwriting became increasingly unclear; lines of words, some of them very faint, meandered up and down the page and crossed over each other. I would examine them under a bright light through a magnifying glass, determined to understand, but frequently frustrated.

I tried to visit him every other weekend through that autumn, winter and spring, and sometimes Dave drove me down in his minivan and came in for a while to see him. As well as his 'fan', he had other friends at the home – he played cribbage with a man who had fought in the Battle of the Somme – and had visits from his friend the chemist, Wing Commander Hayes and Old Bowen. Now and again he would say that he wanted to go home – the rent was still being paid from his pension – and to drive the Cresta – which Ann was looking after – and when we said he wasn't yet well enough, he would shake his head and quickly seem to forget.

Early in that summer, of 1969, a doctor recommended that he have minor surgery because he was becoming incontinent. There was a risk in such an operation, but otherwise he would soon have to leave the home for a geriatric ward, where dealing with incontinence was part of the routine – and where he would have a bed instead of a room and encounter, once again, those who were crazy as well as old.

~

On the day after his operation I found him lying between crisp, white sheets in a long, white-painted ward. The room was filled with sunlight, and outside the windows were treetops and a flat blue sky. Two rows of beds, all of them neatly tucked and with the same intense whiteness, stretched towards a vanishing point beyond the furthest wall. Only one bed was occupied, half-way along on the right. His head was on the pillow and his eyes were moving rapidly; his cheeks were sunken and he looked much older and more tired than he had just a week before. He didn't notice me straight away. I leaned over him. 'Hello, Dad.'

He turned his head towards me and frowned. For a second he didn't seem to recognise me. Then his eyes focused. 'David?' His lips were dry, his voice a low croak. He moved his hand under the sheet.

'How are you feeling?'

He tried to clear his throat but it seemed to be too great

an effort. 'I've been driving my car.' He tried to bring his hand out from under the blankets. I reached over and put my hand on the sheet over his. 'On the road to Cookham.'

'Oh.'

'Yes.'

The only other person in the room was a dark-haired male nurse, whose immaculate white coat matched the whiteness of everything else. He had been at the other end of the ward when I arrived. Now he was standing at the end of the bed. 'Is very weak – your grandfather.'

'My father.'

'Sorry. He will take time to get better, to get strong.' He spoke with an Italian accent. 'Will stay here in bed many days. I look after him. His operation and his anaesthetic, they weaken him.'

'How long till he is up and walking about?'

'Is hard to say. A few days. A week. Doctors decide. Is nice for him to see you, but perhaps not stay too long. He is very tired.'

He smiled and walked quietly away. I turned back to my father. 'He says you need lots of rest. He seems nice.'

My father was looking at me. A smile just showed around his eyes. 'Nice of you to come – a long way.'

'It's not far. I wanted to see you.'

He moved his arm under the blankets. 'Hold my hand . . . please.' I pulled down the sheet, lifted his hand and smoothed the sheet back over his chest. His hand was dry and cooler than mine, but not cold. I squeezed it gently. The lines around his eyes deepened and his mouth moved towards a smile. I felt pressure on my hand and looked down. Those who noticed them had always admired his hands; they were large with long tapering fingers and elegant nails. His hand looked as it always had – bony and deep brown with some dark hairs towards his wrist.

'Who's that?' His mouth was open and he was looking

past me. 'Tell him to go away.' I looked round. The nurse was a few beds away. There was no one else. 'Tell him to stop grinning at me with his monkey face.' He had stopped smiling and looked frightened.

'Who? The nurse? He's over there.'

'That man . . . outside the window.'

My stomach tightened. There was no one outside the window. We were two floors above the ground.

'He's often there, making faces.'

'It's all right. There's no one there. Not really.' I hoped my voice didn't betray my dismay.

The nurse came over, smiling. 'There he is. Get him to go away.' Still smiling, the nurse walked off up the ward. My father seemed to relax. He squeezed my hand again. 'You're a good boy. Look after your old father.' His eyelids started to close. Then he opened them and looked at me. 'Thought I was in heaven when I woke up in here. Everything is white.' He seemed to smile as he shut his eyes again.

I waited a minute. He seemed to be asleep, so I let go of his hand and kissed him on the forehead. 'I'll see you soon.'

I spoke to the nurse on my way out, and asked why my father was the only patient in such a large ward. He told me that some of the men were watching television and others were outside, walking in the garden; the ward was for men recuperating after surgery – some of them were young and stayed only two or three days.

'My father imagined he saw a man outside the window. Has he done that before?'

'Yes. Then he thinks it is me. I come and I go away again. Then he is all right. Is the anaesthetic. In older person it takes longer to leave his system.'

I walked down the stairs and out into the sun. I wondered how much the nurse knew, whether my father would really improve once the anaesthetic had worn off. I had a sense that he would die soon, that this was the last stage of the process that had begun nearly a year before, and I thought about why I was not more upset. Presumably the shock had been his stroke, the end of the life I used to enjoy with him – and its repercussions had become apparent only gradually. Since then, the fumbling, nice man that he had become had not really been him. There had been small moments – a remark or a look, or a phrase on a postcard – but that was all.

I knew Ann had seen him that morning. I rang her from a telephone box and asked whether she thought he would get better.

She didn't know. The doctor had said that he hadn't recovered as they had hoped. She said that perhaps he shouldn't have had the operation, but then reminded herself, and me, of how he would have hated living in a geriatric ward and being completely incontinent.

I had a holiday planned, starting the next weekend. I told Ann that I thought he might die in that time, and that I should cancel it.

She laughed, nervously it seemed to me, and told me not to worry. 'He'll last two weeks.'

Later that week I phoned Ann again. She had been to see him and said he was a little better. I should go away, enjoy my holiday and not worry. She and Madeline would be visiting.

~

Four of us camped on a beach in Corsica, swimming in a turquoise sea, cooking on wood fires and shitting deep among pines. I seemed to be falling in love again. I phoned Ann from a glass cubicle in a square in front of a church. 'Daddy's a little better. Don't worry. Enjoy yourself. Phone me when you're back.'

I got home very late and was woken by the telephone early the next morning. It was Ann. 'I'm glad you're back.

He's not at all well. They've moved him to another ward, on the ground floor.'

'What happened?'

'He's just a lot weaker. His heart and his arteries . . . He's just running down.'

'You mean – he's going to die soon?'

'I don't think he'll last another week. But they haven't said that. It's just that he looks so ill.'

'Should I go today?' It was a Friday, and I had planned my holiday so that I could go back to work on this day. I had things to do; if I didn't do them, the paper wouldn't come out.

'No. Go tomorrow. Or Sunday. I'll phone if he gets worse.'

~

His new ward was busy with patients, nurses and visitors. He was leaning against pillows; the flesh seemed to have left his face and the skin was stretched around his jaw; the yellow tinge that I had noticed two weeks before had deepened. But he smiled and lifted his hand when he saw me.

'Good chap . . . for coming to see your old father.' His voice was low and throaty. 'I've missed you.'

I kissed him, sat down and asked about the new ward.

'I don't like it. They're much more bossy than Ricky . . . and his friends upstairs. They've hidden my stick . . . somewhere . . . so I can't get to the television room . . . and I can't smoke here in bed.' His speech came in short bursts as he paused for breath. He looked at me for a moment. 'If you gave me an arm . . . we could go to the television room.' He pointed to some swing doors, five beds away.

'Are you sure that's all right? Can you walk that far?'

'Easily. Just need you to lean on . . . like a stick.'

'What about the nurses?'

'They won't care . . . and to hell with them if they do. It'll do me good to stretch my legs. Been lying here for days.'

I didn't like the idea, but I couldn't argue with him – he was my father. With my help, he got out of bed and grabbed my hand so that his forearm locked over mine. He was wearing a white hospital nightshirt instead of his pyjamas and his legs were shockingly thin. With one hand on me and one on the bed, he reached the ward's central aisle. There, he put his arm round me so that it rested on my shoulder and told me to walk on slowly. As we moved away from the bed, he slumped against me. I put my arm round his waist and we took a few steps before he started to slide out of my grasp. His legs had given way and I found that I was holding him under his arms from behind. I was taking all his weight, but, as I struggled to hold him up, he paddled on with his feet in an attempt to reach the swing doors. A young male nurse rushed up and took hold of him, taking half the weight off me. 'You mustn't do this. He has to stay in bed. He isn't at all well.'

'I'm sorry. He just wanted to watch some television. I didn't know he was so weak.'

We put him back in bed and the nurse adjusted his pillows so that he was lying down. He looked tired – the few steps we had taken seemed to have used what energy he had. I poured some orange squash, leaned over him and held the mug for him to drink. He looked steadily at me and I saw how sunken his eyes had become and that his eyelids were tight hemispheres. 'I regard awareness as life itself. I am aware. That is all that is worth living for.'

I couldn't remember his using the word before; the hippies and the new interest in Buddhism had made awareness a watchword for my generation, but surely not for his. 'Yes. I think you're right. But what made you say that?'

He smiled. 'Just a thought I had.'

I told him about Corsica. He seemed to listen, but his

eyelids soon began to droop. I kissed him and watched as he fell asleep.

~

I spoke to Ann several times that week – he was sinking fast, she said. I went again the next Sunday.

He was lying in the bed, turned a little to one side – the side with space for his visitors. His body and his arms were underneath the bedclothes. Only his head was visible. Against the whiteness of the pillow, it looked small and the yellowness had turned to brown. His eyes were open but seemed unfocused. There were smears of yellow saliva at the corners of his mouth. I leaned over, kissed his forehead – gently because it seemed fragile – and said hello. There was a sour, acidic smell, unlike anything I had smelled before. As I pulled my head away, his eyes were drawn to my face, and were filled with puzzlement, and perhaps fear, as they wandered around it, apparently wondering who or what I was. Then his eyes settled on mine. 'David?'

'Yes.'

'Is it you?'

'It's me, David.'

'Good.' He closed his eyes. I pulled up a chair, sat down and looked at him. It was obvious that he would die soon. I put my hand on the sheet, where it covered his shoulder. He opened his eyes, but didn't seem to see me, and closed them again. I sat for a few minutes watching him breathe with his mouth half open.

I found a doctor and spoke to him in a hallway. No, he didn't think my father would die today, but within a few days. He was sorry.

I went back to his bed. He hadn't moved. I sat by him a little longer, then kissed his forehead and said goodbye. Again, he opened his eyes and closed them without showing any expression.

As I walked to the station, I muttered, 'How are the mighty fallen.' I said it out loud several times as I crossed a bridge. The shrivelled head on the white pillow was so far from the man I had loved and, occasionally, hated.

~

Ann telephoned me the next evening. He had lost consciousness and wouldn't regain it; the doctors were certain of that. There was no point in my visiting again.

He died two days later. Ann rang me at my office.

'Thanks . . . Thanks for telling me . . . We'll talk soon.'

I put the phone down and stared at it for a few seconds. Then I stood up, stretched and walked around my desk. I looked out of the window at the traffic below, and wandered around the room staring at things on the walls without really looking at them. After a few minutes I sat down and carried on with my work.

26

On a Bridge near Durban

IT WAS LATE JUNE, warm and overcast. As I drove north out of Winnipeg the spaces between the buildings gradually widened. Half an hour from the centre, new stone houses were set well back from the road with a quarter-mile of grass and woods between them. I began to wonder if I was on the right road. The signs said north, but made no mention of Portage la Prairie, Gladstone or Dauphin, the three towns that I recalled seeing in bold type on the Explore Manitoba map. According to the signs the road led to Lockport and nowhere else. I pulled the car on to the verge; I hadn't heard of Lockport.

The map showed that I had been driving north-east. My destination was as far west of Winnipeg as it was north and I had to drive west first, so as to get on the other side of Lake Manitoba. I drove back the way I had come. In one sense I had had little time to think about this trip; I had been working long hours, had left my office late on Friday and been at Gatwick early on Saturday. In another sense, I had had all the years since that grey March day when, on a whim, I had called in on Uncle George. After all that time I was at last rushing towards Swan River, perhaps a little unprepared.

I didn't even know what kind of car I was driving, just that it was grey and twelve years old, had the steering wheel on the wrong side and no tape deck, just a radio. It had been the only car the rental company had available. A man had hoovered the inside while I waited and I was glad that it was old and had a few small scrapes; the man had said that it was reliable and had made no apologies. And, except for the *Rough Guide to Canada*, my heavy old Nikon and some Neet Deet mosquito repellent, I had brought nothing that I wouldn't have taken on holiday in England.

I drove back, past the well-spaced houses with the plate glass and the shiny new jeeps, and into a stretch where the buildings were wooden and dilapidated, behind broken fences and rusting pick-ups; they were close together, there were children playing, and they made me think of my grandfather Tom, who I was sure had lived in a log cabin. I realised that I was driving more slowly, looking around. There was no need to rush; I was on the edge of a new city, away from my office and the hustle of London. The man had glanced at my map and guessed it might take nine hours to drive to Swan River, though he had never been there. I had already wasted an hour, but what did it matter if it took two days, or three; there was no one telling me what to do, no one with any expectations.

I turned right on to a multi-lane ring road, the kind that encircles every modern city; Portage la Prairie was among the names on the signs. I settled into driving at about fifty-five and thought again about my grandfather. I had read through his letters soon after my father gave them to me and hadn't looked at them again until a few months ago. Then, in order to understand them thoroughly, I had transcribed them on to my computer, peering at his elegant copperplate through a magnifying glass to decipher words that were hard to read.

I had brought the typed transcriptions with me – as well as the original letters – and had read through them once again on my flight from London. There were eight letters, three written in London between 1902 and 1906 and five later, from Durban, Manitoba. In October 1902 Tom wrote to Sis thanking her for a letter telling him that she and Cliffie were well. He told her that he had no money at all, was using his last stamps and had tried to get work 'of any kind, for anything' but had failed. From the end of the week he would no longer have an address; he was leaving because he couldn't pay the rent and he didn't know where he would go. He ended by saying: 'I don't know what you will tell Cliffie about me but, if ever anybody's heart bleeds, mine is now doing so with sorrow at what I have brought about by my thoughtless and bad conduct.'

In December 1905 he sent Cliffie a letter, which was intended to arrive on his fourteenth birthday. Cliffie received it after his mother died, in 1942 when he was fifty. Tom told him that 'your Father has not forgotten for one moment his dear boy' and that it was his 'constant hope and prayer' that he was 'being treated with kindness and growing up to be an honest and straightforward man'. He acknowledged that he was not allowed to know where Cliffie lived, but asked if they could meet soon at Liverpool Street Station; there were things that he wanted to tell him that he could not put in a letter.

I took the slip road on to Trans Canada Highway One and settled down in the slow lane. I held tight to the wheel as monolithic radiator grilles filled the mirror and trucks the size of houses swung past enveloping me in a maelstrom of noise and turbulence. I turned on the radio; a woman was giving advice about shopping for designer clothes in Winnipeg. I turned it off.

Tom's last letter from London had been written on 3 August 1906 to a nameless friend of his brother Bertie, who had helped him before by giving him a suit and who had agreed to help fund his passage to Canada. Tom wrote very politely, enclosing the £4 bill for his passage and asking for extra money to retrieve his clothes from a pawnbroker. He told the man that he was 'quite destitute and starving – and subsisting on what is given me by others little better off than myself'. He gave an address where 'letters are taken for me but my sleeping here or anywhere else is most erratic' and asked if the man might persuade his brother to send him 'a few shillings to get food. I can put up with being out at nights but it is hard to starve.' He ended: 'If I am incoherent you must excuse me as I am in a weak state although, I hope, well enough to pass the doctor on board ship.' The existence of this letter among the others, that were all to Sis, Cliffie or Uncle George, had puzzled me, but then I thought that Bertie's nameless friend – whom he addressed as 'Sir' – probably passed it to Uncle George with the bill for Tom's passage, because they had agreed to split the cost.

I turned the radio back on, pushed the tuning buttons and found a station that was playing Blur and Alanis Morissette. The road was flat and straight, like the surrounding country. This had to be the prairies. I drove faster. Portage la Prairie, which had seemed romantic and faraway on the map in London, passed quickly by, an orange smudge, pierced by a few concrete high-rises. I turned off the Trans Canada on to a two-lane road signed to Gladstone, Neepawa and Dauphin.

The sky was dull grey and getting darker, the country green all around; patches of conifer broke the uniformity. There was little traffic, and T-shaped telegraph poles stretched out ahead for miles. I stopped the car, got out, stretched and looked around. A red pick-up whooshed past. I watched until it became a dull point two or three miles ahead and disappeared over a distant ridge. I was on the open, north American road, and belonged for a few hours in the myth driven by movies and fuelled by rock music. I looked at the car. It was a Ford; some chrome lettering read 'Tempo'; it was old and anonymous, which suited me.

I drove on, pushing buttons on the radio and thanking Tom Reynolds for bringing me here. The road climbed gradually. After an hour's driving a storm broke. Even with the wipers on double speed, I couldn't see out of my Ford. I pulled to the side of the road, cut the engine and stared at the dark, swirling water inches from my face as the country music station played soft. When the rain eased, I drove to the next diner and sat across from a short, fat man in dungarees whose upper lip bumped into his nose as he ate.

Gladstone was a village, a mix of red brick and timber where the road bent west beneath wooded hills. The sun came out as I drove past the malls and filling stations of Neepawa and Minnedosa and turned north on to Highway 10. The road climbed, dipped and twisted through cultivated valleys and hills, as I listened to oldies from the 1960s: Crosby, Stills, Nash and Young; Mick Jagger yelling 'No Satisfaction'. Suddenly there was white light on the horizon and clouds like dirty smoke overhead. Rain fell again, fiercely and briefly, and the sky was a thin blue as I drove into a town with wooden sidewalks and weathered square-fronted buildings like main street in a western. I stopped for coffee and browsed through the histories of Manitoba in a second-hand bookstore, looking for mentions of Swan River. There was just one; it told me that the first homesteaders arrived in the valley in 1898, a century ago – before then the area had been visited only by trappers and fur traders.

I passed a warning silhouette of a moose stamped on a yellow diamond, as the road widened and swept on through an undulating forest. It was mid-afternoon; the sky was blue again and the only clouds were thin white streaks. I turned off the radio and listened to the birds and the silence. I wondered if my grandfather had been in this place, and I thought about Uncle George who had paid half his fare and then told me to follow him. I stopped and strolled by a lake where there were birds and no humans, and watched its ripples sparkle in the sun. I drove on and when I thought I saw a bear by the roadside, turned the car to go back and make sure: it was small and black with a brown snout, a young one, idly pulling leaves from bushes and putting them in its mouth.

From the edge of the forest a straight road led north to Dauphin. I had a vision of Deborah, aged about twelve, in my room in Marlow. Dauphin was the town she and I had noticed in an atlas because it was the nearest place to Swan River; I knew now that it was more than a hundred miles away. It was years since I had seen Deborah; she had married a doctor and gone to live somewhere in the west of England. One day, I might just find her unexpectedly once again.

I saw a road sign and braked. I had been expecting this some time soon, but it was still a surprise. A white arrow on a green ground pointed to the left. Next to the arrow were the words Swan River.

Of course I knew the town was there – maps, my grandfather's letters and the hotel receptionist to whom I had spoken on the phone the previous night proved that – but this mundane notice somehow thrilled me. It wasn't that it showed that I was getting closer, but that it made the town seem like a real place instead of a blurred picture inside my head, a myth that I had been carrying around for most of my life. I got out of the car and used the Nikon, instead of my pocket camera, to photograph the road sign from the best angle, showing the sky, the horizon, the straight road ahead to Dauphin and, to the left, the road to Swan River.

It was eight o'clock, but not cold and the sun was far from setting. The road was straight and empty. Some of the land was cultivated, but there were more woods here than further south and a few miles to the west was a Provincial Park called Duck Mountain. At nine o'clock I stopped to look at the sky and think about someone whom I loved and had left behind in London two days before. It was still light, and low down, where the road ahead met the sky, the thin clouds glowed silver. As I drove on, I tuned to a country-music station and swayed in my seat as a man and a woman sang a duet I had heard a few hours earlier. As the slide guitar faded, I listened to the voice of the host: 'Vince Gill with Patti Loveless, "My Kind Of Woman, My Kind Of Man".'

The clouds thickened and daylight faded. When I reached

the sign that announced Swan River there was darkness on the ground and the silver in the sky had turned to gold.

I passed a filling station and anonymous lots displaying combine harvesters, tractors and pick-ups. A giant supermarket loomed unlit behind a car park. There were streetlights ahead. The place seemed to be flat and there was no sign of a river, or a valley. I drove through traffic lights, the first I had seen since leaving Winnipeg, and saw a sign to The Pas and Flin Flon, towns even further north. I knew that the hotel I'd booked into was a little way down that road, but I drove on towards the streetlights; I wanted to see Swan River now, at least from the window of my Ford.

A sign said Main Street. There were three or four blocks with shops and business premises on both sides of the street – I saw another hotel, two or three eating places, a bank and the office of the *Swan River Star and Times*. Main Street crossed a broad level-crossing without gates – and the last streetlight was beyond a small cinema and another place serving food. I made a U-turn and drove slowly back through the town towards the hotel. A few yards down the railway track from the level-crossing was a corrugated-iron tower, which I guessed was a grain store; otherwise the buildings were low with flat roofs.

The hotel was modern and sprawling, with space for cars on every side. I checked in and went straight to the bar; it was ten o'clock and they would soon stop serving food. It was carpeted and crowded, and filled with people of all ages chattering. I drank bottled Molson Dry and looked at a copy of the *Swan River Star and Times*, as I waited for a half-pounder with bacon and cheese. No one took much notice of me. It seemed to be the kind of place where they were used to strangers passing through.

The front-page story was about star pupils at local schools who had won prizes and places at Canada's universities. Inside, a teenage boy had drowned in a remote lake in the Duck

Mountain Provincial Park and there was a call for improved safety measures. There was a preview of the annual Swan River Rodeo the next week – I felt sorry that I would be back in London by then – and a feature on 'Swan River Past', divided into ten, twenty-five and fifty years ago this week, a past that was too recent for me. The burger arrived on an oval plate with plenty of salad and too many chips.

My swift trip up and down Main Street had given me a sense of anti-climax. It seemed to be a long strip of garish signs – new buildings dumped along a road. There seemed to be nothing old, nothing that would have been there when my grandfather was here, and I wondered if it would have seemed different if I had come sooner. It was 1998; Tony Blair and New Labour had been in power for a year, Spurs had been saved from relegation from the premiership by David Ginola and the brief return of Jürgen Klinsmann. It was twenty-nine years since my father had died – and thirty-eight since Uncle George had tapped my knee and told me to come to this place. 'When you're grown-up and can afford to travel,' he had said. Perhaps it was appropriate that I had delayed so long, until I was forty-nine. I had been busy and had thought little about Swan River or my grandfather for thirty years. Now I had five clear days to make amends.

~

The sky was dark and there was a cold wind as I strolled about Swan River the next morning. My impression from the previous night was accurate; the buildings were mostly post-1960, low and square. I was surprised to see a tourist information centre – in a pristine log cabin that looked as if it had just been built. I took away a brochure with maps of the town and the Swan Valley, sat with it in a café and learned that people came to the region to camp, hike and hunt in the nearby provincial parks, that in winter there was skiing on Thunder Hill, and that Swan River was the valley's trading centre but was surrounded by eight smaller villages. It was as though the writer thought that the town would have little appeal to tourists – although I saw that there was a museum further up the road past my hotel – and was letting them know that there were attractions nearby. The eight villages were listed and shown on a map. One of them was Durban.

I ate fried chicken, drank a Coke and lingered over coffee. I was almost deliberately delaying the next step – driving to Durban. Though Swan River had been the goal specified by Uncle George, Durban was where my grandfather had lived. If this trip had an epicentre, Durban was it.

It was south-west from Swan River. My grandfather had written that it was a twelve-mile walk; it was twenty miles by a road that ran between large fields of young green wheat, a foot or so high. A single-track railroad ran close to the road for much of the way, and there was a long, low ridge to the west which I identified as Thunder Hill. I passed new-looking farmhouses with conical grain stores made of corrugated iron or plastic and occasional fields of brown cows. Otherwise, the rippling wheat was broken only by clumps of poplar and willow and by old grey-timbered shacks and barns that looked as if they could have been there in the time of Tom Reynolds.

I turned off the main road. Durban was half a mile away. There was a level-crossing ahead, a few trees and a tall, square, wooden tower, similar to the one by the railroad in Swan River; I knew now, from the tourist brochure, that these buildings were called grain elevators.

I left the car and walked around. Durban was a collection of about twenty-five disparate buildings, ranging from a handful of dilapidated wooden shacks to ten or twelve well-kept houses of various ages. An old church, built of boards from which cream paint was peeling, was locked and looked little used. There was a post office, small and made of concrete, but shut. Several buildings seemed to have been abandoned and left to decay. Two men were unloading timber from a lorry by the grain elevator, another was mending a roof. One or two pick-ups drove south through the village. Children shouted somewhere, dogs barked.

It was still early afternoon. I drove south between fields, away from Durban and the main road, towards some low hills. The tarmac soon gave way to a rutted mix of mud and yellow gravel. Further on, the road crossed another at right angles, and further on again, another. I turned left and drove around for an hour on dirt roads which seemed to have been laid out on a grid. Every mile or so I passed farm buildings buried among trees. I stopped to photograph an old grey barn, and again at a solitary church among a clump of yew trees, where I lingered over graves grouped into families and read the inscriptions on the tombs of young children.

I stopped the car near a wooden bridge over a narrow stream, and read through my transcriptions of my grandfather's five letters from Durban. They were all sent to Uncle George's home in Upper Clapton and three were addressed to him.

The first, sent in October 1906, states, with no embellishing details, that he crossed the Atlantic on the SS *Pomeranian*, with a single box containing a few clothes and other possessions, and travelled by train from Quebec to Winnipeg and on to Swan River with an Irishman whom he met on the ship. He walked from Swan River, and at Durban got work on the new Thunder Hill branch of the Canadian Northern Railway. He spent the whole of September living under canvas beside the track and is now, temporarily, living with his foreman in Durban in a bungalow, which Tom helped him to build. 'The life I am leading is awfully rough, but the grub I get is, and has been, good and in quantity.' He says that the district is strong on temperance and that there are no pubs. 'What drink is obtained is got on the quiet so I have not had any since leaving Winnipeg.'

The next letter is to Sis and written almost two years later

– there may, of course, have been others not handed down to my father. It begins with a conciliatory paragraph and expresses the 'hope that we might be reunited', but goes on to grouse about 'other people's damned cussedness and selfishness that has brought about our separation'. He asks her to send him photos of herself and Cliffie 'which I have over and over again kicked myself for not getting before I left the Old Country'.

He describes himself as 'one of the original pioneers' in a pioneer town in a beautiful valley where there are several forests and the houses are made of wood. 'Life inside one of these houses is not all too bad.' The summers are delightful – though care must be taken to avoid mosquitoes – and in winter the cold is severe but 'it is such a dry cold that you don't really feel it like those cold miserable days in London that I mind so well'. In winter men do the outdoor work while women tend to stay inside, 'but the women, ladies or girls, are always willing to go any distance to a dance or social'. He says that it is not unusual to travel ten or fifteen miles to a dance in a sleigh with a team of fast horses. 'It is glorious driving so long as there is no wind.'

The next two letters are both to Uncle George, and written in March and October 1909. Both include lengthy complaints about George's failure to send him news of Sis and Cliffie; he says angrily that he'll cause trouble by appealing to certain unnamed people unless he receives the news he regards as his right, and threatens that he might well, at some time, return to London. In the March letter, he writes of the previous winter which has been the longest and coldest for ten years, but says that he is acclimatised and didn't find it as hard as his first winter. At its worst, it was 64° below zero. 'I did feel that bad, and was nearly frozen in my bed in my little wooden house, in which I live all alone of course. I had to get up at 2 a.m. to put on a big fire of wood or should certainly have been dead in the morning. Some surprise has been expressed by my neighbours that I have managed to get through the winter so well but, as I tell them, I am all right.'

The last letter from Tom was written on 30 November 1909 to Cliffie, and is a sorry rant, with no information about his life in Durban. He is obsessed with the idea, alluded to in some of the other letters, that Cliffie should have a good opinion of him and that he has not been told the truth. He writes as though he knows that Cliffie won't see the letter, but that Uncle George – and perhaps Sis and Old George – will. 'I suspect that you have been told some tale or yarn about me which is very far from the truth . . . I can and will satisfy you that my character in London is as good as it ever was . . . I am determined to have communication with you and if this letter is suppressed I shall make it exceedingly unpleasant for those who do it . . . I have got to that stage of my feelings for certain people and for their treatment of me that my sole and principal object in life is to get some satisfaction out of them and I will get it in spite of what they do or do not do.'

I got out of the car and stood on the bridge. The letters contained all I had known about Tom's life in Durban before I came here. Despite the dances and the good, plentiful food, he sounded lonely and, as the years went by, increasingly unable to forget the past. I imagined that he had gone on drinking. If he had reformed, would he not have returned to London with pride and tried to be close to his son, if not his wife; or, if that had seemed too difficult or too painful, would he not have seen his old life – from a sober perspective – for what it was and have abandoned old grudges and looked forward? Drink could be got on the quiet, and, because he hadn't thrown off the anger he felt towards Sis and her family, I found myself hoping that he had got it. But also, perhaps, that here, away from Sis and with a full stomach, he was able sometimes to stop at that early stage of an evening when he could still taste the drink and it was giving him some pleasure.

I had learned almost nothing more about his life by visiting the town; it must have changed totally since he was there. But Durban was in the middle of the valley and, but for some woods which had been ploughed for wheat, the valley was the same now as it was then. He had praised the valley. It was flat and wide – probably about five miles across, north to south – with low ridges, still covered with trees, to the south and west. I looked around and contemplated the dome-like sky. The horizon was visible in every direction; I felt I was at the centre of a hemisphere. He must have gained something from this space, homesteaded by pioneers and so different from Norfolk Road or the streets around his office in Westminster.

The clouds had lifted; the sky was pale blue with streaks of white in the north and grey over the hills in the south. The air was clear, the light was pure. Did he find consolation in the horizon or the sky or the air? Or was I searching too hard? Why was I so keen to establish that Tom's life had not been relentlessly miserable? Perhaps because I thought he was a good man until his marriage and had been treated unfairly. Perhaps Uncle George had thought that too; it would have been perverse of him to send me to this remote place just to witness Tom's misery. Had he expected me just to pay some kind of homage? Or was I supposed to learn something?

There was one more letter, but not from Tom. Like his, I had transcribed it and printed it out on an A4 sheet, but I fetched the original from the car and reread it. It had been sent from Durban to Uncle George on 9 December 1910 by a man called R. W. Glennie; it said that Tom had died of tuberculosis and other diseases in Winnipeg General Hospital the previous day. The letter was well phrased and compassionate, and conveyed that Mr Glennie had been a good friend.

Tom had asked him to write to George and to his brother, Bertie, if anything happened to him, and had left some 'books and trinkets' with him. Sadly, the Health Officer had ordered that these be burned along with Tom's clothes and blankets. There was nothing more that Mr Glennie could say, except to offer his condolences.

27
Loon Lake

I WAS THE ONLY visitor to the museum. The curator asked where I was from and I told her, adding that my grandfather had lived in Durban for four years from 1906. She asked his name and said she would look at her records to see if there was any information. There were some old photographs of Durban in the drawer of a cabinet; I was welcome to look through them.

I spent most of the day there. It was a spacious L-shaped room crammed with pictures and memorabilia, and outside was a field of genuine old buildings that had been transported intact from their original locations, many with their entire contents. Swan River's first general store was there, filled with tins, jars, packets, farm implements and clothing; plaster hams hung from the ceiling and the owner's living quarters were at the back, as though he, his wife and a tribe of children were about to return. It had been built ten years before my grandfather arrived, and at first had served only trappers and fur-traders. I looked at the floor – he must have travelled back to Swan River from time to time and trodden there – and at the worn counter where he would have put down his dollars and cents.

There was a school, a church, a blacksmith's shop, a telegraph office and a complete railway station – with platform, rails and a two-car train. I looked closely at two log cabins. One was clean and plainly furnished and had belonged to a homesteader. The other was a trapper's cabin, with space only for a table and a bed, both of which had been roughly knocked together from unplaned wood. The trapper's clothes were hanging on nails, and he had just two or three fur blankets, a kettle, a frying pan and a pair of rifles. The place was full of dust and cobwebs. I imagined my grandfather in such a place in midwinter, a bottle of whisky and the odd book and trinket beside him, trying to keep warm.

Inside the museum I stared at innumerable images and objects, and captions that told stories. There was a photograph of a family named Reynolds; they were standing beside a covered wagon in which they had brought their goods from Ontario in 1898. It had a lengthy caption: the father and eldest son came first, staked their claim and built a home; almost a year later the mother arrived with the four younger children, and father and son went to meet them at a river crossing; the eldest daughter, who was fifteen, was so excited at the sight of her father and brother on the facing river bank that she ran into the water thinking she could wade across; she stumbled, was swept away by the current and drowned.

I sifted through drawers of photographs categorised by subject – Durban, Swan River, the railroad, house-building, threshing, daily life, leisure, football, curling – in search of a man with a large moustache who looked like Marlon Brando in *Viva Zapata*. There were one or two possibilities, including a photograph of four men standing, facing the camera, on a railway line; the man on the left had a moustache. Ann, the curator, lent me a magnifying glass.

In the Durban drawer there were two pictures from the early 1900s. One was a view along Main Street, shot from the ground. The other could only have been taken from the top of the grain elevator; the street and the valley beyond were covered with snow, and in the foreground, two horses were pulling a sleigh. The street was straight and broad and lined with two-storey buildings that butted up close to each other and to the sidewalk. On both sides of the street the buildings were formally regimented in a line and of roughly the same height. It was not unlike the High Street of an old town in England, except that the buildings were wooden and their roofs were flat; there was no resemblance to the place I had visited the previous day.

I could read the signs on the two nearest buildings. 'The Durban Stores' was built to Georgian proportions with cornices and a flagpole. Facing it, on the corner, was an equally elegant edifice. The sign was on the side around the corner from Main Street. I looked at it through the magnifying glass: 'Pool Room'. I smiled to myself; Tom would surely have been a regular. Behind the street to the east I could see smaller houses and shacks. Perhaps one of them was his home.

Ann photocopied some of the photographs for me. She hadn't found any references to Thomas Reynolds, but she had written down the phone number of a man she thought I should call. He was the author of a history of Durban.

'Really? There's a history of Durban?'

'We used to stock it. Stuart wrote it a few years back. It went out of print, but he may be able to lend you a copy. He's a nice guy.' Despite what she said, I imagined an overly intense academic with wire-rimmed glasses and a jutting chin.

He lived in Swan River in a quiet street off Main Street. The house was new and built of brick and had a neat front lawn like its neighbours. Stuart was tall and lean with close-cut grey hair around a tanned, bald dome. I guessed he was about sixty-five. He smiled in greeting and introduced me to his wife before taking me downstairs to a basement room with armchairs and bookshelves. He fetched us each a Molson, and we drank from the cans as I told him about my grandfather and his letters; I tapped the folder I had brought. He thought for a few moments and said that he didn't know of my grandfather. The only Reynoldses he was aware of were the ones whose daughter had drowned, and they had lived in another part of the valley.

'There were a lot of bachelors back then.' He spoke

almost as if he had been there. 'Lived in shacks close together. You got any other names? People he knew? Mentioned in his letters?'

'Only one. R. W. Glennie.' I spoke the name slowly and precisely, without much hope of his recognising it. I picked up the folder. 'There's a letter from him. He wrote to the family in London in 1910 to tell them my grandfather had died.'

'You got the letter? Let me see it.' Glennie's original letter covered two sheets of paper. Stuart scanned the first page, lifted it aside and looked at the name at the bottom of the second. He looked up at me and gently slapped his knee. 'Bob Glennie! Well, I'll be damned!' His face broke into a wide grin.

'You've heard of him?'

He was holding the letter up and peering at it. 'Bob Glennie! December ninth, nineteen ten. I'm damned!' He looked at me again. 'I knew Glennie. He was my neighbour for thirty years. He moved to BC – that's British Columbia – in nineteen forty-five.'

I was amazed, and doing mental arithmetic. How old was this man with the kind eyes and slow smile?

He read Glennie's letter carefully and put it down. 'Tells me a lot about your grandfather. If he was a drinking man in London, then he went on drinking when he was here. Lots of them drank. It was sort of illegal. But they drank – every night, in the back of Honsinger's livery stable. Glennie drank. When his house burned down, the only thing he rescued was a crate of whisky.'

Stuart was eighty-four; he had been born in Durban in 1914. His grandfather, his father and his uncles had come to the district from Ontario in 1899 and established themselves on homesteads. I asked if he had been a farmer himself. He looked a little insulted and said, 'I *am* a farmer,' and told me that his sons, both in their sixties, now ran the family farms near Durban.

Though he hadn't known my grandfather, he had known a lot of people who surely would have known him, and he had a full understanding of what the town had been like in the years my grandfather was there, the years just before he, Stuart, was born. The town I had seen the day before contained just the faintest relics of the place Tom had known – wooden buildings were liable to burn down and were easy to demolish if you wanted something new.

A building boom had begun in Durban in the summer of 1905 in anticipation of the arrival of the railway that autumn. From that date, the place had been a lively pioneer town and in many ways surpassed Swan River – though the pendulum was to swing back again with the arrival of large grain businesses in the 1930s. Stuart confirmed Tom's assessment of himself as a pioneer. 'Oh, sure,' he said with a drawn-out lilt. 'A man who worked on the railroad here in those years was a pioneer.'

The town, back then, had two hotels, two dance halls, a pool hall, a curling rink, a doctor, a drugstore, a barber, a blacksmith, two butcher's shops, three groceries, two hardware stores, two banks, a school, a church and a Chinese café. Stuart explained that every place that could call itself a town had at least one Chinese café. The Canadians had encouraged the Chinese to come to work on the railroad; they were good cooks and it became commonplace for them to stay in a town and set up in business, after the railroad moved on.

Though only three or four hundred people lived in the town, it was the trading and supply centre for a large area which, by 1906, was homesteaded all over. A train and a stream of wagons with big teams of horses arrived every day except Sunday, and a hub of the town was Honsinger's livery stable on the west side of Main Street. Fifty or sixty horses were stabled there every night while their teamsters probably ate a Chinese meal and slept in one of the hotels. From the same premises Robert Honsinger also sold farm machinery, furniture and insurance, and his business partner, a man called Phil Zinger, ran an undertaking business. It was a two-storey building and the upper floor, accessed by an outdoor stairway and known as Honsinger's Hall, was used for dances, and for shows by visiting entertainers – and from early in 1908 as a venue for Newell's Moving Pictures which brought movies to the town for two days every month.

Most evenings Honsinger himself would sit at the back of his livery stable mending harness, and there the town's drinkers would quietly congregate, to drink, chew tobacco and chat. 'Honsinger had spittoons like in the hotels. They mostly chewed their tobacco,' Stuart said. 'Your grandfather would have been there, for sure. All the bachelors went there – almost every night. Jack Macaulay, Jack Sedgwick, Jim McNab. There were others. They did that when I was a boy, and they were there from 1905, 1906, when the town got going. They lived in little shacks to the east of Main Street. They knew each other, helped each other.'

He shook his head and smiled when I asked if Tom's shack would have been like the trapper's log cabin at the museum. 'There were no log cabins in Durban. They were all board. Where there's a sawmill, you get board – and there was a sawmill up the track on Duck Mountain. The roof would have been single pitch . . . you know, sloping just one way. Whole thing would have been about eighteen feet by twelve, with a stove with a pipe to the roof . . . and two plates for cooking.'

I asked what kind of furniture he would have had.

'It would have been rough. Basic. A washstand – probably a plank on apple boxes – a board bed with a straw mattress.'

'Where would he have put his clothes?'

'Nails. They hung them on nails.'

'What about the floor? Would he have had a carpet?'

'No.' He smiled again. 'Bare boards . . . or maybe a piece of linoleum, lino.'

We talked for three hours that evening, and arranged to meet again. In the meantime I read his book, forced the Ford to the top of Thunder Hill and went to Durban again, where I studied the sleepers and rails by the level crossing, wondering whether Tom had helped to lift and lay them.

I also visited the *Swan River Star and Times*, and was surprised and thrilled when the receptionist said they had back issues since the paper's foundation in 1900 and that I was welcome to browse for as long as I liked. She even made me a cup of coffee as I rested the old newspapers on a filing cabinet in the cavernous back room, and stood reading beside an idle, but gleaming, printing machine.

The early editions were a large, broadsheet format, yellowing pages with fraying edges bolted together by year between sheets of cardboard. From 1906 the *Swan River Star* had a correspondent in Durban who supplied news every week. I turned slowly through his reports for 1906 and 1907. Much was happening in the town and many names were mentioned, but I grew increasingly pessimistic as week after week there were pie socials and quadrille club gatherings and people named who were visiting just for a few days, but no Tom Reynolds. Could he have been so anonymous, have made no mark whatever in a town of just three or four hundred people? But then, like an unexpected encounter with an old and close friend, there he was, on 20 August 1908, two sentences: 'Mr Thomas Reynolds is about to open his boot making establishment. Repairs and patches a specialty.'

Two weeks later the correspondent reported that the machinery had arrived and been successfully installed and gave some detail: 'A little difficulty was experienced at first with the cross arm of the cylinder shaft connecting the bob winder, and with the eccentric – but Mr Reynolds being a very eccentric man he was soon able to set matters right. He was ably assisted by Mr Frank White.'

In September there was more: 'The boot and shoe factory is working overtime. Many people were awakened rudely the other morning from a healthy sleep. Could someone invent an automatic, hammerless, double-back-action cobbler with a pleasing disposition?'

That was all – in 1909 and 1910 he had done nothing to catch the attention of the Durban correspondent – but it was enough. I was exhilarated – the three tiny items confirmed my grandfather's existence in the town; he had been a little bit more than an anonymous bachelor; he had made an impact, woken people early and got himself in the newspaper.

But, at the same time, I had a concern. I made photocopies and showed them to Stuart. Could it be that Tom hadn't been very popular, that he had drunk alone and been shunned by the other bachelors?

Stuart laughed. 'They wouldn't have minded him being cantankerous. Lots of them were like that. They had come to get away from something, to start a new life. That was very common. Lots of them had secrets, stuff they didn't talk about. In fact, Frank White . . .' He pointed to the photocopy. 'I knew him well. He ran the hardware section of Harvey's Store till it closed . . . in 1935. He was the best hardware man in the valley. He could fix machines, make you anything you wanted. A good man. He wouldn't have helped your grandfather if they hadn't been friends.' He paused. 'Frank White had a secret. He came here from Australia, but originally he was from Ireland. When he died . . . around 1937, they found out he had a wife and children in Ireland. No one knew.'

~

At eleven o'clock on my next to last night I stood in a car park outside a steak house and stared at the sky. There were strange colours to the north, and overhead it was blue, shading to grey. A star dropped and vanished near the horizon.

I didn't feel like going to bed or watching Wimbledon highlights on the television in my room. I drove towards Durban – I wanted to see that valley at night; it was only twenty miles. On the way I tuned the radio to country music and saw just two other cars.

I walked north for twenty minutes along a track half a mile from the town. In front of me the sky was rimmed with a pink brown glow, and streaks of two blues, light and dark, stood out higher up, motionless against a dark grey wash that dimmed the brightness of the stars and stretched over my head to the horizon in the south. Dark rod-like trees were silhouetted against the sky, and the fields winked with glow-worms; it was so quiet that I thought I could hear them. As I walked back to the Ford I remembered that Bob Glennie's homestead had been next to Stuart's, somewhere close by, in the fields behind me; I wondered whether Tom had ever walked home this way, after a late drink with Glennie – and seen a sky like this.

I felt I had found out a lot about my grandfather and his life here. The vision I had had for so long had changed almost totally. The man I had imagined to be lonely, freezing and miserable was undoubtedly all those things some of the time, but in a thriving pioneer town there had been cures for those complaints that he would not have ignored or refused – and he had sufficient energy and faith in the future to start a business.

It was unlikely that I could find out more. I had one day left, Sunday, and planned to spend it walking around a lake I had read about in the tourist brochure.

I was woken by the telephone. A voice said, 'You still there? How you doing?'

'Fine.'

'You gonna be there today?'

'Yes. Who's that?'

'Harris. Stuart Harris. Thought we might meet and talk.'

I hadn't recognised his voice, but I was pleased – flattered – that he wanted to see me again. He drove over and we had coffee in the breakfast-room.

He said he had been thinking about my grandfather and Frank White. 'I didn't tell you before. Something was bothering me, but I've worked it out now. Your grandfather wrote that he was working on the railroad and sleeping beside the track. He arrived in 1906. The railroad from Swan River reached Durban in October 1905. The next stop is Benito, and the first train arrived in Benito on Christmas Day 1905, so when your grandfather arrived the railroad was already built. It would be possible, but unlikely, for someone to live in Durban and work on the next piece of track, Benito to Arran, but they didn't start on that until 1910. I checked.'

He paused to swallow some coffee. 'OK. I remembered that when Frank White first came to Durban, he was employed to fence the railway line. They had regulations: the whole line, Swan River through Durban to Benito, had to have a four-wire fence on cedar posts, with upright wires every two feet, on both sides of the line. It was to keep animals – and people – off the track. It was a heck of a job. Four men did it for months, from summer 1906 through freeze-up and on into 1907. Frank was the foreman.'

He pointed his finger at me, and I began to see his drift. 'Your grandfather said he was working on the railroad in 1906. He was – *fencing* it. And he said he lived for a while with his foreman, who was building a house. He did. Frank White was his foreman. Frank built a house at that time, on First Avenue South; he lived there till he died.' He smiled. 'And, when your grandfather went into the boot and shoe business, who helped him set up the machinery? Frank

White.' He slapped his hand gently on the table and looked up at me. 'What do you think? Adds up, doesn't it?'

'Certainly does. That's fantastic . . . And Frank was a pillar of the community, a popular man, wasn't he? That's the impression I got from your book.'

'Frank? Oh sure. A lovely man. Great sense of humour. Always telling jokes. A bachelor – at least that's what everyone thought. He ate out every day, in the hotel or the Chinese café . . . That's another thing I thought: they were both – your grandfather and Frank – escaping from some kind of unhappy marriage. Maybe it drew them together, even if they didn't talk about it.'

We talked a while longer and I walked with him to his car. I asked why the place was called Swan River. I had strolled in the sun along the river at the edge of the town, but had seen no swans; the town's emblem seemed to be a crested bird called a loon. He shrugged and said he hadn't seen any swans here in all his eighty-four years, but that an early explorer had called the river Swan River because he thought he saw some swans on Thunder Hill. He laughed. 'And who are we to say he didn't?' We parted saying how much we had liked each other's company. He seemed to have enjoyed talking to me and puzzling over my grandfather, but I knew that my gain was far greater.

~

The next afternoon, on my way to catch a plane from Winnipeg, I stopped by a lake in Duck Mountain Provincial Park. A pair of loons drifted back to back, the only living creatures in a mass of rippling greys and silvers that mirrored the washes in the sky. As I watched, one of the birds turned and aligned itself in the other's wake, and together they set off in slow procession towards the further shore. My father came into my mind, how he would have enjoyed this trip, driving on empty roads and gazing from the tops of hills, and how much he would have had to say to Stuart, about yields and straight ears and the big grain companies. And then I thought about my mother, who had died only four years before, in 1994, after a long, somewhat uneventful second marriage; and about my daughters and what I would tell them about their great-grandfather.

I found again that I was silently thanking Tom for bringing me to the north of Manitoba. He had been desperate to prove to my father that he was a man of good character, perhaps because he thought that he had nothing else to pass on. Now, without knowing me, he had passed something on, of which his story was just a part. And I thought that I could see what Uncle George had had in mind.

Acknowledgements

The content and shape of this book owe much to the wisdom of Peter Straus at Picador, and to that of his colleague Becky Senior who has been tremendous, providing copious cogent insights and pivotal suggestions. William Styron, a master of euphemism, describes a fictional editor in *Sophie's Choice* as having a sharp eye for 'the onanistic dalliance'. He could have been describing just one of Becky's many editorial skills. Any onanistic dalliances that remain are my fault entirely.

My daughters, Martha, Grace and Rose, delivered whole-hearted enthusiasm when I left my job to complete *Swan River* and write for a living; they should already know that they are a large part of my inspiration. I thank them, and their mother, Philippa Campbell.

My half-sisters, Madeline and Ann, and my half-brother-in-law, Adrian, dug deep into their memories and spent many hours talking with me about the past. My half-nephew, Geoffrey Rippingale, wandered with me for hours through the streets and graveyards of East London, uncomplaining and in all weathers, as we speculated about our forebears. For this he has been rewarded only with a drink at the Norfolk Arms in what is now called Cecilia Road; his companionship, insights and painstaking research have been a pleasure and a boon.

My longest-serving friend, David Hunt, has given much energy to stimulating my memory and to reading and making suggestions, and his specialist knowledge of knees – he is now a leading orthopaedic surgeon – has thrown much-needed light on La Frascetti's acrobatic talents. For reading, commenting and encouraging, I would like to thank Camilla Elworthy, Ruth Logan, Liz Calder, Tony Peake, Patrick Walsh, Sarah Beal and Ira Silverberg.

I have been helped by seven Canadians, four of whom, Candace Savage, Marilyn Biderman, Rob Sanders and Colleen Macmillan, have never been to Swan River, but knew that I should go and encouraged me practically and spiritually. Shauna Jackson-Osatchuk, editor of the *Swan River Star and Times*, and Ann Dubreuil, curator of the remarkable Swan Valley Museum, helped me greatly and graciously when I was there. Stuart Harris gave me time, wisdom and the benefit of an increasingly rare and valuable possession, a lifetime's local knowledge. He also gave this story an ending and in so doing has become a treasured friend; to him I owe something truly incalculable.

I am blessed with a third professional editor. Penny Phillips has been ever-present, dispensing love, humour, encouragement and the willingness to read and comment at all times of day and night. But for her, Swan River would still be only a town in Manitoba. I owe her so much that it is fortunate that she is my wife, and that I have the rest of my life in which to attempt to repay her.